with my best wishes

signed by the author
on publication of this book

Henry Leach

ENDURE NO MAKESHIFTS

'The sea has formed the English character and the essential England is to be found in those who follow it. From blue waters they have learned mercifulness and a certain spacious tolerance for what does not affect their craft; and they have also learned – in the grimmest schools – precision and resolution. The sea endures no makeshifts. If a thing is not exactly right it will be vastly wrong. Discipline, courage and contempt for all that is pretentious and insincere are the teaching of the ocean and the elements – and they have been qualities in all ages of the British sailor.'

John Buchan

ENDURE NO MAKESHIFTS

Some Naval Recollections

by
Admiral of the Fleet
Sir Henry Leach

LEO COOPER
LONDON

First published in Britain in 1993 by
LEO COOPER
an imprint of
Pen & Sword Books Ltd,
47 Church Street, Barnsley, South Yorkshire S70 2AS

Copyright © Sir Henry Leach, 1993

A CIP catalogue record for this book is available
from the British Library

ISBN 0 85052 370 2

Typeset by CentraCet, Cambridge
in Linotron 10pt Plantin

Printed by Redwood Books,
Trowbridge, Wilts

To Mary, without whose constant,
staunch and loving support so much
would not have been possible

CONTENTS

ACKNOWLEDGEMENTS

My grateful thanks go to Lord Tweedsmuir for allowing me to use the title drawn from a passage in one of his late father's books, to David Bolton of The Royal United Services Institute for Strategic Studies for permission to reproduce my lecture, to Vice Admiral Sir Ted Horlick for letting me draw freely from his lecture on Merchant Ship conversions and other important ad hoc work at the time of the Falklands War, to 'Uncle JAK' of *The Evening Standard* for reproduction of some of the mickey he has taken out of me over the years, to the Syndication Managers of *The Times*, *The Daily Telegraph*, *The Evening Standard*, *The Sun* and *The Argus (Cape Town)* for permission to use some of their material, to cartoonist Smiles and the literary executor of the late Marshal of the Royal Air Force Sir William Dickson (neither of whom have I been able to contact) for the inclusion of some of their works, to Elizabeth Money-Kyrle for taking on the typing after my wife died, to Sir Frank Cooper for his professional advice on security and to Christopher Verey of the Ministry of Defence for security vetting, to Jill Black and Michael Shaw for patiently reading my manuscript and introducing me to the world of publishing and finally to Tom Hartman and Leo Cooper for their courage and support in producing the finished article.

ILLUSTRATIONS

FOREWORD

This is not an autobiography nor complete memoirs. It recounts, broadly in sequence, certain events which occurred during my main working life. For reasons of similarity or security there are large gaps; thus the fascinating problems with which I had to deal in a number of appointments are conspicuous by their absence.

I derive no pleasure from retrospective criticism of others; where I have been critical it is to set the record straight or to point up a lesson to be learned. Most of the stories are against myself.

There are those who have exhorted me to fill in the gaps, to set out, unexpurgated, the full facts and lock it up for release when the statutory 30 years have elapsed. I have not done so: neither I nor the subjects of such disclosures will be around to support or contest the issues; in baring my own soul I should be exposing those of others, and I have no particular right to do so; it is no bad thing to leave scope for future historians to speculate; and anyway some things are best left *unsaid*.

45 years of active service among super people in an organization called The Royal Navy gave me enormous fun; this book is an attempt to put something back and share some of it with you.

1

A BEGINNING AND AN ENDING

And the stately ships go on
To their haven under the hill;
But O for the touch of a vanished hand,
And the sound of a voice that is still!
Alfred Lord Tennyson

'Oh well, it'll be all right when he's in the Navy,' said my father.

'That's what you always say,' retorted my mother, 'but have you ever discussed it with the boy?'

'Er no, I don't think it's necessary.'

'But I really think you should.'

'Very well, I will.'

I was blessed with exceptional parents to whom I was devoted – more so than perhaps I realized at the age of ten. They had married young and there could not have been a more devoted couple; twenty years later they might have been thought to be on their honeymoon. Home (Yarner), on the edge of Dartmoor near the village of Bovey Tracey, was a very happy place.

Mother was beautiful with raven black hair, a lovely neck and clear grey eyes set in a rounded face above a humorous mouth. She was highly intelligent, soft-spoken and very strict, but always scrupulously fair, so that I knew exactly where I stood; a brilliant organizer, resolutely determined, and with a bubbling sense of humour and appreciation of the ridiculous. She herself had a strong streak of naughtiness and was always game for a bit of fun. She had the guts of ten and little would stop her in the particular pursuit of the moment – especially if she knew she was right (as she normally thought she was!).

'If I say "it is" it *is*,' she often used to say, adding 'even if it isn't!'

Father was a big man in every sense, well over six foot, broad and strongly built in proportion. Prematurely bald, he had a kindly, oval face from which projected a large nose and a firm chin. He was affectionately known by many of his sailors as 'Trunky'. In his time he won the Navy Racquets and Tennis Championships and was a devastating slow left-arm bowler on the cricket field as well as being much in demand at rugger and hockey. His natural eye and sense of timing made him a crack shot with a twelve-bore and a skilled fisherman. Somehow he seemed to radiate an aura of calmness, gentleness, kindness and humour; he was never edgy or got in a flap; everyone liked and respected him for his steely sense of purpose and code of values which underlay his character. He was a charming no-nonsense man.

But father was now committed to a personal discussion on my future which he did not relish. And so, one winter's night before I was even eleven, he came up to my room to say goodnight. The discussion was strictly limited to our exchange of goodnights, no other subject was broached; he switched out the light, left the room and shut the door. Moments later he just cracked the door open again, stuck his head round and speaking rather quickly muttered:

'I take it you have no objection to joining the Navy?'

Instantly withdrawing his head and slamming the door without waiting for a reply he stumped off downstairs to report to my mother:

'I've discussed it with the boy and it's all fixed.'

The matter was never raised again in my family and at 13½ I went to the Royal Naval College, Dartmouth, proudly wearing the uniform of a Naval Cadet. Now, more than fifty years later, I can reflect on the outcome of that Careers Interview and reply:

'No objection.'

Dartmouth in the thirties was much like any other good Public School. I got an excellent general education, orientated away from the classics, but learned little about the Navy. So that when the war-clouds gathered in September, 1939, and the Training Cruiser (to which I would normally have gone on leaving Dartmouth) was transferred back to the Fleet, the curriculum at the College had to be modified to train the young Cadets in preparation for operational life at sea.

In the summer of 1940 my Father was Director of Naval Ordnance at the Admiralty. As such he played a prominent part in the procurement of weapons for the Fleet. It was a busy time but he managed a few days' leave.

'Which ship would you like when you go to sea?' he asked one evening as we were returning from a few hours' fishing in the River Bovey.

'That's all right Dad,' I replied, 'it's all organized. I've put my name down for the *Fiji*.'

She was a brand new six-inch-gun cruiser of the latest class and most of my particular chums were hoping to go to her.

'Hmm,' grunted my Father. 'That doesn't sound quite right to me. Better to have a thicker roof over your head before the next summer months.'

'But Dad,' I expostulated, 'it's all fixed and my buddies are going there.'

'No, no, I'll get it changed,' he replied.

He did and I was appointed to *Prince of Wales*, our newest battleship still under construction at Cammell Lairds in Birkenhead. So began a chain of curious coincidences.

In December I left Dartmouth for the last time, having collected the Special Subjects Prize for those aspects of work which would otherwise have been done in the Training Cruiser. In the final academic exams I achieved a good 2nd Class Certificate and I felt my priorities were right. So, bless him, did my father!

Just before Christmas he turned up unexpectedly at home one Saturday evening. We were in the middle of family tea in the dining room.

'Didn't you get my letter?' he asked, since everyone was looking so surprised to see him.

'No, not a word, but anyway it's super to have you home,' replied my mother.

'Oh, well, I'm off to sea,' said father.

Mother's face fell. 'I see,' she said quietly. 'Are we allowed to know where and when?'

'No, I'm afraid not.'

'But are you pleased with the prospect?'

'Yes, very.' And nothing more could we extract from him.

I was still very ignorant about such matters but experienced a strong hunch which I couldn't explain that father was to be Captain of the *Prince of Wales*.

When I left home to join my first ship in early January, 1941, *Prince of Wales* was still not sufficiently completed to take midshipmen and I was temporarily re-appointed first to the Cruiser *Edinburgh* and then to the battleship *Rodney*. Those early days were full of uncertainty and change: short periods spent in a variety of different ships. To some a green Midshipman was an encumbrance unlikely to enhance the busy conduct of the war; to others he was the seedcorn of the future and a potential trade-off in the present if you were prepared to risk giving him opportunities and responsibility. The divergence largely differentiated between the good ship and the commonplace; it still does.

In the course of the next few weeks my father did indeed assume command of *Prince of Wales* so I could no longer go there. To have done so would have invited allegations of nepotism or (much more likely) to have suffered unduly harsh treatment to negate such allegations. I ended up in the Cruiser *Mauritius*, sister ship of the *Fiji*, and found myself the only ex-Dartmouth Entry in a gunroom otherwise composed entirely of ex-public school midshipmen, a situation which exposed me to broader, different points of view and did me a power of good.

Within days we left Scapa Flow for Greenock, there to pick up a convoy and escort it to Freetown in West Africa. In Greenock was the *Fiji* with my friends laughing their heads off at my predicament. Their laughter was short-lived; later that year *Fiji* was sunk off Crete and almost all the gunroom were killed.

Mauritius now started to develop a serious defect. She was one of the first big ships to have a degaussing system incorporated on building as an integral part of her structure. This system, essentially a series of loops of electric cable laid right round the hull through which was passed electric current, was the latest antidote to the magnetic mine and effectively cancelled out the ship's residual magnetism. But it had been the practice to construct the firemain – a series of interconnected pipes also running right round the ship and fed with water from the sea under pressure by special pumps – of copper. Before long it was found that the interaction of the electric current in the degaussing loops and the salt water in the firemain reduced the latter to copper sulphate and resulted in extensive leaks and bursts. This situation caused us to proceed south to Simonstown for repairs.

There we experienced the full meaning of the word 'hospitality', which nowhere is more generously interpreted than by the South Africans. Under the tireless drive of the South African Women's Auxiliary Service every officer and man in a ship's company of some 750 was fixed up with a home to go to in town or country, quiet or boisterous, sporting or with girls, according to his taste. The leading light in this marvellous organization was Lucy Bean, a seemingly mild but charming woman whose genius lay in getting things done, however unlikely, and without fuss.

Later she was to become editor of the Women's column of *The Argus*, one of the main South African dailies. Her efforts generated a debt we were never adequately able to repay.

South Africa had not yet entered the war and most people were eager to stand by Britain and do what they could to help. In Cape Town every day at noon police on point duty blew their whistles and in the shops and public places similar noises were made so that all traffic and movement ceased for two minutes – observed in silence to remember the war. Some less responsible elements endeavoured to prolong Boer War attitudes (though most were far too young to have had any personal memories or experience) and displayed sympathy more towards Germany than Britain. They made futile attempts to break up silent periods by singing, shouting and other noisy demonstrations but were disdainfully ignored and made to look foolish.

One morning my Captain sent for me.

'I thought you would like to know that I have just received a signal saying that *Prince of Wales* has sighted the *Bismarck*.'

This was thrilling news; the chase had been on for some days but hitherto little information had come through. My father had been instrumental in opening fire on the *Bismarck* in spite of his Admiral's instructions to engage the *Prinz Eugen*, which the Admiral had misidentified. But the German gunnery was very accurate; *Prince of Wales* was hit several times and nearly everyone on the bridge was killed. Miraculously my father survived, though he had been flung right across the bridge by the blast and was ruptured and briefly knocked out. Extricating himself from the blood and shambles he took stock of the situation: his ship was not yet worked up; several of the main armament guns were not yet operational and indeed experts from the makers were still on board trying to remedy this; the enemy had clearly 'found the range' and were straddling *Prince of Wales* continually. He broke off the action.

The correctness or otherwise of this decision subsequently provoked some controversy. Admiral Sir Dudley Pond, First Sea Lord and a notorious backseat driver, instructed the Commander in Chief Home Fleet, Sir John Tovey, to court martial my father for withdrawing from action. But this was quickly rescinded when the C-in-C announced unequivocally that if the First Sea Lord were to proceed he would strike his Flag and appear in Court as Prisoner's Friend. Father was awarded the Distinguished Service Order.

This saga emerged later and anyway I had little opportunity to reflect on the action for *Mauritius* was now temporarily repaired and soon we put to sea again, this time bound for operations in the Indian Ocean. These lasted for several months and involved much seatime. Our tasks varied from trying to intercept and destroy enemy raiders, maintaining a presence near strategic islands and supervising the initial setting-up of Port X on Addu Atoll in the Maldive Islands, later to become the RAF Staging Post Gan. But the firemain defect blew up again, this time more seriously, and in October the ship was taken in hand for a proper refit in the Naval Base at Singapore.

Singapore – Gateway to the Pacific. Dominating the Straits of Malacca it lies on the most direct route by sea from the West to China, Japan and the Far East. The island is full of contrasts: the modern high-rise blocks of the business and shopping centres, and the rustic simplicity of the picturesque native kampongs; the impeccable bungalows of the well-to-do, and the squalid ramshackle huts of shanty town; the flooded streets and gushing monsoon drains after a tropical downpour, and the arid dustiness of the laterite secondary roads after only a few hours in the scorching sun. Over all hangs the pervasive, distinctive smell of the East – a mixture of spices, boiling rice, fruit, fish, exotic blossoms and lush tropical vegetation. Lying only three degrees north of the equator Singapore is hot, very humid and almost devoid of seasonal change. In 1941 it was the enervating effect of this year-round high humidity coupled with the relative cheapness of living well and the ready availability of good native servants that inclined the Westerner to lethargy and indolence. The Services were no exception.

The strategic importance attached to Singapore by a British Government 8000 miles away in the face of the imminent Japanese threat was reflected in the Armed Forces stationed there. The Navy could draw on a few obsolete light cruisers and a handful of elderly destroyers – together now with *Mauritius*, but non-operational in dock. Subalterns of the Regiment with which I stayed spent their working hours (0900 to 1300) riding motor bicycles round the rugger field ('always useful to be able to carry a dispatch'); HMS *Queen Elizabeth*'s former 15-inch guns pointed nostalgically, if inflexibly, to seaward. The RAF was equipped with Vickers Wildebeeste biplane torpedo-bombers which, if put into a shuddering dive, could nearly equal the speed of a high performance car today; Brewster Buffaloes provided fighter air defence but could only be operated in daylight.

Not that the evident thinness of the red line occasioned much local apprehension; far from it. Up country in Malaya, where I stayed, the British rubber planters gathered of an evening at their club to discuss the situation.

'What d'you make of it?' one asked.

'The Japs? Well, not much,' another replied.

'Those Nips?' a third chipped in. 'They couldn't do a thing if they tried.'

'Reckon it's all a bluff,' was the unanimous summing up.

'Boy – another round of stengahs.'

And so the evening settled to its familiar pattern with thoughts of war as remote as they were uncomfortable.

Then, early in December, Force Z (*Prince of Wales* and *Repulse*) arrived at the Naval Base and the tempo of life quickened somewhat. The despatch of these ships from Britain and each stage of their passage out to the Far East had been much publicized. The world watched with interest and incredulity; the Japanese licked their lips. It had been intended that the Fleet Carrier *Indomitable* should be with the Force, but she had grounded in the West Indies and no replacement was made available. Clearly the importance of organic air power at sea had not yet been appreciated by Whitehall. In retrospect it is fair to describe this whole operation as a classic example of political expediency leading to the misapplication of too little force too late. This was starkly in my mind when, 41 years later as First Sea Lord, I found myself tendering advice to the Prime Minister on the Falkland Islands crisis.

★

Shortly after the big ships arrived at Singapore I returned from my brief leave in Malaya and dined with my father in *Prince of Wales*. For dinner in the Flagship I had put on Mess Undress (evening uniform equivalent to a dinner jacket) and on arrival on board was surprised to find father, who was meticulous about his dress, still in tropical open-necked shirt and shorts. Though his usual cheerful self he seemed a trifle subdued and I could tell that a nagging anxiety was never far from his mind. Not having seen each other for nearly a year – and a highly eventful year for us both – there was much to talk about alone in his cabin and we quickly slipped back into our old, easy, very close relationship. He had a nearly-finished letter to my mother on his desk and had left space for me to add a tailpiece; it was the last letter home he ever wrote.

After dinner we sat together on the sofa and talked.

'Cigarette?' he tentatively enquired. 'I don't know what bad habits you've fallen into this last year.'

'Thanks,' I replied, taking one. 'You're quite right – I have!'

'What RDF' (Radio Direction Finding – later to be renamed Radar) 'do you have fitted?' he asked next.

'I don't know,' I said after a moment's thought and feeling rather ashamed of my ignorance. In retrospect perhaps it was excusable; I had been in *Mauritius* for nine months and kept watch regularly on the bridge and in the main armament director control tower; never in all that time had I heard the term RDF even mentioned. How quickly that was to change.

'I expect you've got Type 79,' father speculated. This was one of the earliest sets, mounted at the masthead and entirely hand-operated; it gave some rudimentary warning of aircraft approaching at high level.

It was not long before we turned to the subject which was clearly absorbing all his attention: the position of Singapore and the mounting Japanese threat.

'What d'you make of the situation out here?' my father asked.

'Let 'em come,' I replied without thinking. 'Let's have a crack at them.'

Father suddenly looked very grave.

'I don't think you have any idea of the enormity of the odds we are up against,' he said.

And he was right; I hadn't.

We agreed to meet at the Naval Base swimming pool two nights later and I left.

Our poolside meeting proved to be prophetic. It was very hot that evening as there had not been the usual afternoon rain-storm. Being a poor swimmer I merely sploshed about to get cool. Towards 1830 my father remarked, 'I must be getting out soon. I've promised to meet Bill Tennant, Captain of *Repulse*, for a drink before we go back on board.'

'Am I in on that?'

'Yes of course, but don't be too long. I'm just going to swim a couple of lengths. You never know when it may not come in handy.'

Gin and tonic had not yet caught on; the popular drink out there (apart from whisky) was John Collins or Gin Sling. I had not previously met Captain Tennant but took to him at once. Tall, well set-up and with a kindly weatherbeaten face much lined by life in the open from which looked out two shrewd eyes of clear faded blue. He spoke softly and when he did his whole face and eyes creased into lots of little wrinkles. A real countryman as well as a sailor, at home with birds, wild animals and nature.

It was obvious that the two Captains were close friends and held each other in mutual respect. That they were under considerable strain at the prospect which had all the ingredients of a one-way mission was also not hard to discern for the talk was rather desultory – of trivialities and of home. We parted and two hours later Force Z sailed.

I never saw my father again.

I was now temporarily assigned as a Plotter in the War Room in the Naval Base. It involved keeping the positions of British and Japanese ships in the area up to date on a large wall chart. My duties gave me access to most of the incoming operational signals but it was hardly an exacting task since our own ships were virtually all in Force Z and our intelligence on the Japanese Fleet was minimal; but at least it kept me in close touch with events as they developed. From time to time the Service Commanders wandered in together, looked at the wall chart, saw no significant change, had a short chat, muttered, 'About time for a stengah old boy', and wandered out again. It was all very relaxed.

At that time half a squadron of Australian-built Beaufighters was flown in. This was an important reinforcement because these aircraft had a night-fighting capability. But only their Australian pilots could operate them by night and only those same pilots were available to return to Australia to fly up the other half-squadron. On the decision rested a gamble between half a loaf and the risk of no bread. The risk was accepted and the pilots sent back; while they were away the enemy struck.

Force Z sailed from Singapore in the belief that it would get full shore-based air support. Later a signal was received in the flagship stating that with regret the Force must now be prepared to get only weak air support due to air operations elsewhere. Later still, during the afternoon preceding the action, a further signal made clear that there would be no air support at all. The significance of the critical change seemed to make little impact on the Force Commander who continued to steam in a north-easterly direction. Only at about 2000 that night was it decided to turn back and head for

Singapore but, curiously, at reduced speed. No clear aim seemed to have prompted this manoeuvre until an intelligence report of an enemy landing at Kuantan, some 200 miles to the south-west, was received. At this, course was altered to investigate and speed increased.

When dawn broke over the Kuantan area next morning and the Force reached its new objective there was nothing there. Further time was then lost in meandering about in the vicinity in case something turned up. It didn't.

In the middle of the forenoon of that 10 December the Japanese re-located Force Z and attacked with bombs and torpedoes. Nearly 100 aircraft were involved; no request for air support was made from the Force. In the course of the next two hours *Prince of Wales* and *Repulse* were both sunk with heavy loss of life. Subsequently wave after wave of enemy aircraft flew over the survivors in the water and the rescuing destroyers but released no weapons. The Japanese conducted an honourable action from which they emerged with professional credit. They displayed resolute courage and skill, and magnanimity in victory. From talking to them since it is clear that they were amazed at the ease with which they had wrenched the British Lion's tail.

That night when the destroyers arrived back I wandered anxiously along the jetties seeking news of my Father among the weary, shocked, oil-soaked survivors as they came ashore.

'Any news of Captain Leach?' I asked the first batch.

'Sorry, no,' came the reply. 'We're from *Repulse*.'

'Anyone from *Prince of Wales*?' I asked the next lot, but they too were from *Repulse*.

At last I came to a group from *Prince of Wales* and put my question to them. They looked at each other then back at me and shook their heads.

'Was he your father?' asked one older Able Seaman.

'Yes,' I replied. 'Can you tell me if he got away?'

He put his arm around my shoulder and gruffly said, 'He's not here, son. You'd best get back to your ship. There's nothing more you can do.'

I thanked him and dejectedly trudged the mile and a half to the Fleet Shore Accommodation to try the wardroom for news among the officers.

By the time I got there a number of officer survivors had arrived. Again I went from group to group with my question but nobody seemed to know anything and my spirits dropped still further. With mounting hopelessness I approached the last group in the room; they too shook their heads.

Then a big man who had been sitting alone looked up and came over to me. He was, I later discovered, Lieutenant Commander Skipwith, *Prince of Wales*'s First Lieutenant. Gently he took hold of my arm and drew me aside.

'Are you . . .?' he asked.

9

'Yes,' I replied.

Poor man, he was very tired but staunchly faced one more unhappy task in that long, tragic day.

'I'm afraid I have bad news for you,' he said. 'Your father and the Admiral were the last to leave the ship. It was then too late.'

'Do you mean . . .?' I started to ask.

'Several people approached them in the last few minutes,' he went on. 'They urged them to leave as nothing further could be done, but got no reaction. The Admiral stood motionless, stunned by the shock of events; his Flag Captain stood beside him. In life their relationship had been neither very close nor very warm; they were together at the end.'

'Later,' went on Skipwith with infinite sympathy, 'your father was seen in the water looking very blue.'

'Go on, please,' I said. 'Tell me all.'

'He had . . .' he paused, then collecting himself, 'his neck . . . was broken.'

We looked at each other blankly.

'Thank you, sir,' I mumbled.

'I'm very . . . sorry,' he said chokingly. 'He was . . . a fine man . . . and we all loved him.'

I nodded blindly. 'So did I.'

2

OUT

'From the sublime to the ridiculous is only one step.'
Napoleon Bonaparte

Officer Under Training – colloquially known as 'OUT'. Then, as now, the career of an OUT followed a broadly similar pattern. Leave Dartmouth. To sea in the Fleet as a midshipman for about 15 months. Then professional courses as a Sub-Lieutenant at various naval shore establishments for about nine months. Finally back to sea to qualify for Bridge Watchkeeping and Ocean Navigation Certificates and generally to consolidate theory by practice.

But of course in wartime it was different. Midshipmen were required to stand watches in various parts of their ship's armament as well as the normal acquisition of bridge watchkeeping experience to train them as Officers of the Watch in due course. Depending on the level of threat in the area in which the ship was operating, it was usual to maintain about one-third of the gun armament closed up constantly. This led to a pattern of four hours on watch, eight hours off – otherwise known as 'one in three'. In an area remote from likely enemy activity the degree of readiness might be relaxed to one in four. Where the situation was tense and action could occur with little warning at any time, the readiness was tightened accordingly.

Opportunities for the formal instruction of OUTs in wartime were thus limited. On the other hand when on watch you learned a lot from talking to those of greater experience and you really got to know sailors at all levels. Overall you acquired your knowledge the hard way, on the job, and gained a wide variety of experience which served you well in the future.

In December, 1941, at Singapore little attention was paid to training. Apart from the incredulous few who still could not bring themselves to realize that the war was on their doorstep, the thoughts of all were concentrated on escape and survival. The recent shattering loss of *Prince of Wales* and *Repulse* did not enhance the prospects.

The position of *Mauritius* gave increasing cause for concern. Her defects had saved her from sharing the fate of the bigger ships but would they now hold her in a trap when the Japanese invaded – as soon they surely must?

Strenuous efforts were therefore made to reassemble stripped machinery and restore at least the ability to move if not to fight. They were not helped when, a couple of days later, we awoke one morning to an eerie silence in the Dockyard in place of the usual clatter and bustle. There had been an air raid the previous night and the native labour had panicked and run off into the ulu. We now had to fend for ourselves.

At last we were ready – or ready enough. The plan was that we should move from the Dockyard out into the stream to await nightfall, then slip down the Straits under cover of darkness. There was not a man on board who did not expect that at dawn next day we should be subjected to the full treatment by Japanese aircraft and submarines.

Chief Petty Officer Dawson, the Chief Boatswain's Mate and senior Seaman rating, was no exception to this philosophy. He was a great big man, broad and thick and tough. With his sunset complexion and shock of nearly white hair his presence was felt whenever he was around without his having to proclaim it. He was as quick to spot when an inexperienced young sailor was trying (even if unsuccessfully) as when he was not; the latter got short shrift. He was at once the father figure to be loved and the personification of authority to be feared. He himself feared nothing and spoke according to his beliefs. But that afternoon something was wrong and he was quick to sense it. Men were gathered in little groups about the upper deck when they should have been busy securing the ship for sea. Whenever he approached them they shrugged their shoulders, mumbled something and went through the motions of going about their work. But there was no zest, no spirit in how they performed their tasks. Something was very wrong.

By 1430, when the bugle sounded 'stand-easy', he had had enough of this unhealthy atmosphere and reported to the Commander.

'Sir, do you realize that not a stroke of real work is being done on the upper deck of this ship and we're due to shift berth in one hour's time?'

Startled, the Commander gave instructions for the Hands to be fallen in at the end of stand-easy. This was unusual but the cause of whatever was wrong had to be ascertained and corrected.

It transpired that the trouble stemmed from a cat. Evidently *Prince of Wales* had had a black cat as her ship's pet. Shortly before she slipped from the jetty for the last time this animal had been seen by some to walk ashore over the brow. At the time nobody gave much thought to this but in the light of the subsequent disaster several of the survivors recalled the incident and mentioned it to others. Soon the story was widespread. In *Mauritius* we already had three rather scruffy tabby cats which went by the unlikely names of Hodge, Mousse and Hendriksen. Around 10 December these had been joined by a fourth: it was black and instantly it was assumed to be *Prince of Wales*'s cat. The animal having walked on board us, we would be all right.

We were until the afternoon of our planned getaway when *a* cat, which was black so it had to be *the* cat, was seen by some to walk ashore. At once spirits dropped and work virtually ceased.

'After all,' said those questioned, 'what's the point of working further if we're all dead men?'

Search parties were formed to try to find the cat. They were unsuccessful. Meantime the ship was prepared for sea and, as planned, moved out to a buoy and subsequently down the Straits.

Next dawn broke on an anxious Ship's Company with little stomach for the job. We never sighted an aircraft; we never detected a submarine. At best speed we steamed for Colombo and safety.

That evening at about 1730 when I was on watch on the bridge a loud and rather awesome noise welled up from the forward part of the ship. I was quickly sent to investigate. As I got lower down and further forward the noise, now very loud, began to take on a more recognizable form. It was cheering. The cat had been found – it had been on board all the time. Instantly the human tails which had been drooping so dejectedly went vertically up once more. We never looked back.

There is, I think, a moral to this simple yarn of not so long ago. When people are subjected to stress it is often the little things that count for much.

In harbour it was the normal practice for the Midshipman of the Morning Watch (0400–0800) to go on watch half an hour before the Ship's Company turned to. This enabled him to get a proper grip of the situation before shaking the Commander fifteen minutes later.

One morning in *Mauritius* I was called very late. The agitated Boatswain's Mate who shook me apologized for this lapse and was clearly in rather a state.

'There's a bit of a panic on, Sir,' he said. 'The time's getting on and we can't find the Commander to call him.'

It was pointless to waste time in reproving him for not calling *me*. Flinging on my clothes I went on deck. The Commander was nowhere to be found. He was not in his cabin nor on a camp bed on 'X' Gundeck, his usual place if he had elected to sleep in the open because of the tropical heat. After a further prolonged and frantic search, he was located on the Quarterdeck, right aft in the stern.

Arthur Pedder was a serious, clever man with a streak of ruthlessness in him. More at home in aircraft than in ships, he nevertheless had a sound professional knowledge. But he lacked that warmth of rapport with the sailors which is so important and did not display much towards the midshipmen either. Certainly he would not treat this sort of stupid cockup lightly. What was the best way out of the predicament?

Like a petty criminal I unhesitatingly compounded the felony. Calling him especially softly I reported (as usual):

'Good morning, Sir. 0615. Fifteen minutes to Hands Fall In.'

My scheme depended on his falling asleep again. Quickly going to the Quarterdeck's clock, from which the ship's routine was run, I put it back 10 minutes. I did the same to the Wardroom clock nearby, in case he should crosscheck with that. Then hurrying straight back to the Commander I said:

'Five minutes to Hands Fall In, Sir.'

Fortunately he had indeed dropped off again, but roused himself with a start and clearly sensed that something was wrong. However, at my signal the Royal Marines Bugler sounded off the 'G' on his bugle (indicating five minutes to go) – so the Commander was not well placed to remonstrate and needed to get a wriggle on. I then walked forward to the waist where the Seamen had collected (and had been waiting for some minutes, poor fellows) to chat up the Chief Boatswain's Mate and warn him that the Commander might be 'a minute or two late'.

The Commander appeared, hurrying along, peering at his watch and demanding to know what time anybody else made it. But there were reports to be acknowledged and orders to be issued so that the time problem remained temporarily unsolved. The Hands were told off for work. I discreetly withdrew to the Quarterdeck to await the next scene in the mounting drama.

It came quickly and as expected. Storming aft, the Commander bounced into the Quartermaster's Lobby and checked his watch by the clock there. There was, of course, a 10-minute difference. Puzzled, the Commander flung open the door into the Wardroom and glared at that clock – again discovering the same 10-minute difference. He then vented his irritation and frustration.

'I don't know what's the matter with the bloody clocks in this ship this morning,' he thundered at me, 'but they're all bloody well different.'

'Sorry about that, Sir,' I replied innocently, hoping my inward quaking would escape notice. 'I'll send for the Chief Quartermaster' (who is in charge of clocks) 'and have them checked.'

'Do that,' growled the Commander and stumped off.

Success now turned on whether the Commander behaved as was his custom at this time of day, retiring to his cabin to shave. He did and in a flash I had moved both Quartermaster's Lobby and Wardroom clocks on 10 minutes to the correct time.

Then I sent for the Chief Quartermaster.

My sleight of hand had been evident to the Gangway Staff but was never revealed by those loyal souls and was never otherwise discovered. It had been a close-run thing.

Months later when I was about to leave the ship I revealed to the Commander what had happened. He took it very well.

The destroyer *Walpole* had just completed 10 days' boiler clean and maintenance in the naval Dockyard at Rosyth. For months past the ship had been intensively employed on East Coast convoys. Day and night she had acted as sheepdog to the numerous small but important ships carrying from source to factory coal and steel and other cargoes vital to the war effort. In dense fog or under naked sunlit skies, in short, steep, gale-thrashed seas or glassy calm, *Walpole* and the other elderly escorts that could be spared for this task had gone about their risky, necessary business. Regardless of conditions, accurate navigation was crucial to keep the convoys inside the narrow swept channels beyond which a variety of mines dealt swiftly and mercilessly with any stray. By day the enemy bombed and strafed from the air. By night packs of E-Boats, small powerfully armed motor torpedo boats capable of 45 knots, would dash in from the darkness, deliver their lethal load and vanish in all directions. Not a very glamorous war and few actions hit the headlines. But infinitely tiring to the officers and men who had to maintain constant alertness, for the safe arrival of one convoy matched the timely departure of the next. A boiler clean, once every three or four months, offered the sole respite.

This had been a good one. Refreshed and reinvigorated, on the last evening a strong team from the Wardroom had indulged in a final run ashore in nearby Edinburgh. Alas, the blacked-out fair city had had little to offer and everything closed early. But back on board one member of the party proudly revealed that he had acquired a set of pawnbroker's brass balls. With great care and unlimited advice the new owner climbed the foremast and firmly screwed the spoil to the very top.

Next morning *Walpole* and another escort sailed for Scapa. This was a slight change of scene from the more usual run south and probably foretold screening one of the 'heavies' back to Rosyth for maintenance and leave. On reaching the rendezvous it turned out to be the battleship *King George V*, flagship of the Home Fleet until the previous day when the Commander-in-Chief and his Staff had transferred to another ship. The friendly 'good morning' was followed by a routine stationing signal and the little force set course for Rosyth.

Visibility was excellent, the sea was calm and no enemy threat was evident. After a while the observant eye of the Captain of the battleship spotted an unfamiliar object at the truck of *Walpole*'s foremast. Further inspection through binoculars gave no clue as to its purpose and having nothing better to do the Captain decided to find out.

'Chief Yeoman,' he called to the Head of the Visual Communications

Department, 'make to *Walpole*: "What is that object at your foremast-head?"'

'Aye aye, sir,' acknowledged the Chief Yeoman and immediately a signal lamp started to blink out the query.

To the Commanding Officer of the *Walpole*, enjoying the sunshine in his chair on the bridge, receipt of this signal appeared as a slight cloud. He was, of course, well aware in general terms of his officers' activities the previous evening and had been carefully briefed on the addition to his mast. Glinting in the sun it seemed in perfect proportion and filled an otherwise rather empty space. Indeed he rather liked it. But now he had to answer his Senior Officer's question and this created a dilemma. While brevity is the hallmark of naval signalling, he could hardly reply 'balls' to a Post Captain – it would be open to misinterpretation. 'Ikey's Triangle' or 'Edinburgh Memento' seemed trivial and not likely to redound to his ship's credit. After reflection he decided to resort to bluff.

'Signalman,' he ordered, 'reply to *KGV* "RDF Type 236". Oh, and add,' he went on as an afterthought struck him, 'it's very effective!'

On the bridge of the *KGV* no one had heard of RDF Type 236. The Torpedo Officer, who was also in charge of things electrical and electronic, was sent for.

'What's RDF Type 236, Torps?' asked the Captain when his specialist arrived. 'I see *Walpole* is fitted with it.'

The Torpedo Officer did not know. Indeed he had never heard of it before. But he had been brought up never to say, 'I don't know,' and some explanation had to be conjured up.

'Er, I think it is the latest surface detection set, Sir,' he replied, 'designed to give warning of small high-speed craft like E-Boats.'

'Just what we need,' snapped the Captain. 'Are we being fitted with it during our period in Rosyth?'

'No sir.'

'Then I'll make a signal asking the Dockyard to take it on.'

'Chief Yeoman.'

'Sir.'

'Make to Admiral Superintendent Rosyth "Request I be fitted with RDF Type 236 during forthcoming Maintenance Period". And make it Priority.'

'Very good sir.'

Some hours later the reply was received: '*KGV* from AS Rosyth. Regret no knowledge of RDF Type 236. No stores or installation diagrams yet received.'

Again the Torpedo Officer was summoned to the bridge.

'Torps, I'm not going to be put off as easily as this. As soon as we get in I'll send you across to *Walpole* and you can make notes of the installation and hand 'em over to the Dockyard. At least they can wire us up and shorten the fitting time when they do get the equipment.'

'Right sir.'

'Chief Yeoman. Make to AS Rosyth "Your so and so. Request I be fitted for but not with. Installation details will be handed to Dockyard on arrival".

'And make to *Walpole*: "If convenient I should like my Torpedo Officer to visit you immediately on arrival to view installation of RDF Type 236."'

On board *Walpole* time was beginning to run out. Perhaps it had all been a little unwise. But her Commanding Officer was not to be put off lightly either. He sent for his First Lieutenant.

'Number One, we seem to have fallen rather deeper into our own poohtrap than I had intended. *KGV* is sending his Torpedo Officer over on arrival to inspect our "new RDF". I know him slightly. Not a bad chap, if a bit serious. But he likes his glass of grog. Meet him when he comes across, take him down to the Wardroom and give him a few gins to loosen up his perspective before you expose him to our treasure.'

'Certainly sir. Leave it to me. I'll fix him.'

What a blessing to have a resourceful First Lieutenant. *Walpole* would weather the hazard after all. Her Captain sat back contentedly.

Towards the end of the following forenoon *KGV* and her Escorts entered Rosyth. Almost at once the battleship's boat came over with her Torpedo Officer. He stepped on board looking rather dour and evidently not much relishing his assignment. The fact was that he did not really know the first thing about RDF and wiring diagrams had never been his forte.

'Good morning, Sir, and welcome,' said the First Lieutenant jovially. 'Come down to the Wardroom and I'll fill you in on this new set we have. Might as well discuss it in comfort.'

'No thank you, Number One, I am in a hurry. My boat will wait. Please take me straight to the bridge.'

A thin drizzle now set in. It was all that was needed to complete the discomfort of the small group of disconsolate Ship's Officers standing at the back of the bridge and gazing with unseeing eyes at The Brass Thing at the masthead.

The battleship's Torpedo Officer looked very solemn. 'I'd like to go up and inspect it close to. Have you got the Safe to Transmit Boards?'

The Boards, removal of which from the Wireless Office precluded any high power transmission and rendered the masts safe for anyone needing to go aloft, were sent for. The game was up.

Briskly the visitor climbed the vertical ladder up the mast. At the top he paused, examining The Thing intently. Then very slowly he descended.

They looked at him expectantly if miserably. His hands were black with soot from the funnel. His face was devoid of all expression. Not by the flicker of an eye or the twitch of a muscle did he reveal his feelings.

'Thank you,' he said quietly.

'Now you must come down to the Wardroom, sir,' pressed the First Lieutenant, still brimming bonhomie. 'It's cold up there.'

'No. I have to go straight back. My boat alongside please.'

And he left.

In the spring of 1942 I faced my Midshipman's Fleet Board. It was held in the battleship *King George V*, presided over by her charming and very senior Captain Philip Mack, soon afterwards killed in an air crash to the sorrow of all who knew him. The Board took the form of a series of written and oral examinations supplemented by practical tests. One of the latter was Boat-work which involved taking away a Whaler under sail and being put through various manoeuvres. Whalers were standard naval seaboats, used for lifesaving and general work at sea. 27 feet long, Montagu-rigged and manned by a crew of five, they were lively, sturdy craft and handled well under sail or oars.

My examiner turned out to be a large, rather plump, grim-faced Lieutenant who looked as if he needed to shave about three times a day but only managed it once. I think we developed an instant personality clash. To me he seemed humourless, over-bearing and rather scruffy. No doubt to him I was just another young Snotty wasting his time. Overall the circumstances did not seem very conducive to achieving a successful examination result. I stepped into the sternsheets, saluted and reported my name.

'Take the boat away,' my examiner growled, 'and I'll tell you what I want you to do. You're in charge.'

I settled myself at the tiller. All the usual examination tricks were being played: some of the sailor crew were without caps, others had them 'flat aback', yet another was even puffing a cigarette. I squared them off, then rounded on the Lieutenant.

'And you, Sir?'

'I told you – you're in charge,' he gritted unhelpfully.

I took a deep breath. 'Then get down in the boat, sit up straight and hoist your tie close up,' I blurted out.

Evidently this was more than he had bargained for and he was furious. Glaring at me he spat out:

'Leave me out of it. I'm staying here.'

'Oh well,' I thought, 'now I've really upset him. Heaven help me. I'd better get on with it.'

We slipped from the gangway without further ado. There was a stiff breeze blowing and things happened fast. I was told to carry out various

1. My father — killed in action while commanding HMS *Prince of Wales*, sunk by Japanese aircraft off Malaya 10 December, 1941. A great man to whom I was devoted.

2. My mother — strict, fair, full of fun and a greatly loved friend.

3. Yarner — my birthplace and happy early home on the edge of Dartmoor. It had a little bit of everything to do with sport as well as huge, lovely woods mentioned in Domesday Book.

4. HMS *Mauritius*, a 6-inch gun Colony Class Cruiser here shown in her wartime camouflage (1941).

5. HMS *Duke of York* — third of the five *King George V* Class Battleships and Flagship of the Home Fleet 1942-1944

manoeuvres with most of which I was familiar and things seemed to go reasonably well. Then came the final test: back alongside the gangway.

Basically there are two ways of doing this. Approach the gangway at a fine angle and edge up into wind. Or, come in at right-angles, heading for a point a little abaft the gangway and at the last minute put the helm hard down and end up broadside on alongside. If you get it wrong the latter method can involve a smashed boat or gangway but it is quicker and much more fun. My blood was up by this time and I chose the second method. We creamed in and I could feel the tension mounting in my examining officer. In the closing stages he made one half-hearted attempt to intervene but was effectively silenced by my immediate riposte, 'Are you taking back charge of the boat, Sir?'

Fortune favoured me that day and we ended up nicely alongside without mishap. With glowering eyes the Lieutenant told me to carry on to my next examiner.

This was the climax: Captain Mack himself, exhaustively covering all aspects of the duties of Officer of the Watch. On entering his cabin he quickly put me at ease by talking of my father whom he had evidently known well. Then he got down to business. The ordeal was not as bad as I had feared. Most of the questions were predictable and I had done my homework. We had completed the sea aspects and must be nearly at the end of harbour duties. Then came the crunch.

'You have the Middle Watch,' (midnight to 0400) said Captain Mack. 'It suddenly blows up very hard. You are in an open anchorage. What do you do?'

I went through all the usual drill about calling the Commander and Captain, setting an anchor watch in case we started to drag and looking to the safety of the boats.

'Ah, the boats,' exclaimed my examiner. 'What would you do about them?'

'Put the larger ones astern on boat ropes and send the remainder inshore for shelter – assuming I couldn't hoist them.'

'Very good. But now it comes on to blow even more fiercely. The boats struggle back from shore with the disturbing news that there is no shelter there. What next?'

'I'd have to risk it and hoist them, Sir.'

'How? It's now very rough indeed.'

'Spread oil to deaden the force of the waves.'

'And how would you get hold of this oil in the middle of the night?'

'Send down to the Engineer's office, Sir. The Engineer's Writer [a Leading Stoker] always sleeps there.'

'All right. Suppose you have somehow got your oil, how would you spread it?'

A perfectly valid and practical question but way beyond the book. I thought desperately.

'Put the oil in 5-gallon drums, take them up onto the forecastle and pour it over the side.'

'That wouldn't do much good. It would just float down the ship's side.'

'Punch holes in the bottom of the drums, take them out onto the lower boom and lower them on heaving lines into the water, Sir,' I finally hazarded. A brilliant improvisation, I hoped, and one that was really practical. Surely this would do the trick and I could escape to the next question. I had had oil and exhausted my repertoire on the subject.

But it was not the solution required.

'That would be much too close to where the crane plumbs for hoisting boats,' pronounced Captain Mack. 'There would be insufficient time for the oil to disperse and its effect on the waves would be negligible. Try again.'

I thought hard but knew that I was beaten. It was probably best to admit defeat, so I did.

'Take the drums right forward to the Seamen's heads, pour the oil slowly down the pans and keep on flushing them to disperse it into the sea,' said my examiner. He was clearly delighted to have won that round and yet was so gentle and nice about it.

Later I reported again to Captain Mack to hear my results.

'You have gained a very good First Class Certificate,' he said, 'with a special commendation on your Practical Boatwork. Well done,' and he shook me warmly by the hand.

I never saw him again, nor the swarthy Lieutenant.

Because it had been badly damaged by bombs the Torpedo School, HMS *Vernon*, was transferred from Portsmouth to Roedean at Brighton. By then the girls had been evacuated elsewhere but certain signs of former excellence remained to tickle our fancies. In each dormitory was a bell-push and prominently displayed beside it the exhortation 'Ring For A Mistress'. By the time we arrived there neither the bells nor the mistresses were in working order.

Though we worked at Roedean, most of us Sub-Lieutenants slept in St Dunstan's a mile or two further along the road towards Ovingdean. The St Dunstaners had also been evacuated and extra bunks had been installed in all the rooms to take the increased numbers. Each floor at St Dunstan's was readily identifiable by an embossed knob on the bannisters and there were guiderails leading to all parts of the buildings. These facilities could have encouraged nightly excesses among the bright lights of Brighton but wartime conditions severely restricted any such inclinations.

Despite the war our instructional work normally ended at lunch-time on Saturday. One weekend Sub-Lieutenant Peter Bennett and I decided we would take advantage of nearby London and go up for a theatre and an evening's fun. Noel Coward's *Blithe Spirit* (with Margaret Rutherford playing Elvira) was running and for this we had obtained tickets by post. Rashly assuming that overnight accommodation would present no problem, we arrived at Victoria at 1620, giving us (as we thought) ample time to book in somewhere and get to the theatre by half past five – which was the time at which the curtain rose on the evening performance because of the difficulties of the blackout.

'Take us to the nearest hotel please,' I said airily to the taxi driver and off we went.

It was full and we were turned away. The same with the next one. And the next.

The time was now 1710. The taxi driver said he'd exhausted his repertoire of nearby hotels. And we were getting desperate.

'Come on,' I said. 'Surely there must be *some* other hotel close by – we've only been to three.'

'Oh well,' replied the driver facetiously, slightly narked by my disbelief, 'there's Claridge's just round the corner.'

This innuendo was lost on us in our youthful ignorance. 'Then what are you waiting for?' I said sharply. 'Take us to Claridge's – and fast.'

Five minutes later we were standing up to our ankles in the thick pile carpet and surrounded by the palatial luxuriance of the reception desk at Claridge's. A tall, willowy, supercilious receptionist with slicked black hair and a toothbrush moustache was playing the now familiar record that he was full up. With measured glances of extreme disdain he also made it quite clear that he was not accustomed to doing business with Acting Sub-Lieutenants – except perhaps royalty. Over his head the gilt and marble clock showed 1720.

I had had enough and blew my top.

'You miserable little squirt,' I gritted at him, using the familiar term of endearment practised by my sometime Science Master at Dartmouth. 'There you are simpering away behind your cosy desk and lying in your teeth that you're full up. And here are we,' I went on, having by now worked up a head of steam, 'out in the bleak, freezing Atlantic fighting the war for the likes of you. And you have the nerve to try to turn away shipwrecked naval officers. Why even the clothes we stand up in,' (I played my master, not qute honest, stroke and pulled out the front of my ill-fitting uniform monkey jacket) 'are borrowed.'

The ensuing pause was brief and loaded.

'Room 537,' he said.

We dropped our grips, ran to the waiting taxi and made the show just in time. It was a magnificent performance.

Later, after a good supper, we assessed the prospects of our 'evening's fun'. The thing to do, we knew, was to go on to a night club. But since neither of us was a member nor had been to one before we were not too clear how to set about it.

'Do you,' we enquired of several taxi drivers in succession, 'happen to know of a really fun night club that's not too expensive?'

'Ho! Ho!' was the standard reaction. 'I know what *you* mean. *I* don't know no brothels!' And nothing would persuade them to the contrary.

Eventually we entered a rather dubious-looking establishment called, unbelievably, 'The Slip-In'. To pass the gigantic black chucker-out on the door cost us £12 and a good deal of adrenalin. Inside the floor was of plate glass, lit from below; these were the only lights. The band was sleazy but poor. The company unattractive. It had really been a great mistake. We sipped a drink and soon after 0100 left, thankful to brush past Tarzan without being taken apart. And so back to Claridge's.

Tired but buoyant after the vagaries of the evening, no longer did the haunt of Kings and Sheiks hold any fears for us.

'Room 537. We're booked.'

Up in the lift we glided. Along a thickly carpeted, beautifully panelled, dimly lit corridor we padded. The door of Room 537 was thrown open and we stepped through. We passed through a small hall, an exquisitely furnished sitting room, into a large and sumptuously appointed double bedroom (mercifully with twin beds). Beyond lay the bathroom: black marble and mirrors surrounding a sunken pool equipped with an infinity of gold fittings. We arranged a call for 1130 and tumbled into bed. Sleep came quickly.

Later that morning came the call: the knock at the door and jingling telephone perfectly timed, the trolley laden with a magnificent breakfast, six different newspapers. Not *quite* the same as St Dunstan's or indeed any other aspect of naval life that we had yet experienced. Too different? We did not let such thoughts disturb the eating of that delicious breakfast at leisure in bed. Then there were the papers to browse through. And, finally, of course, the bath of a lifetime.

In due course we dressed and took stock of the situation. It was now 1245 and a tiny trickle of cold realization was beginning to run down our spines. What had we done? What staggering sum would we be charged? How on earth were we going to get out of the pit we had dug for ourselves? Anyway we might as well be hung for sheep as for lambs and it was now lunchtime. The cost of lunch could hardly make much difference on top of everything else. We went downstairs.

The Restaurant was crowded, mainly with elderly women wearing that unmistakable look of grannies or maiden aunts. The Palm Court four-piece orchestra strummed Strauss discreetly from the dais. There were very few uniforms and none naval. The entry of two Sub-Lieutenants caused the surprised turning of some heads and the raising of several curious lorgnettes. By the time we were seated at our table all traces of hunger had evaporated and our spinal trickles had become rivulets. We ordered dressed crab and light white wine and discussed our fate in pessimistic mono-syllables.

By 1400 there seemed little point in further prolonging suspense. When execution is imminent it is best to get on with it. Pale with apprehension and with legs like jelly we went up to the cashier and asked for our accounts. They came to twenty-nine shillings each.

I next stayed at Claridge's 16 years later on my wedding night. Their benevolence was less marked.

The Torpedo Course was the last in the series, the other main ones (Gunnery, Navigation and Signals) having been completed previously. Together with my Fleet Seamanship Board I had achieved the target of five First Class Certificates which led to my award of a prize '£10 worth of books or instruments'. I applied for a sword (which in those days was an obligatory article of uniform and cost precisely £10) but was informed that it was not an instrument. Next I tried for a telescope (also a necessary article) but that too was disallowed. Finally I ended up with a bundle of extraordinarily dull text books. But I was now a confirmed Sub-Lieutenant and could look forward to getting back to sea.

3

THE LIGHTER SIDE OF WAR

'It's being so cheerful keeps me going'
Anona Wynne (ITMA)

A bright winter's sun tempered the frosty crispness and tried unsuccessfully to melt the late traces of snow as I climbed the long gangway on to the huge quarterdeck of *Duke of York* in January, 1943. For once the waters of the Firth of Forth were mirror-calm and the colours of the hills around Rosyth, all greens and browns and mossy softness, were at their most beautiful.

The battleship lay at a buoy, the epitome of the newest, the best and the most powerful in the Royal Navy. She was a sister ship of the *Prince of Wales*. Dominating her long, sleek fo'c'sle were the six massive 14-inch guns of the two forward turrets. Then came the superstructure, towering upwards to the bridge, air defence position and main armament director control tower. Amidships the eight twin 5.25-inch turrets of the secondary armament flanked the two tall, upright funnels on each of which were mounted searchlights. Further aft the mainmast merged into more superstructure, secondary armament directors, and finally the quarterdeck with the after 14-inch turret. In between, everywhere, bristled close range anti-aircraft guns: multiple 2-pounder pom poms and 20mm Oerlikons. 35,000 tons of the ultimate in power and naval technology, with her dark grey hull and light grey upperworks glinting in the clear light she was a sight to stir even the most insensitive. This handsome giant was to be my floating home for the next two and a half years.

Partly for domestic convenience and partly from tradition the officers in a big ship were divided into three separate Messes for eating and general off-duty living. Midshipmen slept in hammocks (like the sailors) but the rest had cabins of varying degrees of comfort and numbers of inmates. The more senior officers, ranging from lieutenants to commanders, messed in the Wardroom – a large compartment just forward of the quarterdeck. On the deck below was the Warrant Officers' Mess housing those officers who, after years as ratings, had merited well-deserved promotion by reason of their experience and specialist expertise: older men and the salt of the earth from whom us youngsters learnt a great deal. Opposite the Warrant Officers' Mess lay the Gunroom with the Sub-Lieutenants and Midshipmen. The Captain's and Admiral's quarters (known as 'the cuddy') were right aft in the stern.

My appointment was as Sub-Lieutenant in charge of the Gunroom. There were forty-three of us including ten other Subs (two of whom were 'under report' for various misdoings); one of the Reserve Midshipmen had already been subjected to three Boards of Enquiry in the East Indies Fleet. It was a mixed bag – mixed in age, in experience, in attitude and in conduct.

I was soon put to the test. One of the Royal Naval Volunteer Reserve Sub-Lieutenants had become thoroughly disenchanted with the way of life in a battleship which spent quite long periods in harbour; keeping watch on the quarterdeck bored him rigid. He yearned for more seatime, more excitement and the greater variety of activities in a small ship. He had continually applied for transfer to a destroyer but invariably his applications had been turned down. Now he was desperate and determined to get his way by fair means or foul. The 'normal channels' had been exhausted.

That night he made his way aft to the cuddy where the Captain was giving a dinner party to thank the local shore and dockyard authorities for their hospitality and help during the ship's stay at Rosyth. On reaching the cuddy door he dropped to the deck on his hands and knees and, taking a deep breath, started to scratch up and down on the door with his finger nails. It was not long before the Captain called out.

'Come in.'

He ignored this and went on scratching.

'COME IN,' roared the well-known voice from within.

Still no reaction.

Irritated, the Captain strode to the door and flung it open. Instantly the Sub rushed past him on all fours into the cabin, barking like a dog. One brisk circuit of the cuddy was sufficient to paralyse the guests and send flying various small tables laden with glasses and coffee cups before half knocking down the Captain and rushing out.

At this I was sent for and given clear instructions. The officer left the ship next morning.

Sailing for the first time under the Forth Bridge in a battleship was an awe-inspiring experience. As the massive structure of the bridge drew near it seemed impossible that the radar aerials on top of the tall masts, towering upwards above the great bulk of the ship, would not be knocked off. Indeed as far as practicable they had already been lowered slightly to provide a better margin of safety and of course the state of the tide had been carefully checked. Even so the whole venture looked improbable and I confess to breathing a sigh of relief when we slid past underneath with feet to spare.

Scapa Flow had not changed when we arrived there two days later.

Treeless but softened by rolling cushions of heather and batches of grass close-cropped by the few miserable sheep; utterly desolate and yet with a wild beauty of its own when the gales ceased and the sun shone.

My Action Station was in the main armament Transmitting Station (or Fire Control Room as the Americans more lucidly called it). Deep down in the bowels of the ship, it was a large compartment fitted with an intricate maze of mechanical calculating machines. Into them were fed electrically from the Director Control Tower high up above the bridge the target's present position (observed visually through binoculars) and its estimated course and speed. The machines computed the target's movement during the time of flight of the projectile (i.e. from the moment of firing to the moment of splash) and hence its future position when the projectile landed. This was then converted to the necessary aim-off in both elevation (vertically) and training (horizontally) required by the guns to hit the target. By following the pointers in their receivers the turrets were trained on to the right bearing and the guns elevated individually for the range in use.

It was a fascinating nerve-centre presided over by the Dagger Gunner, a Lieutenant risen from the ranks and with a lifetime of gunnery experience behind him. Basil Charlton was a man of brilliant intellect in his early fifties; sharp as a needle, he had a curiously young face despite its deep lines and his thin sandy-white hair. His piercing light blue eyes missed little and although he would conduct his side of a conversation briskly and concisely, he gave the impression that his mind was really elsewhere on other, higher things. His depth of knowledge of the more intricate aspects of gunnery was profound. He was also remarkably clever and versatile with his hands and in the course of a few four-hour watches would produce an immaculate pair of chamois leather gloves or a board with a whole range of old fashioned knots in fine cord, many of them unknown in the Navy of 1943. I was the only other officer in the Transmitting Station, the remainder being Royal Marine Bandsmen following a long-standing tradition. The secret of success lay in knowing the right corrections to apply to ensure hitting the target under varying circumstances coupled with close teamwork. By the time we arrived at Scapa I had been fully integrated.

It was as well, for after a few days we hoisted the flag of Admiral Sir John Tovey, Commander-in-Chief Home Fleet, and sailed in a hurry on operations. Intelligence had been received that the German battleship *Tirpitz*, sister ship of the *Bismarck*, had left her Norwegian fjord base and might either be about to attack one of our convoys bound for Russia or else attempt to break out into the Atlantic through the Iceland–Faeroes gap to intercept convoys from North America. For days and nights we carried out sweeps through the likely areas, accompanied by our escorting destroyers, but the search was in vain. When it was finally abandoned we put into Hvalfjord in Iceland to refuel from a tanker sent there for the purpose.

That night I was due to keep the Morning Watch (0400 to 0800) on the quarterdeck. It was bitterly cold and blowing half a gale so that conditions were marginal for the tanker lying alongside. On taking over I found my predecessor, an excellent RNVR Lieutenant, Jimmy Nesbit (and in fact the Senior Watchkeeper) in a bad state of nerves.

'What's the matter?' I asked.

'My God,' he replied, 'I reckon I've had it.'

'What on earth are you talking about?' I demanded and then he told me his problem.

'I'd just taken over the watch,' he said, 'walked round the upper deck, checked the wires securing the tanker, looked at the boats and everything was quiet and correct. You know how freezing bloody cold it is out there so I popped into the Wardroom to warm up by the electric fire for a few moments. I suppose it was about half past midnight when the Quarterdeck Messenger came in and said, "Sir, the Commander-in-Chief is on the quarterdeck in his pyjamas and wants to speak to the Officer of the Watch'."

Nesbit was tired and cold and hadn't really hoisted in what the Messenger had said.

'Go away,' he replied 'and leave me alone.' He went on warming himself.

A few minutes later the Quartermaster (a Petty Officer and senior member of the Gangway Staff) entered with the same message. The situation was plainly ridiculous and Nesbit became irritated.

'Get out,' he said 'and stop bothering me with all this silliness.'

The Quartermaster withdrew.

Some time afterwards the Admiral's Orderly, a young Royal Marine specially selected for his smartness and bearing, appeared in the Wardroom, crashed to attention and gave a quivering salute.

'What's up with you, then?' enquired Nesbit.

'Sir,' stammered the young Marine, 'the Commander-in-Chief wishes you to report to him in his cabin immediately. And sir,' he went on, 'he . . . seems rather angry.'

A tiny icicle began to form at the base of Nesbit's spine. Could there be more to this after all? Admirals' Orderlies didn't normally go about in the middle of the night with messages purporting to come from the C-in-C unless something was up. Oh Lord! Had he got it all wrong? 'I'd better go down,' he thought and followed the Orderly aft to the cuddy.

On the way he wracked his brains for some convincing explanation which would fit the facts and extricate him from his apparently impossible predicament. He could hardly say he'd been doing rounds because evidently he hadn't; nor that he had not got the message because evidently he had –

all three. The plain truth was that he was cold and tired and it was all so absurdly improbable that he had dismissed it out of hand without thinking it through – but he couldn't possibly say so to his Commander-in-Chief.

Or could he? There wasn't a more promising alternative. 'Lumme,' he thought, 'I'm really for it this time.' They reached the Admiral's Quarters. The door of the Day Cabin was open; just inside, feet well apart, arms akimbo and now attired in a dressing gown, stood the C-in-C.

'Are you the Officer of the Watch?' he snapped.

'Yes sir.'

'Then why the hell didn't you report to me on the quarterdeck when I sent for you earlier?'

'Well sir . . .' started Nesbit, desperately dredging his shock-numbed brain for a last minute let-out. And then, finding none, he blurted out,

'The Messenger and the Quartermaster both said you were on the Quarterdeck in your pyjamas and . . . well sir, here we are in Iceland in the middle of winter and it's blowing fit to bust – it seemed so ridiculous that I knew it couldn't be right so I sent them packing. It was only when your Personal Orderly . . .'

'Get out,' thundered Jack Tovey.

And gratefully he did.

To this day Jimmy Nesbit has never learned why he had been sent for. Nor have I.

In the summer of 1943 my Captain sent for me. George Creasy exemplified all a good Naval Officer should be: professionally able, intelligent, firm, kind, good-humoured, a gentleman to his fingertips. With his grizzled grey hair, shaggy eyebrows, steely grey eyes and jutting chin he looked what he was, a real seagoing commander. The Ship's Company of *Duke of York* adored him and when he was promoted to Rear Admiral used to cheer him whenever he appeared in public.

'Good morning Sub,' he said as I entered his cabin. 'I've been looking into your future. My secretary has worked out that you should be getting your second stripe [i.e. be promoted to Lieutenant] at the beginning of October; you could then either go to a destroyer or stay here and take on "A" Turret and the Forecastle Division. What do you think?'

This was a bombshell but the choice was not difficult. A 'destroyer' might, in practice, mean anything from a local escort vessel operating around the coast to a Fleet destroyer working from Scapa. But at the age of barely 20 to relieve an RN Lieutenant with 7 years' seniority and assume responsibility for 40% of the main armament of the Home Fleet Flagship in war, together with the welfare of the men who manned and operated it, was not a chance to be missed. In addition *Duke of York* was a highly efficient and happy ship. I opted to stay.

'A' Turret proved to be an absorbing task. Below the massive turret housing the four 14-inch guns and the only part visible at upper deck level was the trunk or barbette forming an integral part of the revolving structure. This central tube extended down to the bottom of the ship and through it the ammunition was fed to the guns. At the lowest level, to provide maximum protection, was the Cordite Handing Room with the four magazines forming the sides of a square round the central barbette. Each magazine contained sufficient cordite charges (propellant) for two hundred rounds per gun. For ease of handling the charges were broken down into four sausages, each weighing three quarters of an hundredweight. They were stowed in aluminium cylinders, withdrawn by hand and fed into a hydraulic lift which raised them to the height of the Cordite Handing Room. This difference in level allowed the various electric and hydraulic leads to pass from the fixed structure via a swivel to the revolving structure. To prevent a flash-back from an explosion from reaching the magazines the hatch between magazines and Handing Room was sealed by a heavy brass door, pushed up automatically by the hydraulic lift. Once in the Handing Room the charges were again manhandled across from the fixed to the revolving structure and fed into the main cordite hoist.

Shells were stowed at the next higher level. The arrangements between the Shell Rooms and the Shell Handing Room were similar to those for cordite except that every movement was by hydraulic grab or ram; with each shell weighing three-quarters of a ton no manual handling was possible.

At a certain stage it was necessary to open out each set of shell and charges from its concentrated central hoist to allow for the greater distance apart of the guns. As with a garden fork the 'handle' opened out to form the four 'prongs'. This was achieved at the level above the Shell Handing Room, known as the Traverser Space. Ammunition from the central hoist was traversed outwards to align it with the separate route for each individual gun.

The machinery in this compartment was powerful and fast-moving. Not long previously in another ship of the same class an Ordnance Artificer working on the hydraulics had slipped and as he fell, grabbed the nearest thing to hand; it happened to be the Traverser Lever and within two seconds the Traverser had whipped across and squashed him as flat as a swatted fly. An interlock was then installed to prevent a similar fatal accident.

From the Traverser Space the shells and cordite charges were hydraulically rammed through connecting tubes into the Gun Loading Cages at the bottom of the gunwell in the turret itself. Thence they were raised to their final loading level and rammed into the breeches of the guns.

What with the whine of the various hydraulic pumps, the squelch of the control valves being moved, the clang of the flash doors at every stage and the rattle of the rammers and the cages, a loading cycle was a noisy operation and called for good drill since few orders after the initial ones could be heard above the din. It was important that the many different operations at the various levels during a loading cycle were closely co-ordinated and performed in the correct sequence. Visual observation was not possible at all stages because of the multiplicity of flash doors. Were a gun to be loaded with cordite but no shell, for example, this would not be visible and would result in ineffectual delay in action. Or if two shells were inadvertently rammed into the same breech there would be a ghastly jam. To prevent such accidents and the consequent damage to men or machinery a series of 'interlocks' were fitted throughout the turret. There were over fifty of these, each making it impossible to carry out the next element of a sequence until the previous one had been properly completed. But if something went wrong it sometimes became necessary to trip an interlock manually and accept the consequent risk.

A Petty Officer was in charge of each stage of the loading cycle and another, or a Leading Seaman, in charge of every self-contained compartment such as a magazine. An experienced Leading Seaman or Petty Officer was Captain of each gun. The Captain of the Turret was a Chief Gunner's Mate, the highest gunnery qualification open to a rating and one backed by lengthy training and much experience. He occupied a position towards the rear of the gunhouse from where he could take charge of the loading cycle and drill generally. The Officer of the Turret, a Lieutenant or Lieutenant-Commander, sat in a bucket seat between the two centre guns at the front of the gunhouse. His view of the world outside was limited to a periscope which projected through the roof of the turret; most of the time it was drenched in spray or caked in salt or ice. From gunhouse to magazine fifty men manned each gun and the combined total equated to the Ship's Company of a Fleet Destroyer.

'Ammunition is perfectly safe until you forget that it is dangerous,' ran the old adage. Daily inspections of all magazines and shell rooms were obligatory at sea and in harbour and only a strictly limited selection of officers and ratings were authorized to draw the keys of these compartments which were invariably kept locked when not manned. The complexity of a four-gun 14-inch turret was considerable and many of the remoter spaces were small and difficult of access. I used to aim at crawling into every nook and cranny once a month. This was a strenuous, sweaty undertaking and for the purpose I would strip to underpants and overalls, and go alone.

One day I was due to take over as Officer of the Watch on the quarterdeck for the Afternoon Watch (1230 to 1600). Other affairs had crowded out my forenoon and it was nearly midday when I suddenly remembered that I had not yet carried out my magazine rounds. If I was quick there would still just be time. Flinging off my clothes I scrambled into my overalls, grabbed a torch, checked that the keys were still drawn (indicating that the Sweepers in charge of cleaning those compartments were still on the job) and hurried off to my turret.

Nobody was about when I arrived in the Cordite Handing Room but the doors to the magazines were open and I climbed into the first one to start my inspection. All was well and I passed through to the second. Nothing untoward there either, but when I came to emerge into the Handing Room I found the door locked. This caused me slight surprise but no anxiety since I could easily retrace my way back into the first magazine and get out from there. This I did, only to find that the exit there was also locked. The situation now became more ominous: I was locked up in my own magazine and nobody knew it. At that moment all the lights went out.

Still there was no real cause for concern. The lights were always switched off when the magazines were not occupied for fear of fire; but I had my torch. Again because of fire risk there were no telephones or other means of communication inside magazines. However, it was now noon; at 1315 the Ship's Company would have finished their dinners and would restart work; the Magazine Sweeper would again draw the keys and open up; I should miss my lunch and be very late on watch but it was entirely my own fault and in fact it would make quite an amusing yarn on which to dine out. Served me right for going it alone. I leant against the bulkhead and waited philosophically.

Then a more disturbing thought struck me. That afternoon the Ship's Company had been granted a special Make-and-Mend (half holiday). Nobody would open up at 1315; indeed nobody was likely to turn up until 0730 next morning. The prospect was now much more bleak and already the penetrating chill from being in an unheated steel box, well below the waterline, in Scapa Flow during winter, dressed only in a pair of thin overalls, was beginning to sap my confidence. There was nowhere to lie down; nowhere to sit; nothing even to lean against except cold steel. I had to get out. But how?

There was only one conceivable way; to follow the route of a cordite charge, climb into the lift, prize open the heavy flash door and crawl through into the Handing Room. From there I could move freely about the turret, get access to external telephones and summon help. I set about my escape.

Though slight of build it was a tight fit as I wormed my way into the narrow tunnel that housed the lift. If possible the darkness there was even more intense. Switching on my torch I struggled to lift the flash door and quickly discovered the fallacy in my plan. The door was some three foot square and made of three-quarter-inch solid brass. In the course of numerous attempts to lift it, not helped by lying prone on my back, able to use my arms only from the elbows down because of the confined space, I raised it at best about nine inches leaving insufficient gap through which to crawl. By now I was panting from my exertions, sweating streams in spite of the cold, and temporarily exhausted.

As soon as I had recovered I slithered my way back into the magazine and armed myself with one of the brass tools for unscrewing the lids of the cordite cases before returning to my prone position on the lift. With this tool I hoped to ease the flash door up higher and, more importantly, jam it in the open position to enable me to clamber through. The manoeuvre demanded nice timing for I only had the strength to hold the door in the up position for a few seconds; and I only had two hands! Settling myself in what I thought was the optimum position on the lift I took a deep breath and set to.

Switch on the torch. Place it where it will throw light on the job. Position the case-opening-tool ready for wedging the door. Now for the door itself. Lift . . . shove . . . arch the back . . . push . . . brace the feet . . . it's moving, it's gone up three inches . . . six inches . . . nine inches . . . keep going, strength ebbing, speed up . . . got to get it up another nine inches, one last effort, *heave* . . . it's there, quick, in with the wedging tool . . . got it, sink back exhausted.

CRASH! Pitch blackness. Silence.

Oh God, what's happened? I fumbled around with aching muscles and fingers too stiff and sore to sense much. The gap had gone, the flash door was down again; no sign of the tool and only the bottom bit of my torch. Evidently in lying back to rest, my elbow had nudged the wedging tool, dislodged it and it had fallen away. In crashing down the door had chopped my torch in half. Phew! 'Count your lucky stars, son,' I thought; 'instead of your torch it might have been your arm, or the soft part of your belly where there's not much bone, or your neck . . .' Ugh. I shivered.

No tool. No torch. No hope? Never give up. There must be another tool somewhere. Try harder.

Gritting my teeth I fought back my aching fatigue and wriggled out into the magazine again. My only remaining chance, so slim as almost to be discounted, lay in once more jacking up that bloody flash door even by a couple of inches so that I could hear if anyone came down into the lower quarters, and call for help. What a travesty of optimism! But there was no alternative. No way could I attempt to escape again.

By now I was jittering with cold once more and every movement was painfully slow. It took nearly an hour of groping in the darkness to find another tool, creep back into the lift, prize up the flash door by a narrow crack, and wedge it. With infinite care, my face pressed close to the tiny opening and with every muscle complaining viciously, I stretched out and waited.

Important not to fall asleep – that way hypothermia sets in more quickly. Sleep? How *could* I when my whole frame was shaking like a tumble-drier? Wriggle the toes, clutch and unclutch the fingers, keep moving the inch or two possible – ouch, it's all so *sore* – but must keep the circulation going somehow. I tried to think of what I should have been doing on the quarterdeck; silenly repeated various pieces of poetry I had learned; mentally roamed over a whole range of topics, but always my mind drifted back to feeling sorry for myself. This was absurd. I had only myself to blame for pushing my luck too far and ending up in this pot mess. There was little comfort to be derived from self-pity. It was a long afternoon.

Hours later I fancied I heard a faint noise in the direction of the Shell Handing Room above. Was it real? Or was it just another figment of an overstretched imagination? I pressed closer to the crack and peered out as best I could. Yes – surely that was a chink of light somewhere? I shouted. The light grew stronger. Now I could hear the clang of footsteps on the metal ladder leading down to the Cordite Handing Room beside me. Then the figure of a very young Ordnance Artificer Apprentice came within my limited field of view. Ah the relief! I called out to him to come over to my crack so that I could instruct him what to do. The result was disastrous: the boy, knowing that nobody could possibly be in a magazine at the time, turned ashen white, dropped his toolbag on to the deck and bolted back up the ladder.

It took a full half hour to coax him back, get him to contact someone authorized to draw the magazine keys, and let me out. The time was coming up to 1800.

The Officer of the Watch who had stood in for me took a lot of convincing before he believed my unlikely story and even then he was not amused. And the young Apprentice? I don't suppose he has forgotten his encounter with the Ghost of 'A' Turret. Nor has the Ghost.

In May, 1944, General Montgomery paid a short, informal visit to the Home Fleet in Scapa Flow. He stayed overnight in the Flagship, *Duke of York*, as guest of the Commander-in-Chief, Admiral Fraser.

We were all rather intrigued and pondered on how this funny little man, who sported a blue and white spotted handkerchief in the breast pocket of his British Warm and sacked his Commanders overnight, would go down. We wondered if he would stick to his alleged habit of going to bed at 2200 and being up by 0600 in the morning. Why was he coming all this way and what on earth would the fellow do? Bit of a gimmick all round, we concluded, and were thoroughly disparaging about it.

Next morning at 0915 it fell to me to show him round the gunhouse of my turret and to demonstrate how the huge 14-inch shells were loaded. Neither my Gunhouse Crew nor I much relished the prospect. It was a quick, put-up job and we all felt we had better things to do than give token demos to cranky Generals.

Monty arrived on the fo'c'sle promptly, neatly attired in battledress and the familiar black beret with its twin badges.

'Good morning, sir. "A" Turret ready for your demonstration.'

'Good morning.' He shook hands and fixed me with a friendly piercing eye.

Briefly I ran through what he would see during the loading cycle. He listened with close attention and asked a few questions. It was a crisp yet curiously intimate, personal conversation which seemed to be of intense importance to him.

'Would you like to meet my Captain of Turret and the Captains of the four Guns, sir?'

'Yes please.'

I introduced them and he spoke individually to each one for perhaps two minutes.

Then we stood back and watched the loading cycle. As usual the noise was such as to drown all further conversation. When it was over and the rattle and clatter of machinery had ceased Monty turned to me.

'*Thank* you,' he said, 'and good luck.' He left the turret.

We dispersed and went about our various duties. There was not a single man to whom he had spoken who was not now absolutely sure of the real reason why General Montgomery had come to Scapa – to see *him*.

4

NIGHT ACTION

To set the cause above renown
To love the game beyond the prize
To honour while you strike him down
The foe that comes with fearless eyes.
Sir Henry Newbolt

Between 1941 and 1943 more than twenty convoys had been run through to Russia. In the early days these had provided vital military supplies for the prosecution of the war on the Eastern Front. Losses en route had been sustainable, though the risks had been high. Often the greatest enemy was the weather.

In those Northern seas in winter the temperature was normally so low that men abandoning a sinking ship could seldom survive for more than three minutes in the icy water before paralysing numbness overcame them. Fierce gales were laced with driving snow squalls, reducing visibility to a few yards and whipping the angry crests off the waves to freeze on the steel of ships' weatherdecks. Icing was a serious hazard: the guardrails (running round a warship's upperdeck to prevent men falling over the side), normally as thick as a finger, would build up with the ice to the thickness of an arm. The resultant increase in topweight and hence reduction in stability were a constant anxiety. So too was any effective means of reducing it – men with chipping hammers slithering about the glassy decks whenever the sea state permitted. Special oils were devised for the hydraulics and the lubrication of machinery. Canvas covers packed with heavy grease were kept over the muzzles of the guns to prevent the barrels from filling with water and freezing into a solid icebar. The first round fired was always a solid (unfused) shell to blow the obstruction clear but there remained the nagging worry of how much ice had been formed and the possibility of a burst barrel.

Most depressing was the light. In winter, apart from two to three hours of twilight in the middle of the day, it was dark all the time and the strain on Commanding Officers and their Officers of the Watch was substantial. This especially affected the destroyers and escorts with their low freeboard and open bridges. In summer it was light throughout the twenty-four hours and knowledge that enemy air, submarine and surface forces were poised not far off generated an acute feeling of nakedness.

The impact of this hostile environment on the human frame was aggravated by the need for constant alertness, the problems of eating and sleeping during violent ship motion, of getting dry and warm in the few hours before the next turn of duty, and the physical effort of constantly bracing muscles to maintain balance against the heaving structure. The cumulative effect of operating under these conditions was to generate fatigue and stretch stamina to the limit.

By early 1943 the real contribution to the war of continuing to run such convoys had decreased markedly. On the other hand the enemy threat in those Northern waters had been maintained at much the same level. For although the U-Boat threat had been reduced somewhat the surface element (now the battleship *Tirpitz*, the battlecruiser *Scharnhorst* and the pocket battleship *Lutzow* together with destroyers) was stronger than previously. Thus the military case for further Russian convoys had become thin and indeed turned mainly on their value as 'bait' to tempt the German surface forces into action. The convoys ceased.

But there were also political considerations and by the autumn it was decided to re-start the convoys later that year. Paradoxically the conditions for the reception of the ships at the Russian terminal were hopelessly inadequate. It appeared that the Russians, far from being grateful for vital war stocks run through at considerable risk and at the cost of many brave lives, went out of their way to be difficult and obstructive.

The merchant ships berthed at Murmansk, one of the gloomiest towns in the northern hemisphere. Repeatedly bombed by the Germans from airfields just across the Norwegian frontier, it had been reduced to a state of rubble and dejection. In winter the uncaring inhabitants shuffled about like ghosts. In summer the whole town stank with a stench so vile as to be hardly bearable. The disorganization, muddle and inefficiency on the part of the shore authorities were incredible and the effect on the morale of the seamen, who had been through so much to get the supplies through, was deep.

Conditions were no better for the escorting warships. They were allocated an open anchorage at Vaenga, to seaward of Murmansk in the same Kola Inlet. It was a bad choice, exposed to the elements and with unsuitably deep water and a poor bottom for holding so that much of the time spent there necessitated an undesirably high state of preparedness against the weather – short notice for steam which precluded the much needed maintenance of machinery and weapons; and extra watchkeeping for officers and men already tired from their arduous sea passage. The threat of air attack with very little notice was constant and led to a continuous readiness being kept.

Being in Kola was like being in a trap with the knowledge that it might be sprung at any moment. The amount of rest and relaxation obtained was commensurate and nearly everyone was glad to put to sea again where they felt that at least they were 'in with a chance'.

Admiral Sir Bruce Fraser, Commander-in-Chief Home Fleet, knew all this from his Commanding Officers with whom he kept in close touch. Now, with the restarting of the convoys, he determined to visit Kola to see things for himself and to try to sharpen the Russian Commanders into doing better. Flying his flag in the battleship *Duke of York*, he sailed from Scapa Flow with the cruiser *Jamaica* and four destroyers to provide distant cover to Convoy JW 55A which had left Loch Ewe on the West coast of Scotland on 12 December.

At that time I was a young Lieutenant of 20 in *Duke of York*. My action station was Officer of the Quarters of 'A' Turret – four 14-inch guns each firing a shell of over ¾ ton to a range of 18 miles and each manned by fifty men.

Sailing from Scapa was not in itself an event which aroused much excitement. Such sorties from the Home Fleet Base were not unusual and normally presaged a sweep north in support of a Russian convoy or to back up the Carrier Squadron in shore attack operations off the Norwegian coast. But this occasion was marked by an incident which seemed to be particularly significant. A few days before, our own Captain (Brian Schofield) after only three weeks in command, had hurried south to stand by his wife who was desperately ill. Twenty-four hours before we sailed Guy Russell transferred to us from *Nelson*, an unusual occurrence which led the discerning to suspect that something out of the ordinary was impending. Guy Russell was a wonderful man, big in every sense of the word – physically, in leadership, in charm and in his understanding of human nature. He had a well-developed and unique method of registering commendation or reproof to his subordinates, based on his intimate knowledge of London. For the former he would grin and drawl 'Bond Street', while a coldly growled 'that was pretty Whitechapel' had the opposite effect. His repertoire was extensive and contained much finesse.

The visit to Russia, though the first of its kind by a British battleship, was unremarkable. We entered in a howling snowstorm and left a few days later in another one. If there was one overriding impression gained by everyone it was the almost total lack of life. Even the few people with whom fleeting contact was sought seemed automatons who were more dead than alive. In the bitter darkness of those northern wastes, with everything insulated by snow, an eerie, muffled, utter silence pervaded all.

Duke of York, *Jamaica* and their escorts returned south to Akureyri in Iceland to refuel. On the night of 23 December they put to sea again in distant support for the next convoy which had sailed from Loch Ewe three days earlier. It was this latter convoy, JW 55B, leaving as the slower earlier JW 55A arrived at Kola, that it was hoped would provide irresistible bait to the German surface forces lurking ready to pounce in the North Norwegian fjords. Further bait was provided by a third convoy, RA 55A, sailing south from Kola on 22 December with a heavy destroyer escort. To the north additional distant cover came from the cruisers *Belfast* (wearing the flag of Vice Admiral Robert Burnett, commanding the 10th Cruiser Squadron), *Norfolk* and *Sheffield*. This British trap was now set; would the Germans spring it?

From the outset the weather was bad and steadily deteriorated into a full gale from the North East. Visibility was indifferent, not helped by the long Arctic night. It was still in the early days of radar (then called RDF); by today's standards the sets were crude, limited in range, lacking in discrimination and much degraded by sea returns in bad weather. Blind fire (i.e. with no external visual point of aim) by the gun armament was still being pioneered and its accuracy, especially in terms of observing the fall of shot, was uncertain. These factors were relevant when considering the range at which to fight an action under conditions of darkness, high winds and rough seas.

At 2000 on the evening of Christmas Day *Duke of York* went to Night Action Stations. This was a normal procedure at that time and was sensible in that it enabled men to close up at their quarters, clear away the armament in an orderly fashion and then break down to the more relaxed second degree of readiness throughout the night. This avoided a disruptive changeover from a lower to a higher degree of readiness if contact with the enemy occurred unexpectedly. It was very cold and the few radiators inside the turret were quite inadequate for the conditions. The weather had deteriorated further and even a great ship like *Duke of York* was bucketing about in a manner which precluded anyone lying on a camp bed for long. Few slept much. Over all hung an air of expectancy and uncertainty. What was the enemy up to? When would we meet him? Would we meet him at all? Doubts on the latter generated the greatest anxiety.

We did not meet him that night. But soon after the black dawn of a long, dark, storm-ridden Boxing Day, cold and fatigue were ameliorated by definite news of our impending target and for the first time the real prospect of action that day. *Scharnhorst* had attacked the convoys but had been successfully intercepted and had withdrawn, later to attack again from a different quarter and again be driven off. This was a much-needed tonic. Hours of uncertainty and inactivity, not helped by one of the most revolting and inappropriate action messing dinners on record, lumps of soggy pork swilling in fannies full of greasy sludge, had made the most hardened feel queasy in that weather and dulled the edge of alertness and ardour.

Scharnhorst turned south, pursued by our cruisers. This presented the Commander-in-Chief with a dilemma: would she attempt to break out into the Atlantic to carry out further raiding operations like the *Bismarck*? Or would she return to her Norwegian base? Instinct inclined the C-in-C to the latter view and he adjusted course to intercept accordingly. Events were to prove him right.

Bruce Fraser's tactical plan was clear. Unless the enemy opened fire first, *Duke of York* would not engage until the range had closed to 12,000 yards; *Jamaica* would illuminate the target with starshell and was disposed accordingly.

Then came the long-awaited order:

'All positions stand-to.'

In an instant tiredness, cold and seasickness were shed and all hands became poised for their individual tasks.

'Follow Director', and the huge turrets swung round in line with the Director Control Tower.

'All guns with armour piercing and full charge load, load, load.' The clatter of the hoists as they brought up the shells and cordite charges from the magazines. The rattle of the rammers as they drove them into the chambers of the guns. The slam of the breeches as they closed. These were music to all.

Then a great stillness for seemingly endless minutes, disturbed only by the squelch of the hydraulics as Layers and Trainer followed the pointers in their receivers from the Director.

'Broadsides' and the interceptors completing the firing circuits right up to the Director Layer's trigger were closed.

A glance at the Range Receiver whose counters were steadily inexorably ticking down until . . . 12,000 yards . . . the fire gong rang 'ting ting' and . . . CRASH, all guns fired and the Battle of North Cape had started.

I have commented earlier on the indifferent view through a turret periscope, especially in rough weather, but two things of significance stick in my mind. The first was that when *Jamaica*'s starshell illuminated the target, *Scharnhorst*'s turrets were clearly seen to be still trained fore and aft. Astonishingly, after being trailed by our northerly cruisers for the whole of that day, she was caught completely by surprise by *Duke of York* and *Jamaica*. Twenty-seven years later, when commanding the Commando Carrier *Albion* on a visit to Wilhelmshaven, I had a long, friendly and objective talk on the action with a retired Federal German Navy Captain who had been the Executive Officer of the *Scharnhorst* until a few months before her end. In his view his Captain and Admiral were obsessed by the risk of RDF transmissions being intercepted by Direction Finding equipment with which the British were known to be equipped. Although they had considerable faith in the effectiveness of their RDF, they preferred not to use it for this reason.

The second incident was that at an early stage in the action my No. 3 gun misfired, so reducing my turret's output by 25%. The rules for this were unequivocal: wait 30 minutes, open the breech, remove the cordite cartridges and drop them overboard. Entirely prudent for peacetime but arguably too rigid for a war situation in which time and output were crucial to success. I compromised – waited five minutes and ordered the gun to be unloaded and the charges ditched. The God of Battles was with me or I should not be writing this.

Scharnhorst turned east and, despite the best endeavours of *Duke of York*'s Engine Room Department, it became clear that she had the legs of us in those conditions. Steadily, gallingly, the range counters clicked up as the enemy drew away. I cannot adequately describe the growing frustration of those few who were in a position to realize what was happening: to have achieved surprise, got so close, apparently done so well, and all for nothing as the enemy outpaced us into the night. To conserve ammunition fire was checked when the range ceased to be effective on an ahead bearing where the ship's movement generated the greatest fire control errors. The resultant despondency was profound.

Suddenly the range steadied, then started to close. Had we done it after all? We gained rapidly; our own secondary armament of 5.25-inch illuminated with starshell and fire was re-opened with the 14-inch. We closed right in to point blank range. *Scharnhorst* was ablaze from end to end. Men could be seen leaping over the side into the icy sea, and death within minutes, to escape the inferno. It was a terrible sight. Thirty-six survivors, including one Petty Officer but no officers, were picked up by the destroyers and later transferred to *Duke of York*. It was over.

One's feelings? Almost a blankness of shock at what had been done. Some relief that it had gone the way it had. Little exultation – the closing scenes were too grim for that and the remoteness of actions at sea precludes hate between sailors. Pride in achievement. And a great weariness. It had been a long day's night.

But now a new hazard tempered success. *Duke of York* and her Force had insufficient fuel to return to Scapa. Norway was already in German hands. The only practicable course of action was to continue north to Kola. The Arctic night, so freely cursed when seeking the enemy, now became our salvation against the ministrations of the Luftwaffe. In the event these did not materialize. There was a daily German reconnaissance flight at about noon but no attack developed. This enabled repairs to the *Duke of York*'s masts, both of which had been damaged by enemy gunfire, to be completed adequately for the passage home. We returned to Scapa without incident.

In the easy and critical light of hindsight what lessons should be drawn from this vignette, paying due regard to the many and varied developments in technology in the last 40 years? I single out four as being predominant and summarize them in no special order.

First, the influence of the weather. At sea this has not really changed much although the performance of today's radars and sonars are less affected. Seasickness apart, rough weather is always tiring and the stiffer motion resulting from stabilizers does little to alleviate this. Armchair strategists without operational experience should temper their glib pronoucements on setting up Maginot Lines across the Greenland/Iceland/UK gap with the knowledge that in those northern waters for half the year it is almost always dark and for the other half almost always light.

Next, afloat support. The state of the art in 1943 was such that normally replenishment at sea was not a practical proposition. Today it is common-place though still constrained by weather to an extent. But now, as then, failure to make adequate and timely provision of Afloat Support could alter the course of a battle.

Third, notwithstanding modern technology, including satellites, we would do well to appreciate the sheer size of the ocean area even north of the gaps and to remember the scale of forces necessary to neutralize a single high-value target. The position has not changed as much as some would have us believe.

Finally, and most important of all, we need constantly to remind ourselves to take proper account of the unexpected. 'Experts' are continually predict-ing the course of the next war (which please God will be deterred from happening anyway) with an air of precision which is not supported by reality. Nobody has got it right yet and there is no reason to suppose that today's prophets are any better at it than their predecessors. Who could sensibly have predicted that *Scharnhorst* would not radiate her radar and would be jumped? Or that *Duke of York* could enter the lion's mouth of Kola and get away unscathed? The prudent will keep open their options for as long as they can, thereby providing the maximum flexibility against the unforeseen.

5

CEASE FIRING

'Nothing is ever done in this world until men are prepared to kill
one another if it is not done.'

George Bernard Shaw

By the late autumn of 1944 the focus of the war at sea was beginning to shift
away from Germany and the European theatre towards Japan and the Far
East. Preparations for the formation of a British Pacific Fleet under Admiral
Sir Bruce Fraser were put in hand. The flag of the Commander-in-Chief
Home Fleet was transferred from *Duke of York* and the ship entered
Gladstone Dock, Liverpool, to be refitted for the Pacific. At that point I was
reappointed to *Javelin*, a Fleet destroyer also undergoing repairs at
Liverpool.

Any ideas I may have had of avoiding the filth and gloom of a ship in refit
were quickly dispelled. *Javelin* was in an advanced stage of having her third
stern installed, the previous ones having been blown off by mines or
torpedoes. Apart from the Commanding Officer and First Lieutenant I was
the only officer so far appointed. There were few sailors and the ship was in
a total mess.

Throughout most of October and November Liverpool was cloaked in
thick fog and it rained, God how it rained. Trudging daily through the slush
and puddles of the Docks area, whither the overhead railway had clanked its
rickety way from the city centre, was infinitely depressing. If anything
conditions on board were more so. Little light, less heat and everywhere a
penetrating dank cold. The dirt and disruption were incredible and the
prospect of recovery from this all-embracing squalor ill-defined. Such was
the dispiriting environment of my 21st birthday.

The Commanding Officer was a complex character. A regular naval officer
with pre-war experience in big ships he was clever, precise, petulant but
perhaps somewhat lacking in human understanding. He had a considerable
knowledge of how to do things 'by the book' but his intuition and initiative
were less developed. He was a little unsure of himself and, it being his first
command, he could have been forgiven for this had it not been for his failure
to conceal it from his Ship's Company. He lived on his nerves and was not a

natural ship-handler. Later we discovered that his contemporaries had nicknamed him 'The Sheep'. If he had a sense of humour it was rather brittle and incapable of direction against himself.

In contrast the First Lieutenant was a big man with an unusually soft-spoken, equable manner and a good rapport with both officers and sailors. Professionally competent, imperturbable and self-assured he was an admirable foil to the Captain. He was liked and respected throughout the ship.

These two officers were to have a profound influence on what was to be an unusual commission.

Most of the rest of the officers and a high proportion of the Ship's Company were Hostilities Only. Their quality and experience varied but overall they could fairly be described as average for an elderly destroyer after five years of war.

Well before completion date the Captain decided that the progress of work was slowing down and the general state of the ship was deteriorating steadily. With the approval of higher authority he resolved to take the ship away from Liverpool prematurely and proceed to the Fleet Base of Scapa Flow to work up operational efficiency. He was absolutely right. Accordingly one afternoon in late December we extricated *Javelin* from the Dockyard and berthed overnight at Wallasey Stage to await the morning tide. The weather was foul: a full westerly gale, driving rain and bitterly cold. Wallasey is not a comfortable berth. It is exposed and subject to vicious tidal variations. Despite the extensive use of hurricane hawsers most of our berthing wires had parted by morning. Next day we sailed for Scapa.

It was not an auspicious start to a commission in which cold, wet and the malfunctioning of much of the equipment predominated. But at least we were clear of the filth of the Dockyard and a good wash-down and blow-through were much needed. There was a lot of seasickness on our passage north. We reached Scapa several hours late and took several more securing to our buoy in Gutta Sound. Conditions were not easy and were not matched by shiphandling skill. Soaked to the skin and chittering with cold, the Cable Party, roundly cursed from the Bridge for being too slow or parting a picking-up wire they had just been told to hold on to, retired below to eat a supper long since gone tepid in the steamy warmth of their messdeck. Only with considerable reluctance was I given the approval I sought to administer a tot of rum to the now almost numb buoy-jumper.

Of the next fortnight we spent a few days at sea in appalling weather achieving little, and ten days alongside the Depot Ship *Vindictive* trying to make the equipment work. Despite these setbacks the Ship's Company slowly began to meld together as an entity and improvement in performance was noticeable. It was still in the days of compulsory church attendance on Sundays and after conducting the service (there being no Chaplain embarked) it soon became the practice for the Captain to address the assembled company and expound his views on their progress towards efficiency. It was not a very encouraging ritual. The highest commendation for a task done well was a curt 'satisfactory'. Matters performed just adequately were described as 'unacceptable'. Mistakes, whether avoidable or reasonable were 'disgraceful'. As an example of confidence-building and leadership it rated very low. So it was with widespread relief and anticipation throughout the ship that one morning we sailed for the Mediterranean, there to work up properly. Our longer-term future remained somewhat uncertain. Everyone wanted to go out to the Far East and finish off the war. But at least the Mediterranean would provide good weather and extensive practice facilities and the ship would quickly become an effective fighting unit.

0600 on a lovely, sunny morning. The sea a shimmering mirror. Cape Bon ten miles off the starboard bow. No enemy around, no imminent threat. Utter peace and quiet. A slight nip in the air on the open bridge. Good to be alive. *Javelin* slicing through the placid water at an effortless 15 knots. The ship and her company beginning to come properly alive at last. Suddenly a loud explosion and the ship started to lose way. As Officer of the Watch my first thoughts were that we had struck a mine. I called the Captain to the Bridge and rang up the Engine Room to assess the damage. In fact it was not a mine; we had burst one of our two boilers. Fortunately nobody was hurt but there was a lot of steam around and conditions were unpleasant.

As soon as things were sorted out we got under way again and in due course limped into Malta at half-power. But Malta Dockyard was already full to capacity and could not take us in hand; so on we went to Alexandria. Complete re-tubing and extensive associated work was the assessment at the refit conference. A 2½-month job. 'Oh God,' I thought, 'will this ship *never* get running?'

Berthed the other side of the same jetty in Alexandria was another destroyer, the *Bicester*. She was nearing completion of her refit and was then scheduled for the Far East. As is usual under such conditions her Ship's Company wore overalls during working hours and the radio was relayed through the upperdeck loudspeakers. Her routine was relaxed and formal parades ('Divisions' and 'Evening Quarters') put in abeyance. Because her CO was a Commander, he was in a position to call the tune. In *Javelin* things were different. Sailors working on the upperdeck wore full uniform; the ship's radio was not relayed; formal Divisions were held every Sunday and Evening Quarters occasionally. Full normal routine was worked. The contrast was marked. Still more marked was the fact that *Javelin*'s Ship's Company was as yet unworked-up hence still to be welded together as a complete team. 2½ months was a long gestation period.

But, like everything else, the time passed. We played a lot of sport, especially hockey, the weather was warm and Alexandria at that time was the cosmopolitan fleshpot of the whole Mediterranean. Life might have been a great deal worse. If any consciences pricked they were young ones stimulated by the knowledge that the war was still on in both Europe and the Far East and *Javelin* was contributing absolutely nothing to it. Older men were more inclined to take things as they found them and be thankful. Nevertheless there was nobody who was not relieved when the repairs were satisfactorily completed and once again we set about the task of working up efficiency as an operational warship.

At about 1100 one forenoon, in the middle of exercises off Alexandria, the Petty Officer Telegraphist, grinning all over his face, came to the Bridge brandishing a signal which had just been received in the Wireless Office. Since it was unclassified there was no reason why it should not be shown to anyone who happened to be around and he did so. The signal was in fact an Admiralty General Message. It read quite simply:

'The war in Europe is over.'

Several officers and ratings were on the Bridge at the time, including myself. We were, of course, delighted and displayed our feelings with some spirit. All of which attracted the attention of the Commanding Officer, seated in his chair. He was shown the signal with some enthusiasm. It did not take long to read and evidently he did so several times. Then with a deadpan face he turned to the PO Tel. and asked:

'Is this genuine?'

The cold hand of pedantic authority quickly dampened our exuberance.

'Good grief,' most of us thought, 'have we really got to have a great witch-hunt to check that the war is over when the Admiralty has already told us that it is?'

'We will carry on with the exercises,' said the Captain curtly.

Here was a turn-up for the book. The Signal Officer was summoned, a young Australian Sub-Lieutenant RNVR who didn't give a damn for anyone. Instructed to verify the signal he did so.

'You could ask FOLEM, Sir,' [Flag Officer Levant and Eastern Mediterranean, the local Senior Naval Officer at Alexandria] one of us suggested.

But the CO saw through this one. Ever with an eye to the main chance he realized that if the AGM was valid, in challenging it he would appear an ass. Equally if it was a hoax, it would reflect ill on the ship (and him) to bring it to the notice of his Admiral. A Catch 22 situation and he discarded the option.

By this time the news had spread all round the ship. Most of the rest of the officers had come to the Bridge, amongst them the First Lieutenant. He quickly grasped the situation.

'I don't think, Sir,' he quietly put to the Captain, 'that anyone's heart is really going to be in the exercises now or that any real value is likely to be derived from continuing with them. If you are still not prepared to accept the signal why don't you turn back towards Alex and see if any other ship appears to have got the message?'

After some further argument the Captain reluctantly agreed. Course was reversed and we headed back down the Great Pass towards Alexandria. As we neared the harbour we were met by the cacophony of many sirens being sounded incessantly and when closer still we could see that every ship had dressed overall with flags.

Short-sighted? Let us just say that the Captain was the only man in the squad in step.

Not long afterwards we completed our work-up and sailed from Alexandria, a fully operational ship at last. It was long overdue and the whole ship's company was eager to get stuck into a worthwhile job to prove themselves. Unfortunately there did not seem to be any very specific task for us and we spent weeks wandering among the Greek Islands providing a presence in support of the British authorities ashore. Most of the Aegean and the approaches to outlying islands had been mined and accurate navigation to keep within the comparatively narrow limits of the available swept channels was essential to survival.

One of our earlier visits was to Corfu. Here the Germans had remained in control until close on VE (Victory in Europe) Day and clearly the inhabitants had suffered considerable deprivations. Most were very thin, many of the children to the point emaciation, and relations with their late captors were understandably edgy. The one thing they really wanted now was cricket.

Cricket had been introduced to Corfu by well-to-do British travellers in the late 19th century and its roots had gone deep. But the war had put a stop to that and all the local gear had been lost. An early match was therefore arranged. It was held on the Village Brown in the centre of the main town and there was an enthusiastic turnout. Initial scoring was slow as the pitch was rather uneven and every boundary necessitated a prolonged negotiation with the crowd for recovery of the ball. When the tenth wicket fell a battalion of small boys rushed on to the pitch and secured stumps and balls, while a second assault force of old men grabbed all the bats, pads and gloves they could lay their hands on. After considerable delay one of the Town Elders was persuaded to make a public announcement. If the locals would hand back all the gear the match could continue and the ship would undertake to present two complete sets to the town before she sailed. On this basis the match was played out to a convincing (and only marginally manipulated) draw and all were satisfied.

In due course we returned to Rhodes, there to put the finishing touches to *Javelin*'s smartness before being inspected by Commander (D). All Hands worked hard and willingly and the ship was got up like a new pin. The entire Iron Deck was burnished with graphite and black lead until it shone with a lustre like pewter. The barrels of the 4.7″ guns in their twin mountings were chipped down to bare metal and carefully repainted with black enamel except for the muzzles which were polished. The full gamut of peacetime, pre-war tiddliness was applied. By the evening before the inspection there really was very little that could have been improved. As if to provide a climax, the Leader (*Jervis*) arrived shortly before sunset. It was not an impressive entry: a rope's end was trailing over her side amidships and the oily waterlines on her boats had not been cleaned off following her last port visit. We reckoned we would be able to show Commander (D) a thing or two.

Next morning, as promulgated in Daily Orders, the Hands were to fall in at 0530. This was an hour earlier than usual and was designed to provide time for the final touches before the inspection at 0900. But for some reason the issue of those Daily Orders became delayed and they did not appear on the Ship's Company boards until after 2100 the previous evening. As a result they were first seen by the majority of the sailors when they returned from shore leave at midnight. They had worked hard to get the ship up. They had enjoyed as good a run ashore as Rhodes could provide and if the Vino was not quite as palatable as beer its mellowing effect was no less. Now they were tired and ready to turn in. Better take a quick look at Daily Orders before going below to the Mess. Then '0530 Hands Fall In' leapt at them out of the notice boards. It was unexpected. It was unnecessary. It was undeserved. It was too much.

At 0530 next morning only two or three Petty Officers and a handful of sailors fell in. The remainder stayed quietly sitting in their messdecks. This was mutiny.

The Captain was informed and shortly afterwards came up on deck. As Officer of the Day I was sent for'ard to see what was going on and to get the men to fall in. I found them jammed into the for'ard messdeck, waiting for the next move.

'Come on lads,' I called out. 'This is nonsense and won't do. Lay aft and fall in.'

My appeal was received quietly and courteously but was rejected. Several shook their heads and muttered, 'No.'

'I am giving you a direct order,' I said. 'This is your last chance and I shall not repeat it. Get aft and fall in abreast the after tubes.'

Apart from a few shaking heads no one moved, no one spoke. I turned away and walked aft to report to the First Lieutenant. The latter conferred briefly with the Captain and then himself went for'ard.

The next hour was a long one. The Captain strutted up and down the starboard side. Those few sailors who had originally fallen in remained on the port side. Amidships stood a handful of officers. Though there was much to talk about none felt inclined to do so. The minutes dragged by, the sun rose, it got warmer.

At 0630 the First Lieutenant returned. Two minutes later the remainder of the Hands walked aft and fell in. The tension relaxed. It was decided to work for a token half hour and then to send everyone to breakfast early, at 0700. Meanwhile the First Lieutenant conferred with the Captain and the rest of the officers busied themselves with their normal affairs.

0700. 'Hands to Breakfast' was piped together with the warning order 'Lower Deck will be cleared at 0730' (i.e. every officer and man except those actually on watch). At this point I was sent for and instructed to have a certain Leading Seaman brought before me by the Duty Petty Officer, charged with incitement to mutiny and placed under close arrest in the Tiller Flat (the Steering Gear Compartment right aft). Leading Seaman Leverett was a good deal older than most. Tall, dark and powerfully built he spoke and moved with a sort of massive gentleness. He wore three (the maximum) Good Conduct Badges and was an experienced and reliable seaman. Generally respected and liked throughout the ship, he was looked up to as something of a Father Figure. A more unlikely person to stir up a mutiny would have been hard to conceive but . . . he had sat in a prominent position in the front row on the for'ard messdeck. When brought before me he heard the charge with surprise and dignity, and denied it. He had nothing else to say and was duly put in the First Lieutenant's Report under close arrest.

In the Wardroom breakfast was none too convivial a meal that morning. By half-way through it also became rather disturbed. One by one the Leading Hand in charge of every Junior Rates' Mess in the ship came aft and asked to see his Divisional Officer. The message of all was similar:

'I don't know if I'm doing the right thing, Sir, but the lads in my mess have all said that unless Leading Seaman Leverett is released they won't be falling in when Lower Deck is cleared at 0730. I thought you ought to know.'

To complete the irony I was Leading Seaman Leverett's Divisional Officer.

The Captain was informed of the latest development. He signalled Commander (D):

'Request I wait on you 0900. Request inspection be postponed.'

Later, when the Captain returned on board, I was sent for (having recently taken over as Navigating Officer) and told to prepare charts for leaving by the north and the south swept channels. That I was not told where we were going was symptomatic of the level of trust, though it was clear that the northerly route headed us for Malta and the southerly one back to Alexandria.

We sailed at 1100 and headed north, leaving our Leader swinging gently to her anchor. Her boats were still dirty and the same rope's end trailed over the side. No parting signal, only the Officer of the Day and the Quartermaster on deck to return our salute. No sign of Commander (D); he never came on board and indeed we never saw him. Elderly and remote, perhaps it was all a bit too much for him. But as an example of leadership it was mediocre.

A few days later we reached Malta. As we approached Grand Harbour a motor torpedo boat came scurrying out to meet us and an angry Duty Commander from the Commander-in-Chief's Staff came on board.

'Where the hell d'you think you're going?' he demanded belligerently of the Captain on reaching the bridge.

This was a good question since we had received no berthing signal nor any local instructions.

'Turn round at once,' the Commander went on. 'You are to anchor in St Paul's Bay pending further orders.'

And so to the remote beauty of St Paul's Bay the leper *Javelin* went, there to have her disease beaten out of her. For the next fortnight we were to carry out another work-up, exercising at sea by day and by night with minimal and infrequent respite. It was of course a shake-up, calculated to expose any residual traces of dissidence. In effect it was a very wearing time, almost non-stop, for the Captain and the Navigating Officer but not all that arduous for anyone else. For me it was professionally rewarding and enjoyable; the ship achieved much higher standards from the extensive practice facilities off Malta than had ever been possible from the limited and rather desultory programme off Alexandria. It was just a pity that the underlying reason for it all could not quite be forgotten.

Over the ensuing two months preparations were made for a series of Courts Martial. A Lieutenant Commander RNVR, a peacetime criminal lawyer, was appointed for the defence and another RNVR lawyer as prosecutor. The former was as sharp as a needle and turned everyone inside out; the latter was wet.

One evening at about 1700 eight Petty Officers, two Leading Seamen and a number of junior rates were together disembarked into a tender and taken to the local shore depot. At that time of day normal work had ceased and there was little for the rest of the Ship's Company to do beyond giving them a rousing send-off. A singularly inept bit of staff work.

Javelin then moved round into Grand Harbour and berthed alongside the destroyer *Chaplet*. From subsequent conversation with her Captain it was learned that he had received orders to load his close-range weapons and train them on the beam as *Javelin* approached 'in case of trouble'. Needless to say this ridiculous command was ignored.

I mention this incident to indicate the degree of sensitivity towards disaffection (often then regarded as associated with violence) which prevailed at the time. There was the case in a cruiser when at 2200 one night in Grand Harbour the Officer of the Watch on the quarterdeck thought he heard a large splash in the vicinity of the lower boom, where the boats were secured. Having nothing better to do he wandered for'ard, thought he saw something struggling in the water and ordered a boat to be called away to investigate. Just in time they picked up the Master At Arms (ship's 'Head Policeman'). He had been doing rounds of the messdecks to enforce Pipe Down ('Lights Out') when on entering a certain mess someone had grabbed him from behind, thrust a kit-bag over his head and shoulders, and shoved him through an escape-hatch over the side.

Another case was that of a naval ocean-going tug. Her First Lieutenant was a very good, young Sub-Lieutenant RNVR, son of the Engineer Officer in one of the Destroyers. If the tug was due to sail very early the following morning it was the reasonable practice to grant leave until midnight. But on occasion the First Lieutenant would wake at midnight to find a jacknife pricking his throat and the hoarse voice of a drunken seaman demanding, 'Leave extended to 0400 or . . .'

In *Javelin* things were not like that. At no time was any real aggro exhibited. The situation was simply that of men being driven too far for too long, often without real need, and with a complete absence of encouragement. Most of those concerned were wartime only; the war had been won and they yearned for release. Coupled with the lack of accord between the Command and the Lower Deck (and even the Wardroom, come to that) it was too much and the camel's back quietly broke.

There were three Courts Martial: for the Petty Officers, for the Leading Seamen, for the junior rates. All resulted in convictions and all were subsequently quashed. Then followed a fourth, for the First Lieutenant whose minor indiscretion on an isolated occasion had been unearthed during the witch-hunt. He was convicted and awarded a wind-up-the-war DSC the same day. Forty-eight hours later, at noon, I was summoned by the Captain:

'The First Lieutenant and I are leaving the ship at 1400,' he said. 'You are temporarily to take over as No. 1 until a new one is flown out from England. The Captain of *Tanatside* will take over as Captain.'

At 1400 they left, piped over the side for the last time, to go to 'made' jobs in Athens and Jerusalem. It was the end of an era in *Javelin*.

Twice previously I had briefly met the Captain of *Tanatside*. On each

6. HMS *Javelin* in the Mediterranean, 1945. Note the latest fashion in camouflage.

7. The Author mounted on an elderly Police horse demonstrating to the First Sea Lord in the Admiralty Quadrangle the correct dress for a Naval Officer mounted. Coronation 1953.

8. HMS *Newcastle*, Ship's Company, Far East Flagship 1953-1955. A lovely ship and a very fine team.

9. HMS *Dunkirk* — my first command. A 1943 Battle Class Destroyer, powerful in speed and armament but cumbersome to handle in close anti-submarine action due to her single rudder.

occasion he had been drunk. An ex-Gunner, known to his contemporaries as 'Hutch', I looked forward to his arrival half an hour later with considerable misgiving. After he arrived we had a long talk and later he spent some time in the Wardroom meeting the Officers. Next morning at 0900 he spoke to the whole Ship's Company on the fo'c'sle with no other officer present. At the time I regarded this unique approach as a matter of trust and, whether ingenuously or not, made no attempt to find out what he had said. Indeed to this day I do not know.

Within 24 hours Hutch had the entire Ship's Company eating out of his hand.

Not long afterwards we sailed for a visit to Ferryville. That part of the North African coastline is flat and featureless and on approaching it at right angles for the first time it was something of a gamble which way to turn for the final run up to our destination. All of which I had pointed out to my new Captain when calling him early on the day of our arrival. Since leaving Malta he had hardly left his bunk; there had been a good deal to sleep off. In due course we sighted Ferryville as expected and shaped up for the outer harbour entrance which lay between two breakwaters. Despite several calls there was still no sign of the Captain. 'Just passing the breakwater, Sir,' I called down to him desperately as we went through the hole and then abandoned all thought of him as I was busy. The passage to the inner harbour lay down a long, narrow canal strewn with bombed wrecks and with very little room to spare. With some trepidation I negotiated this and faced the uncomfortably small basin at the far end where we had to make a sharp U-turn before berthing. The Gods were with me and it worked out – my first real experience of ship handling. With a sigh of relief I was just about to call down finally to the Captain to tell him we'd got there when a quiet voice from the back of the Bridge ordered:

'Ring Off.'

Before returning to Malta we paid a short visit to Nice on the French Riviera. At the time Nice was mainly occupied by the British and Cannes by the Americans. Both were largely deserted by their normal inhabitants and, except for those which had been commandeered as Headquarters, the hotels were closed. Nevertheless we were readily able to take over the ground floor of a medium sized hotel and to rustle up a local band for a memorable Ship's Company dance. It lasted far into the small hours and involved a heavy expenditure of energy and booze. As the final weld in the new construction for *Javelin* it was exactly what was needed. From now on we would look forward, not back.

While at Nice all-night leave was granted. The rate of exchange between the English pound and the French franc was stupendous and as yet currency regulations restricting the amount changed back to that originally exchanged had not been introduced. In consequence blackmarket dealings in kind were rife. A single seaboot stocking was worth £1; a pair of grey flannel trousers so old and filthy as to be barely wearable outside the garden rated £10; nearly new articles of this sort were off the scale high. The sailors were quickly alert to this and often returned from overnight leave with half their clothes, even their footwear, flogged, having had the whale of a time and made their fortunes.

On return to Malta we found that we had been transferred to the 14th Destroyer Flotilla under a senior Captain (D). Our new Leader, *Chequers*, was in harbour and it was not long before Captain John Ruck-Keene came on board to return our Commanding Officer's call. He was a short, stocky, little man with a grey goatee beard which wiggled up and down when he emphasized a point (which was quite often) and a habit of snapping his fingers at his side as he strutted up and down. He was a pre-war Captain (D) of fiction: hard-drinking, hard-swearing, hard-driving. A great extrovert but less skilled when interpreting a Cathode Ray Tube. After a time I was summoned to the Captain's cabin. As is the naval custom I knocked and without waiting for a reply grasped the handle to enter. Hardly had I done so when the door was wrenched out of my hand and the fierce, bearded face of my Captain (D) was thrust round it.

'What d'you think of Parnell?' he barked.

Parnell (not his real name) was an RNR Lieutenant. He was fat, flabby and characterless but harmless until given a task which mattered when he would invariably foul it up. Though nice enough in his way, as a naval officer he was useless.

'Not much, sir,' I replied.

Wthout another word the door was slammed in my face. Half an hour later the officer left the ship.

During this period the Palestine Patrol occupied much of our time. I will not enlarge on the political justification for this dubious operation but the practical problems were considerable. The object was to prevent the Jews returning 'illegally' to their own country, which they resolutely attempted to do by sea in any small ship they could lay their hands on. It was an unenviable task and few had much heart in it. The immigrant ships and craft were dangerously crammed with refugees and short of using weapons the only way to stop them was by boarding. This was no easy matter when scrambling nets, grappling hooks and any other means of clambering up a ship's side were immediately dislodged and flung back in the faces of the boarding party. Those few who did secure a foothold on deck were received by solid ranks of women and children, counting on the sailor's aversion to bashing his way through such a throng with trenching helves. As the months passed the technique of boarding under such conditions improved; so too did the desperate determination of the refugees. Women lining the sides of the immigrant ships took to arming themselves with hatpins or similar pointed instruments and with them they would jab at the genitals of those attempting to board. It was all very unpleasant.

The 14th Destroyer Flotilla contained a variety of characters. Two in particular were notorious for their voracious appetites and their remarkable capacity at table. They were the gannets of the Flotilla and known as such. One, in *Chequers* (the Leader), was a Lieutenant RN who retired soon after the war. The other, a Sub-Lieutenant RNVR in *Javelin*, subsequently became a senior Civil Servant until his untimely death from overwork in the early 1970s.

As part of the VJ (Victory over Japan) Day celebrations an Eating Competition between the two gannets was arranged. It took place in the Union Bar in Alexandria, a favourite haunt for wardrooms taking a run ashore. The rules were simple: start time 1900; drinks and small eats as desired were provided by the supporters for 30 minutes; contestants to their table at 1930; then eat and drink in competition. The winner to be the one who consumed the greatest number of courses, each accompanied by an appropriate beverage. No time limit but undue delay (other than short-term visits of necessity) to result in disqualification. There was just one bizarre aspect: the sequence of courses was to be in reverse.

Thus the menu started with coffee and creme de menthe, proceeded backwards through fruit and port, rum baba and Sauternes, T-bone steak and claret, curried prawns, rice and beer, to consommé and sherry. A surviving contestant (and both were tipped to be in this category) was to return to additional helpings of curried prawns, rice and beer until, one way or another, he indicated that the limit of his capacity had been reached.

On the night of the competition there was a festive air about the Union Bar. The contestants' wardrooms were well represented and there was no shortage of umpires – themselves indulging in a more normal, less gourmand repast. A good deal of money changed hands.

As predicted by the Form Cards, both contestants completed the prescribed menu albeit with some diminution of vigour and incisiveness of speech. After a brief adjournment (by mutual consent) they re-entered their table for the munch up to the finish. The RN Lieutenant succumbed when half way through his second helping of curried prawns and rice. But the RNVR Sub, a man of bigger (or more elastic) stomach, was bent on a really convincing victory and threw in his napkin only when well advanced into his third helping.

The Sudanese waiters were riveted.

★

In the spring of 1946 *Javelin* was ordered back to the UK to pay off. A few days before we sailed I was re-appointed to the Leader, *Chequers*, to relieve an RNVR Lieutenant who was being demobilized. It came as a bitter blow. I had no reason to regard *Javelin* with much affection; but somehow the traumatic events of the past year and the remarkable metamorphosis of the change of command had culminated in a happy ship, albeit a pretty slap-happy one. It would have been coldly inhuman not to have worked up a real affinity with the ship and her Company after all we had been through. I longed for the application of Drake's famous prayer about 'matters being thoroughly finished' and experienced acute sadness at my departure. I also viewed with some trepidation the prospect of serving directly under my awesome Captain (D).

My apprehension was not entirely unfounded. One evening soon after my arrival in *Chequers*, when most of the officers were ashore in Beirut, and I was Duty Officer, the Captain stormed into the Wardroom. He was in a restless and aggressive mood.

'What,' he roared at the few officers present, 'is the matter with this ship?' We waited in silence for a bit more data.

'Why is everyone so bloody boring?' he went on. 'Come on you lot. Out through the port escape-hatch, swim round the bow and back inboard over the starboard lower boom; a double scotch for the winner.'

As a very indifferent swimmer I was glad that being Officer of the Day I could not responsibly participate in this assault course. The others, stripping off their messjackets, wriggled through the escape-hatch and dived, otherwise fully dressed, over the side. It soon became apparent that another officer was not too good in the water either; by the time he had rounded the bow he was making very heavy weather of it. Bellowing exhortations, Captain (D) started picking up the wicker chairs and small tables ranged on deck outside the Wardroom and hurling them down at the luckless swimmer who was now nearing exhaustion. The fun factor was diminishing rapidly and surreptitiously I ordered a boat to be called away. It was as well. Moments later a chair struck the swimmer on the forehead and briefly knocked him out.

It was during this period that I experienced my only real doubts about continuing in the Royal Navy. The six long years of war were over. Most officers, especially the more senior ones, were pretty tired. Everyone was taking a deep breath and giving a sigh of relief. Certain pre-war, peacetime routines were drifting back, but times had changed radically and few were appropriate any longer. Reservists were chafing that their demobilization was not immediate. Regulars were searching for a lead on the way ahead, on the future, but (at least in the Mediterranean) nobody gave it to them. It was a doldrum period, a vacuum in which any real sense of purpose was almost wholly lacking. And to cap it all, there was the RNVR Lieutenant whom I was relieving about to return home to complete his medical training and with a clear, demonstrably worthwhile lifetime's career stretching before him. I felt unsettled and envious.

Nevertheless my ties with the Navy were already too strong to be discarded lightly. I therefore reasoned that it was timely to take advantage of again serving under a senior Captain to renew, with his backing, my application to specialize in gunnery. This, I speculated, would open up new fields and provide fresh incentive. As the ship's Correspondence Officer it fell to me daily to place before my Captain those letters and papers requiring his attention. It was thus an easy matter for me to slip my request in among the other items. Unfortunately I did not pick a good day for this gambit. Captain (D) had had a good night's sleep and was feeling clear-headed and perky. One of his foibles was to sign his letters with a quill pen. This he did with a flourish and since the nib frequently became crossed a good deal of ink was spattered. My letter came to the top and I placed it before him.

'What,' he demanded coldly, 'is this thing?'

'My application to specialize in gunnery, sir.'

'Don't be a fool. How can you, a promising young officer, want to bow down to the Great God Gunnery? The finest officer in the Fleet did this and the last time I saw him he was fiddling about with some footling bit of fire control equipment which wouldn't work. Bah! I won't have you leaving my ship. Get out of my cabin.' And he tore my letter up.

I bided my time. Came the day when I knew my Captain had indulged in a major thrash ashore the previous night, from which the after-effects were likely to be severe. Picking my moment with care so as to be between breakfast and the first application of the hair of the dog, I took in a few selected letters. The first three were signed in throbbing silence. Then I slipped my renewed application onto his desk; he signed it blindly. One more letter as cover also signed.

'That's all for today, sir,' I said and hastily gathering up the papers, turned away.

But my master was shrewd even when hung over. Somewhere in the fuddled recesses of his mind an alarm bell rang.

'What was that I just signed?' he rasped.

'My application to specialize in gunnery, sir,' I answered and instantly left his cabin.

Of course he could easily have called me back or stopped the letter. But when all was said and done he was a sportsman. He didn't.

6

GUN DISCIPLINE

'Si vis pacem para bellum'
Motto: HMS *Excellent*.

'If you want peace be prepared for war' typified the atmosphere at HMS *Excellent*, Whale Island, Portsmouth, the Navy's premier Gunnery School. After three months having our brains sharpened with basic theory at the Royal Naval College, Greenwich, it was good to get back to the practicalities of life and learn about equipment in service. We had mastered the intricacies of the Cathode Coupled Flip Flop in Radar and the mathematics of the more abstruse calculating mechanisms currently used in Fire Control computers. We had also 'come together' as Long Course 1947 and any disparities (never great) between the Royal Marines, Australians, New Zealanders, Canadians, Indians and British who comprised the course of fifteen had been rounded off. Our minds reeling with newly acquired erudition, we now faced twelve months' hard labour, physical as well as mental, at Whaley.

There were three hierarchical levels amongst the officers on The Island: the Staff, who wore black gaiters; the Long Course who wore white; and the Sub-Lieutenants, who wore green. The Long Course were regarded as 'nearly one of us' and expected to set standards accordingly. On the other hand the Sub-Lieutenants were the lifeblood of the establishment and it was accepted that they would perpetrate outrageous escapades from time to time. Discipline was very taut; no mistake at drill or anything else, however small, was allowed to pass uncorrected. But at all levels there was an underlying warmth and understanding between Instructor and Instructed. The whole ethos was one of work hard and play hard.

Early in the Second World War the United States had grasped the problem of how best and most quickly to instil discipline into raw recruits. Hitherto the accepted method had been Parade Training, involving as it did basic training with the rifle and bayonet; but this was regarded as old hat. For nearly two years a high-powered committee deliberated on better alternatives before rendering its report. It recommended no change! Accordingly for the first three weeks of January, 1947, the Long Course found itself on the parade ground every day and all day, trampling the crackling ice and snow that persisted throughout an exceptionally cold snap. With collarbones bruised from the crash of rifle butts, fingers no longer capable of feeling and feet worn sore by unaccustomed boots, we survived this ordeal. Thereafter heads were held a little higher and shoulders squared a little more.

Our Indian, Chandy Kuruvila, was tall, handsome, cultured and charming. He quickly became a great favourite with us . . . and with the girls. Adept at getting to know new people and making new friends, he was a frequent guest at country houses over a weekend, often being lent horses to ride. He was also rather well off and to facilitate his many social activities he bought a smart new car of distinctive blue.

One Monday morning he was absent. It was not until five minutes before the end of the forenoon's instruction that he tottered unsteadily into our lecture room. He looked ill and the whole of one side of his face was lacerated with cuts and scratches. We escorted him to the Wardroom, gave him a stiff brandy and demanded his story.

'Well chaps,' he drawled, 'the thing was that these people I was staying with for the weekend lent me a horse to ride. It was a huge black animal, very powerful, and only when I had got on board did I realise that it was a bloody great stallion. You see it was feeling a bit randy or something and it bolted with me. I was very scared and thought maybe I'd better fall off before we had a ghastly crash. So I did but it didn't work out quite right; I caught one foot in the stirrup and got dragged. It was awful. Eventually my foot came free but now I am very sore all over.' Indeed he was a dreadful sight and we duly commiserated.

Soon afterwards a few other members of the course wandered into the Mess having taken a different route. 'Chandy,' one of them asked, 'what on earth have you done to your car? The whole of the offside is stove in.' For a moment there was complete silence as we all looked at the Indian. Then the truth came out. Our friend had not been spending the weekend anywhere near the country and had never been near a horse. He had been hitting the night spots in London.

'It was really rather a good weekend, you see,' he explained, 'and on the Sunday night I met a very beautiful girl. We stayed up rather late. When I drove back to Portsmouth in the small hours I was absolutely knackered and I suppose I must have dropped off. The next thing I knew I had swerved off the road, through a hedge, and the car was rolling over and over until it hit a tree and I passed out. When I came to again it was broad daylight and the car seemed to be at a funny sort of angle. So I got it back on to all four wheels, pushed the starter and the engine fired at once. I drove off. Trouble was I couldn't find the hole I'd made in the hedge on the way in so I had to make another one to get out on to the main road. That's why I was a bit late this morning.'

'Whereabouts did all this happen?' we asked.

'The Devil's Punchbowl,' he said.

During the summer we spent a few weeks with the Royal Marines at Browndown, near Gosport, learning about small arms and fieldcraft. It was not a very exhilarating period and got away to a poor start. The opening lecture was delivered by an elderly Colonel who, seeing us dressed in denims, mistook us for a routine class of Royal Marines Subalterns – which became increasingly clear to us as the lecturer droned on. We strung him along, asked some suitably military questions at the end and received some military advice whose relevance was minimal. I don't think he ever discovered the charade.

One day we were subjected to a map-reading exercise. For this we were put in the back of a 3-ton lorry, the rear cover was lowered so that we could not see out and we were driven round and round the back streets of Fareham. After suitable confusion had been generated we were dropped off in pairs with instructions to find our way to a specified map reference from which, after identification, we would obtain the clue to the next point. A sort of treasure hunt, ending up close to base in an attractive little pub. As an exercise it was open to differing interpretations and being a lovely hot day our approach was fairly light-hearted.

Two of the course decided they would cut the exercise altogether and go for a swim. They left the Mess much later and were strolling along the nearby beach when suddenly on rounding a corner they came face to face with our two Officer Instructors, walking in the opposite direction. It was anybody's guess who was the most surprised. Seizing the initiative the Long Course officers quickened their pace, assumed a more purposeful demeanour and respectfully saluted their superiors while rather hurriedly saying, 'Good morning, sir'. By the time the penny had dropped that the beach area was not included in the exercise they were round the next corner and holed up behind a bunch of scrub. However, their absence from the lorry necessitated some deception by the rest of us when their turn came to be dropped off. Stamping our feet to create a din we gave vent to loud exhortations and a stream of advice – to thin air. At which point we noticed it was just opposite a bus stop. The good citizens of Fareham were quite unmoved by this lunacy; I suppose they were used to Naval officers.

A colleague and I tried to sharpen the exercise by imposing an additional rule: never to walk more than a hundred yards at a stretch. We achieved some interesting hitching, improved our salesmanship and reached our terminal inn without overheating or fatigue. Soon afterwards in tottered the first of our Officer Instructors. Tired, disshevelled and dripping with sweat, he sank exhausted into a chair and called for a pint.

'How did you get on, sir?' we tactfully enquired.

'Well,' he replied, 'it was a bit rugged. Such a gorgeous morning, I was all set for a swim but you know how Lucky (the Senior Officer Instructor) always goes on about setting the right example so at his insistence we drearily dragged round the full circuit. Phew!' And he buried his face in his tankard.

Almost at once the door opened again and in stumbled the other Officer Instructor. If anything he seemed closer to physical collapse. Gently but firmly we steered him to the other end of the bar and called for another pint.

'How did it go with *you*, sir?' we asked.

'Oh God!' he gasped, 'it was awful. I'd have been perfectly content to have just a quiet stroll along the beach but you know what Brian is. "We'd better show willing," he said, "and follow up a couple of the clues." So off we strode and you know what that means with those great, long legs of his. After a bit he got his blood up and on we went to the bitter end. Gosh, I'm tired!'

On the Parade Ground mistakes in drill were treated increasingly harshly as the course progressed. The ultimate reward for carelessness or inattention was to be ordered to 'double round the island'. In theory this was a distance of some three-quarters of a mile; in practice it was nearly double that because at each of the main Instructional Sections (and there were four) the Chief of that section, informed by telephone that a victim was on the way, would emerge and order 'About Turn' and go on doing so until he judged it was enough when he would allow you to proceed to the next section. Furthermore it was traditional that no Long Course Officer would qualify unless, whether deserving his fate or not, he had doubled round the island.

Our Long Course was of average physical fitness save one who was definitely somewhat below par in this respect, though in the forefront for intelligence and imagination. He used to torture himself with the spectre of 'being sent round' which he knew was inevitable but doubted he could achieve without collapsing. Towards the end of the course fate struck and round he went. By the time he reached West Battery (the Gundrill Section) his rifle which weighed seven pounds, felt like seventy, his chest was heaving in painful gasps and iron bands were contracting his calf-muscles. He couldn't last out much longer. At that moment the bugle sounded 'Stand Easy' (the mid-morning break) over the broadcasting system. Out from the Battery streamed quantities of sailors, capless, lighting cigarettes, laughing and chattering. This was no time to pay any attention to a white-gaitered Long Course officer who was obviously doubling round the island as a penalty for his parade ground fault. They ignored him. To the victim this was the solution to his problem. Shuffling to a halt the exhausted officer called up the nearest rating.

'Come here my man.'

'Sir?'

'Don't you normally salute an officer when he passes you?'

Staggered at the total unfairness and unexpectedness of this accusation – in the middle of Stand Easy when he was not wearing a cap anyway – the unfortunate sailor mumbled something incomprehensible.

'What is your name?'

'Redgrave, sir.'

'Give me your Station Card' (a means of identity without which the owner could not go ashore). This was duly handed over.

Rested and rejuvenated the Long Course proceeded on his way, repeating the gambit whenever weariness again approached. In all a number of cards were collected and the officer reached the parade ground again having taken an inordinate time but in pretty good shape. Too good, perhaps? Pulling his hair down from under his cap he spat on his hands and lightly rubbed them over his face to simulate sweat. Then putting on an act, with buckling knees and panting breath he reported to the Parade Training Officer.

'Doubled . . . round . . . the island . . . sir.'

'Very good. Join up with your Class.'

'The following ratings failed to salute me, sir. Here are their Station Cards. Request you take the necessary disciplinary action.'

The biter was bit. Next morning, at a time when his other duties required him elsewhere, the Parade Training Officer was stuck at the Commander's Defaulters' table for 40 minutes while each case was dealt with. He was furious.

Of course the buzz got round quite quickly and it wasn't long before the Sub-Lieutenants got wind of it. But they did not play their hand very shrewdly. Early the following week a Sub-Lieutenant who was 'sent round' repeated the performance, including a verbatim copy of the report to the Parade Training Officer on completion.

'So all these men failed to salute you?' the latter queried.

'Yes sir.'

'And you took their Station Cards – these cards?'

'Yes sir,' in a voice eager with the enthusiasm of success at having beaten the system.

'Excellent.' The Sub-Lieutenant felt a glow of self-righteousness spreading over him. A hard look from the Parade Training Officer: 'You're just the man we've been looking for.' The glow became a flame and the Sub-Lieutenant ventured a smile of complacency. 'Now double round again and see if you can find any more!'

That stopped the rot.

★

Only a few months to go before the final exams which were to last continuously for three weeks. A time for concentrated hard work if good results were to be obtained.

Returning from weekend leave at my home in Devon one Sunday afternoon, en route to Chatham for a week's 15-inch turret drill in the Monitor *Abercrombie*, I became aware that my left instep was becoming increasingly uncomfortable. Must have tied the laces too tightly, I thought, and as the train rattled along I loosened them. The discomfort grew. A thorn? A wasp-sting? Inspection revealed nothing beyond a slight swelling and redness. On reaching Chatham Barracks I dumped my grip in my cabin and limped, now in some pain, to the Mess for a nightcap. But after barely half a glass of beer I realized that if I didn't walk out soon I should pass out. I left the Wardroom and turned in.

Next morning when I got up I found I could hardly walk. Any weight on my left foot was intolerable. Moving about the turret, always standing, was purgatory and at lunchtime, feeling dejected and useless, I gave in and reported sick.

Chatham Naval Hospital was much the same as any other Naval Hospital of those times. You went in with one thing, got treated for that plus something else, and emerged much later. Today, of course (as they have been for some time past), things are radically different in the Naval Hospitals. I would confidently trust myself to either of them for any complaint and feel absolutely assured that my treatment would be unsurpassed elsewhere. But then it was different and, whilst I was well looked after over the next few days, an air of uncertainty persisted over my problem. Kindly nurses stuck oh-so-thick penicillin needles into my pincushion posterior. The Medical Specialist passed by my bed, enquired how I felt and moved on shaking his head. The Surgical Specialist glanced at my foot and muttered, 'We'll give it another 24 hours before we cut it,' before passing on to the next bed rubbing his hands with knifely anticipation. Under my sheets I shivered and determined to escape before I became a chopping block.

Next day the swelling was slightly less and I was feeling 'better in myself' as Nanny used to say. My difficulty now was how to persuade the butchers that I was on the mend and extricate myself from their clutches.

'How are we today?'

'Oh better, sir, very much better.'

'Good, good. We'll see how you are tomorrow then.'

'And how are you feeling now?' (from another one).

'Quite a different thing, sir. Almost all right you might say.'

A slight shadow of disappointment that I might yet evade the knife clouded my questioner's brow. 'Hmm. Still some contusion. We'll see.'

Another 24 hours. I turned the record over and played Side 2 with more volume.

'I'm fine. Most grateful. Just an occasional twinge when I walk but otherwise no problem. When can I return to duty, please? I have some very important exams coming up. Today? Tomorrow at latest? I *must* get back.' Thus was my release negotiated for the following day.

But there remained one final hurdle, obligatory in those days for an officer: to see the Surgeon Rear Admiral before departure. The great man was pacing up and down in his spacious room when I was ushered in next morning.

'Good morning, my boy, good morning,' he boomed. 'How are you feeling?'

'Fine, sir, thank you, just fine.'

'Ah good. My people did a good job on you eh?'

'Magnificent, sir. I really am deeply grateful.'

'Not at all, not at all. What we're here for, don't you know? Well, there it is then. Off you go.'

'Thank you, sir. Goodbye.'

We shook hands and, gritting my teeth against the pain of walking the few paces to the door without limping, I left.

Sunday night. What a relief to be safely back in the familiar surroundings of Whale Island. But the problem of curing my foot remained, as did that of getting about my various duties. Squaring my senior Officer Instructor was straightforward. He was a kindly, understanding man and saw the point immediately. Next, I telephoned an old wartime shipmate who had been a Surgeon Lieutenant RNVR with me in *Javelin* and who now practiced across the water in Gosport. From him I obtained the name of a doctor in Southsea who he highly recommended.

The following day, as soon as work was over, I slipped into plain clothes and hurried off to see my unknown medical adviser, to whom I had telephoned for an appointment. He proved to be a plump, bald-headed man with a toothbrush moustache and serious manner; he did not impress me. Nevertheless on the strength of my introduction he examined my foot and noted my case history. It seemed prudent to mention my penicillin treatment 'at a local hospital', but I carefully avoided all reference to Chatham or the Navy.

'I can do nothing without an X-ray,' he said coldly. 'Here is a chit to arrange it and here is a prescription for some ointment to rub into your instep. Come and see me again in a week's time.'

I took my leave, had my X-ray and dutifully applied the ointment. Ointment? Really, who ever heard of such a thing curing a swollen instep with the skin unbroken? My faith in this recipe was zero. Five days later my foot was completely normal again.

My return visit to the Southsea doctor was interesting. On entering his consulting room he looked at me curiously from behind his desk.

'You're in one of the Services aren't you?' was his opening remark. 'The Navy I suppose?'

Now I had nothing to hide. 'Yes,' I replied.

'Why did you come to see me?'

I told him the truth of my imminent exams and their importance and of the hazards of protracted time in a Naval Hospital.

He accepted my explanation. 'Hmm,' he said, 'we do not seem to have been quite straight with each other. When I first examined you last week I thought you had tuberculosis of the bone.'

It was my turn to look surprised. 'It's all right,' he went on, 'you have not. I'm glad your foot is cured. Good night.' And he declined any fee.

January, 1948. The Long Course successfully completed, I was now a fully qualified Gunnery Officer, re-appointed to Whale Island as Parade Training Officer and teaching Sub-Lieutenants. Immediately on my return I was summoned by the Training Commander. Commander (G) was a rumbustious extrovert whose flamboyance had been developed more than his intellect. But despite our gap in age and seniority we were good friends.

'Morning Henry,' he greeted me.

'Good morning, sir.'

'Parade Training Officer. You are responsible for the standards of drill and smartness throughout the Island. They must be kept at the very highest levels. Nothing but the best will do. Got it?'

'Yes sir.'

'From now on your every action should be tempered by injustice.'

'Aye, aye sir.'

'Make it so.' And with a curt nod my initiation briefing was terminated.

It was an interesting directive and a fascinating task. The Parade Training Staff of a Gunner, two Chief Petty Officer Instructors and half a dozen Petty Officer Gunnery Instructors were some of the finest men in the Navy. They were required to give a performance of 100% and looked to you to give a lead at that level. Their highly developed brand of ruthless kindness led to a love-hate relationship with those under their instruction which was unsurpassed. Superb men whose sense of humour kept them sane and whose sense of fairness (albeit tempered by injustice!) ensured their success.

The Sub-Lieutenants were the spice of life. Young, keen, receptive and up to any tricks they thought they could get away with. Classes were of twelve to fifteen and lasted ten weeks. Each was quite different and lectures had to be adjusted accordingly. Preparation of lectures was hard work and had to be meticulous. But after three weeks of such close contact they were your friends for life and the relationship established was a very special one. It was an enormously rewarding and enjoyable job.

Until one morning the First Lieutenant sent for me.

'Ah, good morning Henry.'

'Good morning, sir.'

'Your next class – Egyptian Sub-Lieutenants.'

'Me, sir? Egyptians? Oh no, you must be joking.'

'Why?'

'Well sir I'm not sure that I like Egyptians all that much and if I "temper my every action with injustice" there may be an international incident.'

The First Lieutenant was a great friend but at this point he looked cross and stern.

'You take the Egyptian Sub-Lieutenants. Now get on with it.'

'Aye aye, sir,' and I left the office.

Later I discovered the reason for his untypical irritation. Two other Junior Staff Officers had been assigned this task but each in turn had ducked it on one pretext or another. Enough was enough.

My new class joined over a weekend and instead of going on weekend leave I deliberately stayed at the Gunnery School to welcome and get to know them a bit before we started work. We first met at breakfast on Sunday morning. We were all in plain clothes and while it was impossible for them to know who I was, it was not difficult for me to pick them out. They were fat, swarthy and morose. Their leader (as I knew), though still a Sub-Lieutenant was seven years older than me and already nearly bald. The prospect was not appealing.

But it was a lovely summer's day and after breakfast I went out onto the lawn in front of the Mess where my new charges had gathered and were smoking cigarettes.

'Good morning,' I said to the first group. 'Is everything all right?'

'Hmm,' was the grunted response.

'No problems over luggage?' I put to the next clutch.

'No. Is all right,' they growled.

'Found your cabins all right?' I enquired of the third and last group.

'Yeah,' they grunted.

What a surly lot, I thought, and what a jolly time we're going to have. But for the moment I reckoned there was little future in prolonging this opening gambit.

'Good,' I remarked briskly to them all. 'I'm glad you have no problems. My cabin is No. 18. Come and see me if you want help at any time. I shall be your Course Officer for the next ten weeks.'

The reaction was instant and extreme. Beaming smiles broke out on all their faces. Rising to their feet they pulled out their cigarette cases and extended bonhomie.

'Have a cigarette, sir.'

'Very nice to meet you, sir.'

'What a lovely place this is, sir.'

Yes sir. No sir. Three bags full sir.

Ugh.

Nevertheless we got on quite well for the first three weeks until one afternoon the Training Commander sent for me.

'How are the Egyptian Subs doing, Henry?'

'Early days, sir, but about as well as could be expected.'

'You're not being too hard on them?' (This from *him* of all people!)

'They are being treated exactly as you directed, sir, occasionally plus a little something. May I enquire why you ask?'

'Because I've noticed that all this week their leader has spent his entire lunch hour in the telephone booth and today I eavesdropped to hear what he was up to. He was ringing up his Embassy.'

'Ah,' I thought. 'Here is another pigeon coming home to roost.' Aloud I said, 'I'll try to find out more sir,' and we left it at that.

The trouble I discovered was money. Two of the course were accustomed to receiving from their parents a private allowance of £500 per month (a good deal of money in those days). But in its wisdom the British Admiralty had deemed that Egyptian Officers under training in this country should get the same pay as their English contemporaries. Accustomed as they were to a much more liberal way of Service life this caused my charges a sizeable problem. It was at that point that word came through that sailors in Portsmouth Barracks were complaining to their Divisional Officers that their girlfriends were being stolen by Egyptian Sub-Lieutenants on Whale Island.

As their final exams approached I became aware that there were four quite separate factions within the course of thirteen. Each in turn invited me out to the most expensive restaurant in Portsmouth and gave me a slap-up dinner. Several of them had their wives present, charming cultured girls of great beauty and clearly briefed by their husbands to direct their talents at me throughout. These evenings were convivial and enjoyable but not long after the coffee and brandy they all ended the same way.

'Now sir,' one of them would say, 'what questions are we going to get in our examinations, sir?'

'I don't know,' I answered. 'Your papers are set by one Staff Officer and corrected by another. I have no hand in it. But of course I do know your syllabus, which parts of it are the most important, and your instruction has been framed accordingly. If you get an off-beat catch question you'll just have to do your best but I think you may be assured that the majority will be straightforward and designed to find out what you know rather than what you do not.'

They all passed and we parted good friends.

The senior Supply Officer at HMS *Excellent* was Captain (S) Valentine Duke. Of tiny stature, he had a round, gnarled, walnut face topped by silver hair. His repertoire of invective was extensive and freely used and his great love was sailing naval whalers. He worked, played, drank and smoked hard and seemed to flourish on it.

At the start of one major Guest Night Dinner towards the end of the summer term in 1948, just as the Chaplain was about to say Grace, Valentine Duke quietly slipped out of his chair and under the table. He had had a stroke and spent some weeks recovering in the Royal Naval Hospital, Haslar. He returned in November apparently unimpaired but under strict injunctions to ease back all round on his way of life. However, he was not a man to change his ways and it took only a short time for him to revert to his norm. Despite renewed warnings from his doctors that if he had another stroke it would be the end of him, he continued to live as he was wont. Shortly before the Christmas break he did suffer another stroke and returned to Haslar.

At this point I was sent for by the Training Commander.

'You will be aware,' he said, 'that *Vernon* (the Torpedo and Anti-Submarine School) has recently been exceeding all traditional methods in attempting to outdo the Gunnery School in smartness and efficiency?'

'Yes sir.'

'And that to an extent they have succeeded?'

'I am afraid that is the case.'

'We are about to be presented with an opportunity to correct this adverse trend. Captain (S) is dying. When he goes I have arranged that he will be buried at sea from the Gunnery Firing Ship (*Modeste*). I want you as Parade Training Officer to write the orders for the funeral. You are to cover the full ceremonial in the utmost detail, and submit them to me before you go on Christmas leave. I will arrange to have a master stencil prepared, lacking only the date and my signature, and it will be held in my office against the event. Is that clear?'

'Absolutely sir.'

And so it was. Valentine Duke was nothing if not tough and he hung on grimly for another two weeks. But there was a limit even for him. Early in January he slipped away peacefully and the full panoply of a ceremonial burial at sea from Whale Island was set in train.

The weather on the day was foul: cold, wet and blowing hard. I had put myself in charge of the Funeral Firing Party and apart from the usual problem of picking up the step during the heavily muffled opening bars of The Dead March from *Saul* the shoreside ceremony went without a hitch. *Modeste* slipped from the jetty as planned and made her way down harbour. As we neared the entrance by Fort Blockhouse the ship began to lift to the heavy seas which were pouring through the narrows. The wind was now at gale force, the Funeral Firing Party had difficulty in keeping their feet still while resting on their arms reversed and the ensign draping the coffin kept flapping this way and that.

Suddenly I was assailed by what the Navigation Manual so aptly describes for the onset of a typhoon: 'an indefinable feeling that all is not well.' What caused it? No clue presented itself but my thoughts and gaze had been centred on the coffin. Flap, flap went the ensign. Now the whole windward side of the coffin was exposed as well as the underneath. Something still seemed wrong but I couldn't place it. Pointless to stand and worry. I broke my position, stepped up to the coffin and examined it closely while pretending to adjust the ensign. Immediately the problem was revealed: there were no holes in the coffin. Without them, instead of sinking it would merely float away when tipped into the sea and the superstitious effects on the assembled company would be considerable.

We finally cleared the harbour with the Funeral Firing Party still struggling to keep their balance against the now heaving deck and with a Shipwright busily applying a brace and bit to the underside of the coffin. One of my nine lives.

During the summer of 1948 two destroyers of the United States Navy paid an operational visit to Portsmouth. The Commander-in-Chief, Admiral Lord Fraser, was a great promoter of Anglo-US relations and had a wide circle of friends in their Navy stemming from his time in command of the British Pacific Fleet at the end of the war. He invited both Commanding Officers to lunch with him on board the *Victory*. Having once been his Flag Lieutenant for a week while the real one gained sea experience in a destroyer in the middle of the war when the Admiral was commanding the Home Fleet from *Duke of York* I was also included in the lunch party.

It was a convivial and informal occasion and soon the two Americans were competely at ease. Over lunch the conversation quickly turned to gunnery (Fraser was himself a gunnery specialist) and a vigorous discussion took place over the relative merits of the standard destroyer's gun in the respective navies – the US 5-inch and British 4.5-inch. From the snippets that I overheard it was mutually agreed that there was not much to choose between them. The debate became centred on the weights of the respective shells. One of the American COs was well versed in all that sort of statistical stuff and came out pat with the 5-inch figure. Over the weight of the 4.5-inch the Admiral had more difficulty.

'Hmm,' he said, 'er, yes, well um, let me see, it must be about 60 to 65 pounds. But here's a chap who will tell us exactly – he's just qualified as a Gunnery Specialist – eh laddie?' and he leant across the table looking enquiringly at me.

I hadn't the remotest idea but felt I ought to put up some sort of show. Assuming an expression which I hoped registered great concentration of thought I looked up at the deckhead, paused for a few moments and then looking my C-in-C straight in the eye I replied.

'Yes sir, that's right.'

To my surprise and disappointment it didn't fool Bruce Fraser for an instant.

'You're guessing,' he said at once and, turning to his American guests, added,

'There you are, you see, a newly qualified Gunnery Officer and he doesn't know the weight of the shell from the standard destroyer's gun,' and he burst into roars of laughter. The Americans were politely sympathetic and I felt wildly ashamed.

The lunch party broke up. The Americans departed back to their ships. Lord Fraser kindly offered to lift me back to Whale Island in his car. At the end of Stanley Road he stopped the car and I got out. Waggling his finger at me he gave a final instruction with mock severity:

'You are to go straight to your Captain and report to him that you, a newly qualified Gunnery Officer, didn't know the weight of the shell from the standard British destroyer's gun. HA! ha! ha!' and roaring with laughter he drove off.

That night, over a drink in the Mess, before dinner, I duly reported all this to my Captain, Pat McLoughlin.

'Humph,' he blustered, 'mm, well now, let me see, I ought to know that because I virtually designed that gun with Lord Fraser when he was Controller. Yes, it must be about sixty pounds.'

At that moment Lieutenant-Commander Harold Dannreuther, the Long Course Junior Officer Instructor, came in.

'Ah,' said the Captain with relief, 'here's someone who will know. What's the weight of a 4.5 inch shell?'

'Oh dear,' came the reply. 'I can do a 6-inch, that's 112 lbs and a 5.25", that's 85, but I'm not sure of a 4.5 inch.'

Shortly afterwards Lieutenant Commander George Lamotte, the Long Course Senior Officer Instructor, entered the ante-room. He did not know the weight of any shell. The Captain left and any feeling of shame I might have previously experienced evaporated!

The story got around. It reached the ears of Commander Michael Le Fanu who was Experimental Commander. He didn't know the answer either but he initiated some research with the local Armament Depot at Priddy's Hard and got the precise figure. He then put his workshop onto making an appropriate present for the C-in-C on the occasion of his next birthday. Le Fanu had been Fleet Gunnery Assistant on Fraser's Staff in *Duke of York* during the war and the two were great friends.

The gift took the form of small stainless steel model shell mounted on a perspex base inscribed with: –

'4.5 Shell wt 55 lbs 3oz 6dr'.

To one side of the plinth was a small cylindrical steel segment of similar diameter which could by means of a projecting pin be slotted into the base of the model shell. An inscription by this read:

'Fraser attachment Wt 7lbs 4oz 10 dr.'

Thirty years later when I became C-in-C Fleet I used to visit Lord Fraser once a term in his little house in East Molesey. Aged 90 by then he had lost the use of his legs but not of his mind. The latter remained needle-sharp with remarkable windows of memory; nearly all those windows were wide open. Every Christmas I would take him a special Christmas stocking, mainly of little things to eat or drink, until I ran out of old seaboot stockings and had to make do with cardboard boxes.

Early in 1981, shortly before his 93rd birthday, Bruce Fraser died peacefully in the little Nursing Home just round the corner from his house. It fell to his erstwhile Personal Assistant when he had been Controller of the Navy, Mrs Renée Duncan, to deal with the large accumulation of memorabilia. I had got to know her quite well during my visits for which she had always baked a special cake.

'Should you,' I asked her with some diffidence, 'come across this little joke-model of a 4.5 inch shell when you sort out the effects it would make for me a happy reminder of a great man and I cannot think it would now mean much to anyone else.'

She was not familiar with the object in question but promised to bear it in mind.

Some weeks later during a buffet lunch in the Mall House Flat over Admiralty Arch, following Lord Fraser's Thanksgiving Service in Westminster Abbey at which I had given the address, Renée Duncan handed me a small package. In it, beautifully polished, was the 4.5 inch shell. It stands on the mantlepiece in my study today.

In the spring of 1949 it seemed likely that I would be re-appointed. I faced this prospect with resignation and interest. Resignation because for long years it had been traditional that the Parade Training Officer of last year became the Portsmouth Field Gun Officer of next year; as such he would train the crew and take it to Olympia for the Royal Tournament. Interest, because although I did not expect to be given any choice, I felt that nearly three years ashore was enough for a young Lieutenant and that it was time I freshened the nip at sea. So when summoned by the Training Commander my mind was prepared even though I doubted the opportunity of speaking it.

'Ah, Henry,' the Training Commander exuded his normal flamboyant bonhomie. 'Your next job. How would you like to do the Field Gun?'

'Straight answer to a straight question, sir,' I replied, 'I'd rather go to sea.'

'What?' He was clearly flabbergasted by my unexpected reaction.

'Of course if you tell me to do the Field Gun, sir,' I struggled desperately to retrieve the situation, 'I will willingly do so. But you asked if . . .'

'Enough. Get out of my office.' I had never seen James Farnol so angry.

'But sir . . .'

'Not another word. Out.' I left.

There followed the most extraordinary performance. It would have been dead easy for the Training Commander simply to have *told* me (or any other Junior Staff Officer), 'You are this year's Field Gun Officer. Get on with it.' But for some curious reason this was not done. Instead other officers were sent for and asked if they would like to take the job on. Their reactions were not unlike mine.

'Not sure that it's quite my line sir.'

'Could I have 48 hours to think it over?'

'May I give you an answer after next weekend so that I can discuss it with my wife.'

And each in turn came back with: 'I'd really rather not.'

Finally one of my own Long Course was transferred from Chatham and given the task without the option.

Three weeks later I was again summoned to the Training Commander's office. The interview was bitter-sweet, opening with:

'Good morning. Now, Henry, *since* you didn't want the Fieldgun . . .' long pregnant pause for effect, ' . . . minesweepers.'

I endeavoured to keep a poker face despite my bitter disappointment being pretty sure that minesweepers possessed no effective gunnery capability whatsoever. My surmise was confirmed when James Farnol urbanely exaggerated the importance of the job, explaining that while my contemporaries would be *second* gunnery officer to some flotilla, I should be the *only* Gunnery Officer in mine. It was unconvincing stuff and on leaving I went across to the Experimental Department to check the facts in their equipment manual. An *Algerine* Class minesweeper was armed with a single 4 inch Mk

V gun (obsolescent frigates had Mk XVI so it was the closest to a muzzle-loader in service), and two single 40 mm Bofors which were hand-operated (so that the possibility of aiming them accurately at a modern aircraft was remote). With a heavy heart I went on weekend leave.

Self-pity is an unrewarding indulgence. I had made my own bed; now I must lie on it. With a forced cheerfulness which I did not feel I described my situation to my mother.

She heard me out in silence, then looking me straight in the eyes commented,

'You *are* a fool.'

This needled me. I explained the unassailable logic of being overdue for getting back to sea.

'That may be,' she retorted, 'but at Olympia you would have been very much in the public eye and that never does anyone any harm. As it is you will be banished to these little dirty, hard-drinking ships and . . . oh! I don't know.'

I loved and respected my mother greatly. She was an exceptionally shrewd and practical person. The feeling grew that perhaps she was right.

I steeled myself for the worst.

7

HAPPY DISGRACE

O happy band of pilgrims
Look upward to the skies
Where such a light affliction
Shall win so great a prize.

J. M. Neale

The 2nd Minesweeping Flotilla was stationed in the Mediterranean and based on Malta. During the war parts of the Mediterranean had been extensively mined and a good deal of operational mine clearance remained to be done. The flotilla was currently deployed in the Aegean. It comprised eight Ocean Minesweepers of the *Algerine* class, some still with reciprocating engines, and three *Isle* class Trawlers as Danlayers. The latter had recently been converted to burn fuel oil instead of coal. Apart from the Flotilla Leader (*Fierce*) which was commanded by a middle-seniority Captain and the Divisional Leader (*Rifleman*) which was commanded by a junior Captain, the *Algerines* were commanded by Lieutenant Commanders and the Danlayers by senior Lieutenants.

Although the Minesweepers were also equipped with magnetic loops for clearing magnetic mines and had a limited anti-acoustic mine capability, most of the fields in the Mediterranean were straightforward contact mines. The technique for sweeping them was for a Danlayer to lay a line of marker danbuoys just inside safe water and for the Sweepers, keeping meticulous quarterline station, to clear a path or 'lap'. Each Sweeper towed a special serrated wire, kept at an angle of 45 degrees from her stern by a heavy metal deflector and maintained at the desired depth by a similar deflector in the vertical plane. The end of the sweep wire was marked by a float which kept on the surface. Thus all ships kept in safe water – the Leader by steering close to the line of danbuoys and the remainder by keeping just inside the marker float of the next ahead. At the end of each lap the Flotilla manoeuvred, always in safe water, to transpose the sweeps to the other quarter and enter the next lap, following a new line of dans, in the opposite direction. This called for precise navigation, professional shiphandling and good teamwork. The sweep wires were designed to cut the mooring wires holding the mines to their sinkers on the bottom. When cut, the mines would float to the surface under their own buoyancy, there to be destroyed by gunfire. The weapons provided for this purpose were 0.5 inch Boyes Anti-Tank Rifles, with a deafening crack and a kick like a mule when fired. Shooting needed to be quick and accurate or the surfaced mine would drift away astern and be a menace to passing shipping. On being struck by several rounds, sometimes the mine would sink harmlessly to the bottom; at others it would explode with a spectacular column of blackened water.

There was always an element of risk in such operations: either from a mine having strayed into what was assumed to be safe water (and no amount of sweeping can be 100%); or from a mine caught by the sweep wire detonating on contact with the wire and so damaging the parent ship. To reduce the risk to acceptable proportions the *Algerines* had been constructed with extra accommodation above the waterline to which the Ship's Companies were limited whilst sweeping.

Tactical Control of mine clearance operations was by VHF voice radio. A simple and highly effective system of ecclesiastical callsigns had been devised: the Leader was 'Bishop' and other individual ships 'Vicar', 'Verger' and so on. The Flotilla as a whole was collectively 'Congregation'. By adding the prefix 'the' before a ship's callsign it was made clear to all that the Captain M/S himself or the Ship's Commanding Officer was speaking.

Having gone out to Malta in a Trooper, I took passage to the Aegean in a destroyer and transferred to a Danlayer for the final six-hour passage to the field on which the Flotilla was working. It was in the aftermath of a gale and a high sea was still running. The notoriously cork-like motion of the ex-trawler combined with a lunch of resuscitated corned beef fritters and leaden suet pudding studded with stale dates inclined me to keep my stomach in the fresh air of the bridge.

We reached the anchorage at 2100. The weather was better inshore but it was a dark night. Almost at once the Leader's motor cutter came over to collect me and my gear. Approaching *Fierce*, there was little sign of life on the dimly lit upper deck apart from the familiar figure of the Flotilla Communications Officer, Peter Page, who I remembered from Dartmouth. He appeared to be the Duty Officer since he was wearing a cap. The rest of his attire consisted of seaboots, a pair of the filthiest old grey flannels I have ever smelled and a tattered sweater which had once been white. Swaying and reeling about the sweepdeck, he picked up a heaving line, hurled it in the direction of the incoming boat, let go of both ends and collapsed in a heap on the deck – clearly too drunk to take any further part in proceedings.

I stepped on board. There were no lights and out of the gloom appeared Bison Turner, the Flotilla Gunnery Officer who I was to relieve and who had qualified in the Long Course before my own. Capless but otherwise quite neatly dressed in a sort of yachting outfit, he greeted me with his usual courteous warmth and only a barely discernible slurring of his words. But the aura of alcohol which surrounded him hit one at a range of six feet.

'C-come to the, er, Wardroom,' he breathed at me, 'and have a . . . a jolly good whisky. I'm ssshoor you need one.' I readily agreed and he led the way below. My mother's cautionary words came back to me with great clarity. 'This is what you asked for,' I thought to myself; 'this is what you've got. Best accept it as your new way of life.'

The scene in the Wardroom removed any residual doubts. The table was covered with a dirty, torn sheet, its owner's name still prominent in one corner. At one side sat Harry Janes, the Engineer Officer, still dressed in filthy oil-soaked overalls and with his gloves and torch where one might ordinarily have expected his glass to have been. He was still wearing his cap and was preoccupied with transferring almost liquid corned beef from a cracked bowl in the centre of the table to his mouth with a tablespoon by the most direct route, and he was not doing it very neatly, so that much of his efforts spattered onto the table.

'Evening,' he greeted me curtly. That appeared to be the limit of his vocabulary.

At the far end of the table sat Bill Fitzherbert, the only officer not part of the Flotilla Staff. He was wearing a flamboyant skiing jacket and was engrossed in shovelling the pile of food from his plate into his mouth in a kind of continuous feed action.

'Mmm,' he grunted, momentarily interrupting the food flow, 'how d'you do? Gotta go on watch,' and he crouched lower over his plate to speed up the supply line.

My predecessor guided me to an armchair and sat down heavily on the club fender.

'Whisky?' he enquired.

'Thank you,' I said with feeling, glancing sideways at the recumbent form of a stout officer stretched out on the settee, his face covered by a duffel coat, snoring like an express train.

'Oh don't mind him,' said my host. 'That's Derek Ford, the Navigator, you know. He's on the bridge all day and it's quite a strain so as soon as we get back to harbour he relaxes a bit. He'll be all right again in the morning, or certainly by around midday.'

I sipped my drink appreciatively and we chatted.

'Are we sweeping again tomorrow?'

'Oh yes. We've only got another ten days to finish clearing this field if we are to keep to programme.'

'What sort of timing does that involve?'

'Enter the first lap at first light. That means weighing at about 0530. Back in the anchorage around 2100. Have another whisky?'

'Thank you. Have you had supper yet?'

'No. That'll be in about half an hour. There's plenty of time for you to unpack your essentials and get changed.'

'Into what?'

'Well, I should just slip on a bow tie and otherwise stay as you are for tonight.'

He showed me to my cabin, introduced me to its other occupant – Bill Mann, the Torpedo and Anti-Submarine Officer – who greeted me coolly and immediately launched into a diatribe against the inconvenience of having to double up in a cabin that size. And with a *Gunnery* Officer! With which he stumped off, slamming the door behind him.

I had a quick wash, sorted out a few things and brooded momentarily on my folly. Brooded with resolution, for continually running through my head was the refrain 'only yourself to blame . . . only yourself to blame.'

Fifteen minutes later I cautiously re-entered the Wardroom. It was full. All the officers were there, laughing and chatting away happily. All smartly turned out in Mess Undress.

The whole affair had been a put-up job.

Not long afterwards the Flotilla paid a visit to Izmir (formerly Smyrna) in Turkey. This was a welcome break from the long days of minesweeping and everyone who could went ashore to take advantage of it. For the officers a *Thé Dansant* was arranged in the local yacht club on the evening of our arrival and shortly after 1700 most of us went along to this.

The prospect that confronted us was not encouraging. A sizeable room with huge picture windows, giving a magnificent view of the harbour. In the centre a small, circular, highly-polished dance floor, to the side of which a four-piece Palm Court orchestra strummed Strauss. At one end a tiny bar dispensing extremely fizzy soft drinks of vivid colour; and all around the perimeter little tables at some of which sat plump, elderly locals with their plumper, faded wives, nibbling sticky cakes. The air conditioning was token, the conviviality muted and overall there hung a pall of heavy cloying sweetness. With sinking hearts but resolute chivalry we stepped into the room prepared to do or die.

A quick scan of the social horizon revealed only one promising target: a strikingly handsome woman with a magnificent figure, swept back blonde hair above an attractive, humorous face with clear, slightly mocking, grey eyes. She turned out to be the wife of an English doctor. To her my predecessor Bison Turner homed with unswerving accuracy. Soon they were in happy, laughing conversation and wandering across to the bar. Within minutes, while the rest of us were still stumbling over our introductions and wondering whether tea or lemonade was the lesser evil, Mrs Carruthers had taken charge and organized gin and tonic. Bison – so called because of his remarkable facial resemblance to this formidable beast – was the gentlest of people with a great sense of fun and absolutely unflappable. He was forever quietly teasing people to jolly them along. He was also one of the best (smoothest?) men on the dance floor I have ever seen. Fortified by a glass and a dance of two he was now well advanced in teasing Mrs Carruthers; they seemed to be getting on splendidly.

Evidently he went a bit too far. To the astonishment of the rest of us in their vicinity she suddenly rounded on him and slapped his face. It was a resounding blow which echoed through the room like a pistol shot. Instantly all conversation ceased and a complete hush descended. At that moment the band struck up an old-fashioned waltz. Turner did not bother fingering his smarting cheek, smiled devastatingly at Mrs Carruthers and said firmly:

'Shall we dance?'

Without waiting for a reply he grasped her around the waist and expertly swept her onto the floor. Nobody else ventured to compete with this display and throughout the entire dance they had the floor to themselves.

Next day Captain Keith Walter (the Senior Officer of the Group) gave a lunch party in his cabin on board the Leader. He was a big, well-built, impressive man whose almost outrageous good looks were a source of embarrassment and envy to the Staff and Junior Officers less well endowed when it came to impressing the girls. As is customary in those parts the ships were berthed stern to the jetty and to get ashore involved more or less 'walking the plank' over some of the minesweeping gear before reaching the normal gangway; not difficult but a manoeuvre which called for care and attention rather than panache.

The lunch party was an exclusive little *affaire à deux*; Mrs Carruthers had evidently also caught the Captain's eye at the previous evening's reception ashore. She arrived punctually in a chauffeur-driven Rolls Royce, negotiated the gangway with applomb and presented her magnificent mink-clad figure to her host with a smile to capture kings. I was the Duty Officer.

At about 1530 there were signs that the party was breaking up: was Mrs Carruthers' car alongside, etc? Though a glorious sunny day there was a sharp nip in the air and the gangway staff were wearing watchcoats. No breath of wind stirred the glutinous slurry which formed the surface of the water in that part of the harbour, a mixture of waste fuel oil, garbage and the usual flotsam and jetsam including several dead rats and a sheep; the crispness of the air acted as only a partial antidote to the resultant aroma.

The Captain led his guest aft, deep in continuing conversation. It had been a convivial interlude and Mrs Carruthers had clearly been charmed by naval hospitality to say nothing of the cultured *savoir faire* of her host. But now, alas, it was over. 'Good-bye Captain Walter,' she said with a radiant smile and, gathering her voluminous fur coat about her ample frame, waving graciously with her disengaged hand and continuing to gush, 'thank you, thank you so much, a really lovely party,' she mounted backwards the three steps leading to 'the plank' and with a final genial wave disappeared straight over the side to join the sheep in the oily mush of Izmir inner harbour.

Reaction on board was swift. Without hesitation. Able Seaman Brown, the Quartermaster, stripped off his heavy watchcoat and leaped over the side to the rescue. The rest of us were then witnesses to the paradox of the century. For Able Seaman Brown, though brave and loyal and gallant to a fault, was quite unable to swim. On the other hand Mrs Carruthers was an exceedingly good swimmer. Grasping the helpless Quartermaster in the approved fashion she ably towed him through the rats and muckage to the jetty steps and so to survival. There, having mounted the steps herself and with filthy black water still streaming off her, she turned to the ship with a last triumphant wave and got into her car past the horrified gaze of her chauffeur. The ghastly squelch as she sank contentedly back amongst the ivory-coloured upholstery still rings in my ears.

During the afternoon of our final day at Izmir there was a local race meeting. The course was a little distance out of town and special trains were run to the nearby station, some ten minutes away. As visitors we were given free tickets and mingled with the happy, laughing crowd in holiday mood.

Everything about the racecourse was in miniature but quite perfect. The whole area resembled an emerald saucer of brilliant hue surrounded by steep hills. The flat course was an oval of short, springy turf, the rails everywhere were gleaming white, there was a paddock, a small grandstand and a tote.

As the time of the first race approached, four fine looking horses were led into the paddock and in due course the jockeys, all in resplendent colours, mounted, cantered down to the start and . . . they were off. A spanking pace was maintained throughout the two circuits and the finish was excitingly close. True it took the tote 45 minutes to work out the odds and start paying out; but meantime the run up to the next race was proceeding on traditional lines.

Once more four splendid horses appeared in the paddock (no, they were *not* the same ones: these were clearly fresh and looked different). Four more jockeys in quite different colours took them away and this race, too, was run at a pace which rivalled its predecessor. Somebody won, somebody lost, and three-quarters of an hour later the tote . . .

And so a delightful afternoon passed in sporting leisure. There were six races in all. Perhaps the third and fourth lacked something of the zip of earlier ones and at the finish the horses were a little more strung out. Always four horses, but then the course was small and it was better that they should not be cramped. No owner's colours appeared twice and an atmosphere of keen, happy competition pervaded all.

Until the last two races. For each the start was noticeably less brisk and the finish was down to a rather forced canter. As we left and made our way back on foot over the green hills among the chattering crowd we learned why.

For the entire meeting there had been eight horses and four jockeys. And, lest the regulars look down their long noses, nobody could have enjoyed it more.

Despite the devastating effects of wartime bombing, the brave little island of Malta GC was quick to recover much of its charm and ability to provide fun, both sporting and social. Its dockyard and magnificent natural harbour with its numerous deep-water creeks provided an ideal base for the British Fleet, strategically placed in the centre of the Mediterranean Sea. The Maltese had been closely associated with the Navy for many years and a happy friendly relationship existed. In spring the island was carpeted with wildflowers of every description. In the summer the sun blazed on a sea of such brilliant blue as to defy the dazzling reflections from the white sandstone of the buildings. The whole island was steeped in ancient history and a rather pleasant languor sharpened only by the smell of goats.

The operating pattern of the 2nd Minesweeping Flotilla was ideal. At sea for mine clearance for about two months, then back to Malta for two to three weeks' maintenance of ships and men. No single element of the programme ever lasted long enough to permit the intrusion of monotony or boredom. At sea they worked hard; back in harbour they played equally hard.

One of my earlier social responsibilities was to write my name in my Admiral's book at his charming official house, Villa Pieta, at the top of Guardamanga Hill overlooking Msida and Lazaretto Creeks. Rear Admiral Jock McCall was a great character and a charming man, if a little alarming to junior officers. A week or two later I was invited to play tennis one Wednesday afternoon. On stepping on to the court my eye was immediately caught by a fresh-faced attractive looking girl of 17 the other side of the net. She was introduced to me as Mary and turned out to be the younger daughter of the house. At once I knew 'That's the girl for me'. Nine years later I married her and she has been the most wonderful wife ever since.

But at that time it was not so easy. She was very young and there were plenty of more handsome suitors whose time ashore in Malta was both more regular and more prolonged. Competition was keen.

One evening a car treasure hunt was organized by the First Lieutenant of the Half-Leader, *Rifleman*. The competitors gathered at the house of Colin Lings and his charming wife Jill. There we were given drinks, briefed on the rules of the game and divided into mixed car-loads. The clues were ingenious. Several of them led to selected bars where the follow-up clue could be obtained only through the proprietor over a drink already organized by our host. No laws on drinking and driving pertained there then. Timing was not too critical but we were to foregather finally in a favourite little restaurant at the head of St Paul's Bay between 2100 and 2130. There our host explained that we were next to drive to the extreme northern edge of the island and have a midnight picnic on the cliffs overlooking the Comino Channel which separates Malta from Gozo. That was when the trouble started.

As we left the restaurant someone challenged: 'Race you to Comino.'

It was enough. Into the cars we piled. Doors slammed. Engines started. Horns sounded. Gravel spurted and we were away. In summer the smooth surfaces of Maltese roads became highly polished by passing traffic and their film of dry dust. Corners – and there were plenty on the road to Comino – even if taken at quite a moderate speed caused a disturbing screaming of tyres. That night the screaming of the tyres was matched by the pleas for mercy and care from those in the back seats. I have to admit that the sliding roof of my small Standard car was left on the edge of the road en route but it caused no other damage. We reached the rendezvous briskly and in close order, parked in a semi-circle with our sidelights left on and got out for our picnic. In answer to a call from nature I wandered off into the darkness when suddenly my feet shot from under me and I fell.

The cliffs of Comino rise sheer out of the sea to a height of nearly 100 feet. No wall, hedge or fence marks the danger but then no sensible person would walk so close, especially after dark. All this flashed through my mind as I was falling. So did a lot else. Too late now to propose to my Admiral's daughter. What a silly way to go. Kaleidoscopic glimpses of the past: of home, the garden, the river, Whale Island, the Flotilla – none of them to be seen again. Some apprehension about the immediate future. What would it feel like when I landed? Would it hurt terribly?

It did. My knees hit my chin and I rolled on to my side, twisting my left ankle. I was on a ledge about twelve feet down.

With some help from above I scrambled back up to safety and rather shakily propped myself against the bumper of my car. An hour or two later when we came to move off I was so stiff and sore I could hardly stand up.

Next morning I had occasion to see my Captain. As I entered his cabin he spotted my limp.

'Hello, Guns, what have you been up to?'

It is always best to tell the truth. 'I fell over the Comino Cliffs, sir,' I replied. He regarded me quizzically for a moment.

'Indeed,' he murmured.

Really there was nothing more to be said.

Normally the events which confronted the Officer of the Day (Duty Officer) in harbour were largely routine. But occasionally the orderly serenity of events was disrupted by some saga. One such occurred a few months after I had taken over.

It was a Sunday evening. Once again we were anchored off one of the Greek islands and due to continue our mine clearance operations early next day. The sky was blue, the sun shone, the sea was calm, all was peace.

At about 1700 the Duty Petty Officer came to me and reported that Leading Signalman Musgrave had over-celebrated his birthday at lunchtime and was now fighting mad and threatening everybody who came near him on his messdeck. I knew Musgrave quite well. He was a great big chap of limited intelligence but performed his duties soundly enough. At some stage in his past he had been a Navy heavyweight boxer. He would be a difficult customer to restrain if he became violent.

'Clear everyone off his messdeck,' I instructed the Petty Officer. 'We'll give him a chance to quieten down before we resort to manhandling him.'

'Aye aye sir.'

'And post one of the Duty Hands to watch him and act as a sentry.'

The PO left. Though none too happy with the situation, I did not see what more could sensibly be done.

Minutes later the PO returned, visibly agitated.

'Sir, Musgrave has broken out of the messdeck. He has unshipped one of those heavy circular hatch-covers and is now up on the fo'c'sle swinging it round his head and threatening to "do" anyone who approaches.'

'Fall in the Duty Part of the Watch,' I ordered. 'On the fo'c'sle but keep them well clear. I'll come up.'

This was the least I could do. Continued inactivity would be thoroughly bad for discipline and was unacceptable. Nevertheless I was none too clear how best to deploy the Duty Part nor how effective they would be in the event. I went on deck.

The scene on the fo'c'sle did not inspire confidence. The Leading Signalman was standing by the breakwater on the port side, his feet well apart, swaying to and fro, swinging the half-hundredweight hatchcover in one massive hand like a conductor with his baton. On the other side was the Duty Part, about a dozen men in two ranks, already muttering about the prospect – which they evidently liked no more than I did. It seemed highly probable someone was going to get hurt.

The Duty Petty Officer silenced the muttering, called the men to attention and reported to me.

I stood in front of them, quickly looked at each in turn and gave my orders.

'I have fallen you in,' I said, 'to restrain the Leading Signalman over there and to prevent him damaging himself or anybody else. In a moment, if necessary – and I think it almost certainly *will* be necessary – I shall tell you to get hold of him and take him below to the Sick Bay, using a Neil Robertson Stretcher [straightjacket] if necessary. When I give the order you will have to move fast and act firmly but he is not to be knocked around.'

It was evident from their expressions that they understood all too clearly what was expected of them. But though nothing was said, their eyes told me that if I did give the order they would not obey it. So what next? There seemed to be only one possible course of action.

'Watch me carefully,' I told the Petty Officer in front of the Duty Part. 'Do not intervene unless it is necessary. Stand by.'

I crossed the fo'c'sle and walked towards the Leading Signalman, keeping my eyes fixed on his. When within arm's length I stopped and said quietly,

'Don't be silly, Musgrave. Put that down and come to my cabin. I want to talk to you.'

Without waiting for any reaction, I turned my back on him and slowly walked aft, wondering what it would feel like to have my skull smashed in.

After a few paces I paused and half-turned to see what was happening. He was just behind me, no longer carrying the hatch cover.

We reached my cabin without further incident. He promptly burst into tears.

After fifteen happy months of work and play I was reappointed to Whale Island. By then the Flotilla was back on operational sweeping in the Aegean and it was arranged for a Royal Fleet Auxiliary to bring up the reliefs for myself and Ted Thorne, the Flotilla Communications Officer, from Malta.

As the day of departure approached the good spirit and comradeship of the Flotilla was revealed in many kindnesses. Every Wardroom lunched or dined or wined us out. The friendliness and hospitality were quite marvellous and it was with weary, nostalgic sadness that the two of us watched the RFA run in to anchor. For our part we had set a little joke in each of the ships, carefully timed to 'go off' some 24 hours after our departure.

The Leader's boat returned from the RFA. In it was the new Signal Officer; there was no Gunnery Officer.

It was three weeks before we got back to Malta and found my relief belatedly waiting on the jetty. Not one of the jokes was retrievable and all had gone off as planned. My arrival had been matched only by my departure.

8

CROWNING GLORY

'I never found naval men at a loss. Tell them to do anything that
is not impossible and depend upon it they will do it.'

The Duke of Wellington

After qualifying at the Naval Staff College in 1952 I was suddenly switched
from a *Daring* Class destroyer whose building had been delayed to become
the Staff Officer for the Naval Brigade in London for the Coronation of
Queen Elizabeth II. For this I was seconded to the Gunnery Division of the
Naval Staff, given some rough figures of the numbers and categories involved
and more or less told to get on with it.

It proved to be a fascinating, unusual and valuable experience. Fascinating
because it involved dealing with all three Services, the Metropolitan Police
and the City of Westminster authorities. Unusual because of its immense
variety ranging from demonstrating full dress uniform on horseback to the
Admiralty Board, through writing very detailed orders which left little to
chance, to painting marks on the pavements of the West End streets.
Valuable because it taught me how the Admiralty worked and brought me
into contact with most Directorates of the Naval Staff at a much earlier age
than was customary. This was to stand me in good stead later.

Apart from the Fleet Review at Spithead (which was an entirely separate
organization) the Navy's participation in London consisted of lining the
streets and marching in the procession. The numbers involved totalled over
2500 and presented an accommodation problem. The solution chosen was to
use the deep ex-World War II air-raid shelter at Clapham and for reasons of
domestic and traffic convenience it was decided to conduct a full scale
rehearsal in that area. Any resemblance between Whitehall and the back
streets of Clapham was purely coincidental and in effect it doubled the extent
and complexity of my task. It also led to some interesting situations. In those
days Clapham was not the salubrious area it is today. The incidence of
vandalism and crime of varying degrees was high, a fact of which the local
Police were all too aware. The local atmosphere was 'nothing comes amiss
round here.'

Into this environment I stepped one Saturday morning with my team to

10. My wife Mary, tall, graceful, gentle, wise, with a great sense of humour and the remarkable ability to gain the confidence and love of everyone with whom she came in contact. Totally unflappable, I loved her dearly and she was an enormous and unfailing support.

11. My two daughters — Henrietta (left) and Philippa.

12. "Wife and sixteen Frigates to support." Reflecting the Defence cuts of the early 1970's.

13. HMS *Galatea* — in command and as Captain (D) 27th Escort Squadron and Captain (D) Mediterranean; one of the earlier *Leander* Class (a huge success, if somewhat under-armed) with sophisticated Operations Room equipment and Sonar. With her twin rudders she was the most manoeuvrable ship I ever commanded.

mark the streets selected as representing the Whitehall area for the rehearsal. My team consisted of one Petty Officer Gunnery Instructor from Whale Island, chosen no doubt because he lived in neighbouring Balham and imagined he was getting a bonus weekend at home. Considerations of local traffic, other requirements in London and the weathering of the paint marks confined the work to this particular weekend. Armed with a supply of quick-drying, road-marking paint and a long tape measure we set about our task. The weather was fine and hot; we wore overalls.

The first incident occurred by midmorning. I had parked my car on the Common and having occasion to get something from it I was surprised to find it surrounded by Police.

'Good morning,' I said. 'Is there something wrong?'

'This your car?' one of them asked.

'Yes. What's up?'

'Oh nothing, nothing,' came the casual reply conveying the clear impression that something was.

I unlocked the car, retrieved what I had come for, re-locked it and turned to the Police Officer apparently in charge.

'Is it all right to leave it parked here?' I enquired. 'There's obviously something that is worrying you.'

'Seeing as how you unlocked the car, took something out and re-locked it,' he answered, 'I'm satisfied it is your car. And certainly you may leave it here.'

'But I told you it was mine in the first place.'

'Yes sir, but we get a lot of stolen ones dumped here and we thought it might be one of those.'

As the day wore on it became increasingly clear that our task was open to local misinterpretation. Applying the precept of 'always be nice to the natives' we did our best to answer questions on what we were doing with courtesy and truth – but with only limited success. 'Marking the route for the Navy's rehearsal for the Coronation' did not inspire conviction in the back streets of Clapham.

Around noon a ten-year-old and his young sister appeared to be with us for the duration. Questions and answers were exchanged with speed and good humour and I began to think that we had won at least two hearts in this rather unresponsive community. I was dreadfully wrong.

'Come away, Marie-Anne,' came the final, damning pronouncement from big brother. 'Nasty man – digging drains.'

Towards 1500 a young woman approached me in a highly distraught state. Tears were streaming down her cheeks and from time to time her whole frame was shaken by convulsive sobs. Wringing her hands in despair she was eventually persuaded to blurt out her problem.

'W-what are . . . that is t-to say . . . oh dear c-could you p-possibly t-tell . . . ah, w-would you think it awful of me if I asked . . . w-why are you p-painting all these m-marks on the r-roadside?'

'For the Naval Contingent at the Coronation next month, madam. The Contingent is being accommodated in the deep shelter and will be carrying out a full scale rehearsal here the day before the great event. But what is troubling you?'

At this the girl went into fresh paroxysms of weeping. 'Oh, thank you, thank you, thank God,' she sobbed. 'Oh, it's such a relief', and then a cloud of doubt once more shadowed her face, 'b-but are you r-really s-sure?'

'Absolutely, but do tell me what is wrong. I might be able to help.'

'You are so-so k-kind,' she sobbed and, pulling herself together with a great effort went on, 'you see for months past there have been growing rumours of a major housing re-development plan for this area. And just after lunch one of our neighbours told me that any house with a white spot opposite it would be demolished as part of the plan and oooooohh d-dear we've only just p-paid off the mortgage on ours.' Evidently neighbours in Clapham were an unhelpful lot.

How unhelpful was soon to be revealed. An hour or so later I needed a telephone to make adjustments to our planned programme for next day. At eight houses in succession I knocked on the front door or rang the bell. The owners were clearly to be seen sitting in the next room, yet none would even look up, let alone come to the door. Eventually I got a reaction and an elderly woman gingerly cracked the door open and peered out. Hastily jamming my foot in the opening I gently requested the use of her telephone (indicated by the overhead wires) at the same time flourishing a half crown.

'Have you a card from the Council?' she asked diffidently.

It took several minutes to persuade her that my Naval Identity Card was not an escaped convict's badge.

As the evening wore on it became increasingly obvious that we were falling behind schedule and that our work would have to be speeded up considerably if we were to complete the job the following day. Accordingly I approached a group of small boys playing on the nearby Common and asked,

'Anyone care to help the Navy for the Coronation? Hold the other end of a tapemeasure and earn five bob?'

Immediately four of them were beside me. Selecting the most likely looking one, a bright-eyed youngster of about ten, I quickly showed him what was required and we set to work. He was a sharp lad and we got on quickly, chattering away meanwhile. He assured me that there would be no problem at home so long as he was back by about 2100. 'It's only just round the corner,' he said. We settled for that.

When the time came, 'Thank you,' I said. 'You were a great help,' and handed over his two half-crowns. Then a thought struck me. Next day was Sunday; no school and by now he knew the drill backwards.

'If you've nothing better to do tomorrow morning would you like to come on with me again and earn another five shillings? As early as you like.'

'Oh yes, sir, I'll be there,' he replied. I bade him goodnight and he scampered off.

The Petty Officer and I worked on until darkness fell and after arranging to meet at 0430 next morning, packed it in for that night. Poor man, it was not quite the family weekend he had expected.

Next day dawned dry and hot. We met and continued as planned, but with only the two of us progress was again slow. When 0900 came there was still no sign of my young helper of the previous evening. By now a third pair of hands had become critical and jumping into my car I drove down to the far end of the Common where I had previously spotted a group of kids playing. Sure enough they were still there. Sticking my head out of the window I repeated my very improbable question about the Navy, the Coronation and five bob. Hardly had I finished when a keen, alert-looking boy was in the car, sitting expectantly in the seat beside me.

'We're off to the other end of the Common,' I said. 'Is that all right?'

'Oh yes.'

'Sure your parents won't mind?'

'No. Not at all. I'm often playing up there.'

I was in luck. Off we drove and then got quickly stuck into the task.

But my luck was shortlived. In little more than ten minutes a police car roared up, sirens sounding and screeched to a halt just beside us. Out jumped two policemen, notebooks flipped open, pencils poised. At the time my young helper and I were crouched by the roadside holding the opposite ends of the 100-foot tape measure. Rising to my feet I looked enquiringly at the advancing Police.

'What exactly are you doing sir?' one of them asked.

I told them, adding, 'What is the trouble, Officer?'

'Well, as it happens there's no trouble,' he replied. 'Everything seems to be in order. But we've had a terrible time with this lad's parents.'

At this moment I spotted a familiar face peering out of the back window of the police car. It was my assistant of the evening before. The police then told the full story.

It transpired that amongst the group from which I had drawn my morning's helper had been his younger brother. He had got very excited about my activities, rushed off home, burst into the house and shouted,

'Hey Mum. Brother Jim's just been driven off by a strange man in a red car. What yer going to do 'bout that?'

The parents' reaction was swift and to the point. Mum went into hysterics. Dad nipped round the corner to the nearest callbox and dialled 999.

Soon a police car drove up. A small crowd gathered. Being Sunday morning, everyone was at home. The crowd swelled. Between sobs the distraught mother regaled the police with a heartrending account of the abduction of her firstborn, ending with another bout of hysterics. The police addressed the crowd:

'Anyone else seen this man around? Or his red car?'

Silence. Everyone looked at everyone else. Anxiously the police scanned the upturned faces.

Then from the back of the crowd piped up a thin, small voice:

'Please sir, I know this man.'

The police stiffened.

'I was with him last night.'

The police started to move in the boy's direction.

'He gave me five bob!' That clinched it.

Turning to me the policeman added,

'There's funny things goes on in these parts, sir. So you see why we had to look into it quickly.'

I did. The least I could do now was to offer to accompany the officers back to the stricken parents to reassure them personally that their son was in good hands – and hopefully would continue as my assistant. Though understandably a bit crusty the father was a reasonable man and readily gave his consent. The mother was so relieved she would have agreed to anything. After giving firm assurances that young Jim would be back at home by 1 o'clock for his Sunday lunch we shook hands all round. I apologized to the police for causing them trouble and, accompanied by Jim, returned to the task.

At noon we ran out of paint. How to get more in the heart of Clapham on a Sunday afternoon? Fortunately in the course of my earlier travels I thought I had seen a chap in white overalls doing things to the outside of a pub about a mile away. It seemed the only chance. Leaving Jim and the Petty Officer to finish off the last dregs in the paintpot I drove off to investigate. The man was indeed a painter and I caught him just as he stepped off his ladder having finished the job. He was not very co-operative, being more concerned with getting home for his Sunday lunch.

'Could you sell me some white paint?'

'What d'you want white paint for?'

It was irrelevant but I told him.

'Well I suppose I might.'

'Do you have it here?'

'Oh no.'

'Where then?'

'Back home.'

'And where is home?'

''bout a mile away.'

'Could I drive you there, now?'

'No. No I couldn't do that. I've got to put this ladder away, wash me brushes out and bicycle back.'

'Look, I'm desperate for time.' (Why was I desperate for time? It was all so improbable to an outsider.) 'Couldn't I drive you home, pick up the paint and drive you back here to collect your bicycle?'

'No. I want to go on me bike.' He was digging in and if I wasn't careful I should lose the deal altogether.

Ten interminable minutes later he sauntered out, trundling an elderly bicycle.

'Follow me,' he muttered and off we set. Past the bottom of the Common, down the hill, across the High Street and up the rise the other side. Half-way up the rise my engine gave a dozen complaining coughs and died. The hot day and crawling along at 4 mph had been too much.

Leaping out I flung up the bonnet and peered inside. Nothing seemed to be wrong. Over my shoulder I saw the painter a quarter of a mile away breasting the top of the rise at which point the road forked. Frantically waving my handkerchief I bellowed at him to stop and wait, then turned back to my car. When next I looked up the painter had disappeared for ever and I did not know which road he had taken.

No car, no paint, no means of communicating with my Petty Officer, young Jim not returned home as promised: it was not my day.

One of the more crucial decisions concerned the manner in which the Board of Admiralty should participate in the ceremony on Coronation Day. Precedent indicated that they should be mounted and this was readily agreed by the Boards of the other two Services. But for the Admirals the solution was not so clearcut. Few of them had ever been astride a horse and none of them cared much for the prospect. Indeed the Second and Fourth Sea Lords circulated a sharp minute on this subject:

'This is,' it said, 'a ceremonial occasion of national importance not a circus. We will not ride.'

Research into past records revealed only a letter from Captain Percy Scott (HMS *Excellent*) to the Commanding Officer, Royal Naval Volunteer Reserve in Scotland in 1905. It read: –

'With reference to your signal, there is nothing laid down in the Admiralty Instructions as regards Naval Officers in charge of Seamen, riding.

'Their Lordships have hitherto left it to the discretion of the officers themselves whether they ride or walk, and it is hoped that Naval Officers would not ride unless capable of withstanding the cup-and-ball motion which is so closely connected with equestrian exercise.

'From the records, however, it appears that this hope has not always been realized, and the disappearance into the big drum of the Grenadiers of the Commanding Officer of the Naval Brigade on the occasion of a Naval Review at Windsor, together with a record made by a Midshipman from Whitehall to Hyde Park at the Jubilee Review, has not encouraged Their Lordships to issue an order that Naval Officers should be mounted.

'On such occasions as I have seen Naval officers mounted, the uniform has been breeches and boots, but there is no mention of these articles in the uniform regulations.

'I enclose a photograph of the saddlery supplied, or obtained by the establishment for the use of Naval officers at functions, the extreme height of the pommel and crupper of the saddle is to give extra stability to the officer while astride the horse.

'The only instructions issued here with regard to equestrian drill are, that rolling and pitching are to be avoided as much as possible, the animal's sway should be checked when rounding corners, and extreme deflection never applied except at low speeds. In mounting and dismounting, the Port side only is to be used, and spurs are not to be used to hold on by.

'If not under control, four red lights need not be used, as placing the hand behind the back is sufficient warning to the next astern not to close.

'The animal is steered in the same way as a boat, with a yoke, except that, whereas in a boat the yoke is in the stern, with a horse it is in the bow. The yoke lines are called reins.

'The initial velocity of the animal depends on the Mark and upon the food given; great care must be taken by officers in getting into the saddle.'

However, in the interests of inter-Service symmetry The Board Mounted carried the day. The C-in-C Portsmouth and the Admiral President Greenwich (who had once played polo) were brought in to make up the numbers and the two non-equestrians were given seats in Westminster Abbey. Nevertheless there remained considerable bashfulness on the part of Board Members who were reluctant to make fools of themselves in public when operating in the unfamiliar medium of the saddle. They therefore elected to carry out their riding practice at an hour which they judged would be too early for their friends and critics to be abroad and reported to Hyde Park Horsed Camp at 0700 daily from mid-April onwards.

There was also controversy about the question of dress. Full Dress in 1953 had changed radically from that at the previous Coronation in 1937. Furthermore research into the archives produced the interesting information that dress for a Naval Officer mounted included box spurs and these were specially manufactured by Gieves.

Came the morning when for the first time the Board wore their spurs. They had almost completed their first circuit of Hyde Park (normally they did two) and were approaching a point opposite the entrance to the Camp. The Sea Lords' string was under the guidance of an elderly Colonel in the Blues whose knowledge of riding was considerably greater than his prospects of further promotion. At the tail of the string was the First Sea Lord (Admiral Sir Rhoderick McGrigor); small, rugged and intelligent, he was probably the least experienced horseman present. He was fed up with trapesing around Hyde Park at what the Colonel was wont to call a 'walk-march'. He might have been having his breakfast or reading *The Times*. And he was very, very bored.

What were these damned silly things strapped onto the heels of his Half-Wellingtons, he wondered. And what effect would they have on his mount? Idly he swung his legs to and fro, to and fro, a little more each time until he drove his spurs sharply into his horse's flanks. The result was violent and immediate. His horse sprang forward, flashed past the rest of the string and bolted into the middle distance with its startled rider clinging on for dear life. The remaining horses, agitated by their stablemate's spectacular acceleration immediately started jumping up and down and broke into a brisk canter. In the lead was the Controller (Admiral Sir Ralph Edwards) a tall, heavily built man who rode his steed rather like a mule bringing in the harvest. At that moment they came abreast the entrance to the Camp. The appeal of his stable was too much for the Controller's horse and, increasing to full speed, he altered course sharply to starboard and headed for home. His rider, however, adhering to that wellworn naval precept of following his senior officer's motions, maintained his course. The two parted. The Controller landed heavily on his hatless head and was knocked unconscious for several moments.

The resulting confusion was of the kind that can only occur with a bunch of very senior officers. Everyone attempted to take charge but none was able to do so because of his total preoccupation in avoiding being thrown by his prancing animal; only the Colonel could meet the situation on level terms. Slipping from the saddle he approached the prone figure of the Controller who was already coming round and exhibiting all the classic symptoms of concussion by insisting that he was quite all right. Someone caught the Controller's horse. Someone retrieved the discomforted First Sea Lord. The Board Mounted straggled back into Camp and a furious Controller was escorted by a worried Colonel to the latter's nearby flat. There he hastily poured a half-tumbler of neat brandy and was about to offer it to the shaken Admiral when wartime memories of hot, sweet tea for treatment of shock and never spirits in any circumstances caused him to change his plan. He gulped the brandy himself, put on the kettle and telephoned me.

With ten days to go the Board were allocated the horses they were actually to ride on the day. Quickly it became apparent that the Army had made a mistake in their arithmetic and were two greys short. Desperately they scoured the country to complete the matching number, eventually getting them over from Rhine Army. This led to a final tease by the RAF. One of the latest pair from Germany was a magnificent beast but it was alleged that it had a well practiced if rather unattractive trick. Seemingly docile and of sweet disposition, it would wait for its rider to mount and settle himself in the saddle. It would then gently turn its head right round and bite its rider sharply in the right thigh. This exhilarating bit of gossip spread rapidly and added little to the pleasure of the C-in-C Portsmouth, to whom the animal was allocated.

All was now ready: detailed orders distributed, roads marked in Central London and Clapham, training well advanced and of a high standard. The Company and Battalion Commanders were summoned to the Admiralty for a final briefing and conducted tour of the relevant part of the processional route. The briefing was straightforward and it then fell to me to take the Commanders out on to the streets and point out their precise positions. I led off, down the stairs, through the North Door and out into the Mall by Admiralty Arch.

'This is where the Navy's area starts, Gentlemen,' I said, 'and here (pointing to it with my stick) is the position of the left hand marker of 1 Battalion, A Company, 1 Platoon – this spot here.'

There was no spot. There was no trace of my laboriously applied white paint on either the roadway or the curb. How *could* this be? I had put them there myself and had checked them only 48 hours before. I felt an ass but there was nothing for it but to put on a brave face and continue the tour.

'I am sorry,' I explained rather futilely; 'that is where the mark *should* be but something very strange seems to have happened to it. It *will* be there on the day. Let us move on to the next one.'

We moved on. It wasn't there either. And so on right round the route which the Navy was due to line. At each point (which of course I knew like the back of my hand) I delivered the same fatuous bromide but there was no mark. By the time we had been down Northumberland Avenue, along the Embankment and Bridge Street, round Parliament Square and were coming back up Whitehall I could have wished that the earth would open and swallow me up – as it evidently had my marks. And my audience, many years senior to me and by now hot, tired and frustrated, treated this young Lieutenant-Commander who had clearly tried hard but failed totally with a kind of indulgent tolerance which failed to disguise their unanimous decision for my early reassignment to a mental institution.

Then I saw it. Half way up Whitehall was one of those monstrous fiery furnace things that burn off old road surfaces. With ponderous majesty it was creeping up the curbside obliterating all. In its wake was only blankness. I pointed this out to my group.

'There, gentlemen, lies the cause of our problem. While the damage it has done cannot quickly be restored I hope my credibility can be.'

We soon completed the last quarter-mile of our route and the group dispersed for lunch. During the afternoon I managed to contact the Westminster City Engineer. It transpired that someone had prudently taken the precaution of thumbing up the records of the previous coronation in 1937 to see if there were any lessons learned or relevant recommendations made. There was one. For King George VI's coronation the sun had shone and it was a blazing hot day – so hot that the tar on the road surface of Whitehall had started to melt. When it was all over and the police disposed along the route came to move off they were temporarily immobile: their boots had stuck to the roadway. The subsequent complaints by the Metropolitan Commissioners had caused the City Council to record a cautionary note to beware of this at future ceremonies.

Seventy-two hours before Coronation Day the street marking problem took a new turn. This was the last opportunity I had for finally touching up the painted marks in Whitehall. Hardly had I done so when I learned that the Council street cleaning vehicles would be administering a final wash down and brush up starting at 0300 next morning. It was midnight before I was able to contact the City Engineer. By now we had established a good liaison and he was most co-operative. Quickly appreciating the problem he undertook to do his best.

'But,' he added, 'I am doubtful if I can stop the drivers at this late stage. They have all been given their orders and have gone home to sleep before the early morning shift. I'll try but I'm not very hopeful.'

I thanked him and put the receiver down. I was very tired. Resignedly I thought it through. There could be no question of chancing it and leaving it to the City Engineer; the odds against success were too great. At 0900 that morning I had to be back at Clapham for the final rehearsal, to be witnessed by the First Sea Lord. But that left ample time to hang around Whitehall and intercept the water carts before they started spraying. Would the drivers accept my orders? It seemed unlikely. Better to have a written instruction from the City Engineer. Again I dialled his number; no answer, he had gone home and I did not know where that was. All now depended on personal interception and bluff. Partly for the rehearsal and partly to be more convincing, I changed into uniform and waited.

It was a long night. 0300 came but no water carts: 0400 and still no sign of them. Shortly before 0500 they appeared, three of them. The drivers had received no instructions to cancel their planned operation but all were decent chaps who saw the point and were basically glad to help the Navy. It may even have occurred to them that a naval officer in uniform would hardly have hung around the streets for all that time for fun. Anyway they readily agreed to my request and caused no difficulty. Greatly relieved, I climbed into my car and headed for Clapham.

It was close on 0600 when I got there. The Officers' Mess of the Camp did not open for another hour, so, pulling into a cul-de-sac, I took off my cap, sat back in my seat and promptly fell asleep.

Twenty minutes later I woke up feeling cold and stiff and uncomfortable. Glancing up as soon as I could straighten my cricked neck I saw that the driver's door was wide open and outside stood three large policemen.

'Good morning,' I said. 'What is the matter?'

'You all right, sir?' one of them enquired.

'Yes, fine,' I replied. 'Is anything wrong?'

'Well, sir,' came the answer, 'we get quite a lot of stiffs around here and thought you were just another one.'

To avoid being held up by the huge influx of traffic the small Naval Brigade Headquarters Staff spent the night before the Coronation in HMS *President* on the Embankment conveniently close to the initial assembly point next day. It was a wise move in all respects save one: the traditional loyalty and hospitality of the London Division RNVR whose Headquarters it was. One of the many points of detail which had had to be settled had been how best to obviate the need for men to visit the Heads in the course of a long day of rigid ceremonial. On this I had obtained the advice of the Medical Director General. It was simple and unequivocal: 'Allow no liquid to pass your lips for 24 hours before the event.' And so the Naval Brigade had been advised.

History was made on board *President* that night. I doubt that at any time before or since an Admiral and his Staff had dined without a drop passing their lips. Nevertheless it was a convivial evening and our kind hosts happily made up for their guests' enforced abstemiousness. Conversation was easy and at times quite hilarious. Dinner over, the table was cleared and decanters of port and madeira placed in front of the Mess President. This was the moment of truth and it had not been foreseen. The question was whether to adhere rigidly to medical advice and thereby imply disloyalty to the Sovereign in the presence of our premier Naval Reserve Division or participate in the loyal toast and risk the consequences. We knew we had

92

been pre-empted and that all eyes were upon us. It did not seem a very big risk and by mutual consent we took it – to the extent of a loyal sip.

It was a cold, blustery night and when the Brigade fell in on the Embankment at 0600 next morning the prospect was disturbingly grey and chilly. Half an hour later it started to rain. Unlike the Army whose involvement in ceremonial is sufficient to warrant special waterproof capes which can readily be discarded and collected at the last minute, wet weather dress for the Navy was oilskins. Their use on such an occasion involved the removal of the white webbing belt, adjusting the securing clips to allow for the extra bulk of the oilskin underneath, and an inevitable clumsy bunching up of the folds of this garment when put on outside it. On the spur of the moment I decided that this really was not on and that the sailors would prefer to suffer a bit of cold and wet (to which they were not unaccustomed) for the sake of preserving their innate smartness. Sprinting to the head of the naval column I was barely in time. Already the order had been issued 'wet weather clothing' and Army trucks had already distributed oilskins to the leading Naval Company who were in the throes of struggling into them.

'Stop,' I shouted. 'Take off these oilskins and chuck them back in the lorries. Whatever the weather oilskins are not to be worn by the Navy today.'

Surprised but relieved, the sailors removed their clumsy encumbrances and returned them to the trucks. I was on the way to winning but I wasn't there yet: a Sergeant Driver in the leading truck was already querying my counter-order and the middle distance I spotted a Route Marshal approaching. The situation called for firmness and speed.

'Drive off,' I ordered the Sergeant sharply. 'Drive off down the Embankment. Keep on driving. Go now and go quickly – you are blocking the Assembly Area.'

'But where am I to go to?' enquired the driver plaintively.

'It doesn't matter,' I replied, still more sharply. 'Go anywhere. Go to your Barracks. But GO.'

'But what about all these oilskins?' he complained.

Time was running out. The Route Marshal was fast approaching, waving his baton in agitation. 'Turn them over to the senior Naval Officer present,' I instructed airily (knowing there was no such person), 'but get cracking *now*.'

He went, closely followed by the other lorries. I breathed a sigh of relief. The Route Marshal arrived, rather out of breath and apoplectic.

'What the devil's going on here?' he rasped. 'Where has the wet weather clothing been sent just as I had ordered it? Who do you think you are to countermand my orders?'

'Sir,' I replied quietly, 'the Navy will not be wearing oilskins today. We don't on occasions of national ceremony. Where they have gone is a matter for some speculation but no anxiety. I am the Staff Officer to the Naval Brigade and will take full responsibility for this modified interpretation of the orders.'

Furious, he stamped on.

And it rained. God how it rained. By the time the Procession approached we were all soaked to the skin and our uniforms clung heavily to our bodies. It took three-quarters of an hour for the Procession to pass any given point on the route and it did so twice, on the way to Westminster Abbey and on the way back to Buckingham Palace. During those periods we stood, cold and stiff, at the salute. Those in the Brigade had been training and rehearsing for six weeks; the staff had had half an hour.

Half way through the Procession from the Abbey some hitch occurred and the Procession was halted for a few minutes. Most of the carriages were open and the one just opposite me was occupied by the Sultan of Johore and Queen Salote of the Tonga. Although drenched by the downpour the crowd was in excellent spirits and started chanting:

'Put up the hood. Put up the hood.'

Of course this was not done. But the Sultan, a man of slim stature, was beginning to feel the effects of the deluge and pulling out his handkerchief made to mop his dripping face. In this he failed. From the opposite seat in his carriage a fist like a leg of mutton was deftly wielded by the Queen of the Tonga and knocked his hand away. The crowd observed this with deight and roared its approval.

The Procession got under way again. In due course the Board of Admiralty (mounted) passed. The impression conveyed was that Their Lordships were just under control but with not too much in hand. As they wheeled at the top of Whitehall to go through Admiralty Arch the First Sea Lord's horse got a bit restive, broke into a jog and started to move sideways. His discomforted rider did not know how to correct this. He transitted Admiralty Arch 'beam on' and was well into the Mall before he managed to straighten out. Which caused a wag in the crowd to call out,

'Wot price the Cruel Sea now, Guv'nor?'

It was a famous occasion and a huge success. I do not know what became of the oilskins.

9

SUGAR AND SPICE

'Ganging along the Scotstown Road
To see the Blaydon Races.'
Northumberland Ballad

July, 1953. The Coronation past, I was appointed as Gunnery Officer to the *Birmingham*, flagship of the 5th Cruiser Squadron in the Far East. Like her sister ship *Newcastle*, she had recently completed a major modernization which involved enclosing the bridge, air conditioning most of the superstructure, installing an entirely new fire control system for the secondary (Anti-Aircraft) armament and replacing the obsolete close range weapons by up-to-date 40mm Bofors. These fine 10,000-ton ships with their main armament of nine 6-inch guns, secondary armament of eight 4-inch guns and numerous close range weapons, were a Gunnery Officer's dream. With their raked funnels and masts and splendid proportions they also had the most beautiful lines of any ship in the Navy. I was thrilled at the prospect.

Three weeks later my appointment was changed; to *Newcastle*. Since the ships were identical and each took on the extra duties of flagship in turn this did not seem to matter. And yet, as I later learned, it may have been significant. Though of the same class, same age, modernized to the same standards at the same time, somehow it seemed that *Newcastle* generally had the edge over her sister. Over the years it had been *Newcastle* that had got the greater number of promotions, produced the better gunnery performance, won the regatta and the football. It was not that *Birmingham* was other than a very good ship; but *Newcastle* was consistently exceptional. This is one of the inexplicable things about the Royal Navy and its ships. Most HM Ships are pretty good and any exceptions are fairly quickly sorted out. But some are superemely good and, despite changes in Command and Ship's Company, go on being that way. To serve in one is a great privilege and enormous fun. Such was *Newcastle*.

The tail end of the Korean War was still on and while direct confrontation with the enemy was now largely confined to ground patrols there remained a vestigial threat to seaward and from the air. A degree of alertness beyond that which was normal in peacetime was therefore prudent. At sea the pattern of operating had become fairly regular: four to five weeks patrolling off the Korean coast, usually in the vicinity of Pang Yong Do, followed by a break for human and machinery maintenance in one of the forward operating bases, Kure or Sasebo.

Korea was still officially designated a War Zone and ships proceeding north of Hong Kong landed their practice ammunition and carried their full war outfits. This, coupled with superb practice facilities, provided a unique opportunity to test fully the gunnery systems. Under peacetime conditions, however accurately you shot the most you achieved in anti-aircraft fire was a puff of smoke indicating a near-miss; off Korea if you got it right you shot the target down and the effect on morale was significant.

The new system installed in *Newcastle* was electric, the forerunner of electronic computers still shortly to come. To set it up effectively involved some hours of painstaking tuning of a number of components, all of which were interacting. Perfectionism achieved in one could result in unbalancing one or more of the others and accurate shooting resulted from achieving an overall compromise within fine tolerances. In short it was a 'Go/No Go' system, the performance of which could generally be predicted before fire was opened. This led to some caustic comments from my Captain (St John Tyrwhitt), a most experienced Destroyer Commander and a brilliant shiphandler.

'It's all very well, Guns,' he would complain, 'but in a real war situation the enemy wouldn't wait for you to finish twiddling your wretched knobs before he attacked and where would we be then?'

In vain I sought to explain that the older systems with which he was familiar could not compete with modern high speed aircraft and that it would really be a fluke if they shot the target down. Whereas our system, when it was fine tuned, would get a high kill rate. True there were times when the computer wandered off-tune; it was then no better (nor any worse) than its mechanical predecessors.

'Hum,' he would grunt in considerable disbelief. But he loved to see the targets tumbling out of the sky.

In the summer of 1954 we embarked the Commander-in-Chief (Admiral Sir Charles Lambe) for an official visit to the main United States Pacific Naval Base at Pearl Harbor, Hawaii. It was the first such visit by a British C-in-C or by a major RN warship since the end of the war with Japan and considerable importance was attached to making it a success. To this end, 24 hours before arrival we hove-to in glorious weather and painted ship overall, working from 0600 until darkness fell.

At 1100 next morning we entered harbour. The ship looked a dream and with the Ship's Company lining the side for the ceremonial entry and the Royal Marines Band playing martial music on the quarterdeck, she was a fine sight. Our gleaming, pale grey paint contrasted spectacularly with the rather sombre dark grey of the US ships.

The jetties in Pearl Harbor are laid out like the letter 'E' relative to the shore line, only with many more 'tails'. At the root of each jetty was a sloping ramp up which could be driven landing craft. Approaching our berth we were suddenly confronted by a large American Carrier leaving harbour unexpectedly. Whilst there was never a close-quarters situation or any real risk of collision, quick action by *Newcastle* was needed to get out of the way of the less manoeuverable Carrier in time. The Captain immediately ordered 'Half Astern' and over the next few moments increased the power until revolutions for 16 knots had been rung on. The ship quickly lost way (we had previously only been doing 8 knots), the engines were stopped, the Carrier slid past and the way to our berth was again clear.

'Half Ahead together,' ordered the Captain and quickly we turned into our berth. Captain, Navigating Officer and Officer of the Watch all forgot that revolutions for 16 knots were still rung on and we shot into the berth as if emulating a landing craft on the fast approaching ramp. In rapid succession the Captain ordered more and more revolutions astern and eventually, with only a few feet to spare, we shuddered to a stop. As an example of big ship berthing it must have been one of the most spectacular on record and those waiting to greet us on the jetty were astounded at what they took to be a smart manoeuvre. We did not enlighten them. 'Our Captain does not care for wasting time,' we explained!

The welcome itself was stupendous, the centrepiece being a large contingent of Hawaiian dancing girls swishing their grass skirts and wriggling their tummies (and everything else) as only they can. The sailors were transfixed and there was some difficulty in getting the berthing wires doubled up and the ship finally secured. Then began individual ceremonies with lais, the gorgeous waist-long necklaces of exotic frangipanis and orchids. Delivered by charming young girls of dazzling good looks, the recipient of these favours had the enviable custom of responding with a tender kiss on each cheek followed by one on the lips. It is a very moving little ceremony and by the time it is over, with nostrils full of the heavy scent of the flowers now strung around your neck, even the most reserved of Englishmen can probably do better than discuss the weather.

Five days (and nights) of glittering glamour and enormous fun passed. On the sixth morning we were due to sail at 0900. Officers and men alike were by now in an advanced state of emotional rapture equalled only by severe physical exhaustion. By 0600 cars and taxis started streaming down to the jetty. The tender farewells were legion and the exchanges of lais astounding. The tempo increased and persisted right up to the moment the brow was hoisted out. The whole ship resembled Covent Garden.

Up on the bridge most of us had collected three or four lais. What to do with them? Traditionally they had to be kept around the neck until the ship was opposite Diamond Head at which point the owner had to go right aft, cast each lai individually into the foaming wake, give a last nostalgic look at the distant shore – and then he would return. But we were due to make a ceremonial exit at the end of an official visit, for which protocol did not include advice on looking like an advertisement for Growmore in a Garden Centre. And the Captain, though a splendid sportsman, was austere. A masterly compromise was reached: we removed our lais but hung them over nearby voice-pipes, ready to hand, and awaited the arrival of the Command.

With two minutes to go a huge mass of flowers slowly ascended the bridge ladder. Above it were just visible the top of Captain St John Tyrwhitt's head and the tip of his nose. Hastily we grabbed our own lais and put them back on. As the Captain later wrote in his Report of Proceedings: 'Seldom has it fallen to a Naval Captain to take his ship to sea at the end of an official foreign visit with £140 worth of orchids round his neck.'

When Diamond Head drew abeam we all went down to the quarterdeck. Standing right aft, one by one we cast our lais into the sea astern with thoughts and hopes as mixed as they were nostalgic.

During the next 30 years I went back three times.

On leaving Hawaii *Newcastle* returned home eastabout through the Panama Canal – to recommission. We were at Portsmouth for three weeks during which leave was given and the majority of the Ship's Company changed. New Captain (Dick Honeywell), new Commander (Michael Pollock – later to be First Sea Lord) and most of the Wardroom except for the Navigating and Gunnery Officers. Led by the Commander the new Ship's Company marched from the Royal Naval Barracks (now HMS *Nelson*) down to the jetty alongside where the usual Service was conducted, culminating in the re-hoisting of the White Ensign and breaking out of the Commissioning Pennant. So started one of the finest, most successful and happiest commissions of any big ship. Soon afterwards we sailed for the Mediterranean to work up.

The new 'Magpies' were a splendid lot. So-called on account of their black and white chequered shirts on the football field (colours derived from their parent town on Tyneside), they set to work with a will. But it soon became clear that they were largely unfamiliar with the equipment and a good deal of time had to be spent on basic training. Moreover the equipment itself, despite every effort to operate it daily and keep it tuned to optimum performance during the long passage home, had suffered from the inevitable fallow period during our time in Portsmouth. It was to correct just these short-comings that the work-up was designed and by the end of six weeks of varied and intensive effort *Newcastle* had once more become an efficient ship, raring to go. But it had been hard work and for my part I was very tired indeed.

The evening before we left Malta to return to Singapore via the Suez Canal, the Captain called a small meeting in his cabin. Timed for 1700, its purpose was to draft an outline future programme for the ship once she had reached her Station. Neither he nor the Commander had had recent experience of the Far East and the knowledge acquired by the Navigating Officer (Peter Mitchell) and myself during the previous commission was therefore tapped. We sat on hard, upright chairs set very close together. The hot Mediterranean sun streamed through the open scuttle. The Captain opened by a general discussion with the Commander. It was too much for me: my fatigue got the upper hand, my eyes closed momentarily and I fell asleep. Only seconds later I came to again but the damage was done. Everyone was looking at me, my Captain especially intently and from a distance of only a couple of feet. Clearly he had asked me a question but since I had not heard it there was no possible way in which I could give a sensible or even relevant answer.

'Wretched fellow,' I thought to myself, 'how could you have been such an idiot? What sort of impression will your new Captain have of his Gunnery Officer who behaves like this? Yours may *have* been a promising career but it's now at an end. There's absolutely no way out of this predicament.'

But the other half of my mind rebelled. 'Come on,' it said. 'Never give in. If in doubt attack. You haven't a hope in hell but it's worth a go.'

Looking intently into my Captain's eyes I said:

'That's a very interesting question, sir; but I'm not sure that I've got the full import of it. Would you mind saying it again?'

Dear, kind, simple soul that he was my Captain obligingly repeated the question. It could not have been easier or more straightforward and I quickly answered it. Discussion turned to other matters. The crisis had passed and I had got away with it.

Or had I? An hour or two later over a drink in the Wardroom the Commander suddenly rounded on me. He was as sharp and observant as the Captain was gentle and benevolent.

'Henry Leach,' he barked, 'I have seen some people do some things. But to fall asleep in a hard-arsed chair in front of your own Captain at a range of two feet in the middle of a question – that beats all!'

By now the Korean War had almost ground to a halt and *Newcastle*'s operational tasking was increasingly redirected to the suppression of Communist Terrorists (CTs) in Malaya. From time to time we would be allocated a sizeable area of jungle (1500 square miles was typical) and a considerable period (up to 24 hours) in which to bombard with our 6-inch guns.

Occasionally an Army Spotter flying a light Auster aircraft was briefly attached to us, but generally it was left to the ship to work out the details of how best to distribute high effect shell randomly over the specified area so as to keep the CTs on the hop. Usually a single gun was fired, the gun being changed to equalize wear, and except at night when the flash of a well-placed air burst could be seen in the tree tops there was nothing to indicate the result. If a Spotter observed a target, however, a whole turret (3 guns) would be used. There was no offshore threat to the ship and she would either anchor or steam slowly up and down off the target area. It was not a very exciting form of action and it took up a lot of men for a long time. Thus it was important that as far as possible other work went on about the ship, for safety reasons due warning being broadcast that the next round was about to be fired. The phrase 'next bang now' soon became a byeword and outside working hours every member of the Ship's Company – Stoker, Electrician, Artificer, the lot – was encouraged to visit the firing turret and personally take part in the bombardment. Most rather enjoyed this novel experience and felt they were doing something worthwhile.

An exception was the Principal Medical Officer, Surgeon-Commander James Dow. A huge Scot, six foot three and broad and thick, he belonged to that former school of Principal Medical Officers (PMOs) whose performance was more notable on the rugger field or at the Wardroom bar than in the operating theatre. He detested anything to do with gunnery. He also had a sort of prophetic sixth sense as had been proved on more than one occasion when we were about to make an ocean passage.

'Sharpen up your scalpel,' he had said to the young doctor. 'I fancy you may have an appendectomy this trip.' Three days out we had one.

On another occasion we were anchored in the Johore Strait, bombarding throughout the night. Just before 2300 when the wardroom bar closed the tide turned, the ship swung and it became necessary to check fire and close up the after turret before continuing. Miserable, the PMO had ordered a final treble whisky to alleviate the impending disturbance to his rest. On my entering the wardroom to discuss something with the Commander he rounded on me in disgust and growled:

'Bloody Gunnery Officer. I'll stop you firing your blasted guns even if I have to get a stomach ulcer to do it. Bah!' And he drained his glass with a flourish. A few minutes later we re-opened fire with 'Y' Turret.

Shortly before 0200 we had to cease fire, raise steam in a hurry, and proceed at speed up the Strait to land a young Stoker with a perforated stomach ulcer. True to his threat the PMO had won that round. But by 0600, with only two hours to go, we were back in our bombardment position and had re-started firing. I had won the next!

★

Some months later we were again anchored for bombardment, this time off the west coast. Our priorities were varied and at times conflicting: throughout daylight hours we were requested to bombard; we had to paint the ship's side prior to taking the Commander-in-Chief to Rangoon and the Sultan of Selangor had been invited to lunch on board. Rationalizing these issues was not helped by a strong tide which turned in the course of the forenoon so that the unfortunate sailors on their overside stages had to stop everything and transfer to the other, disengaged side as the ship swung. The firing plan was adjusted so that bombardment would cease at 1230 giving 15 minutes' grace before His Highness arrived.

At noon the ship swung radically and 'Y' Turret had to take over the firing. By 1215 the ship still swinging, we were firing over the stern. Range was fairly short; the elevation of the guns was not great in the area of the quarterdeck the blast effect was considerable. At 1225 two things happened. Our recently acquired Spotter saw a band of CTs running for cover and called for rapid fire; this meant three gun salvos reloaded as fast as possible and he got it. The other thing was that the telephone in the Operations Room rang; it was the Captain (who had already expressed anxiety about damage through firing on an aft bearing). He was inarticulate with rage and concern for his lunch party.

'G-G-Guns,' he stuttered, 'you must st-st-stop this instant. I'm standing in the cuddy, it's a total shambles, the deckhead fan . . .'

At that moment the Spotter, wild with excitement, announced that we were right on target, the gun ready lamps came on (indicating re-loaded), 'Aye aye sir,' I replied to my Captain, 'I am ceasing fire immediately' – at the same time mouthing 'shoot' to the Communications Number. 'Ting-ting' went the fire gong. 'Crash' thundered out the final broadside. Fire was checked and, cursing all ceremonial in the middle of action, I went aft. Though feeling slightly Nelsonic I hardly expected a hero's welcome.

I did not get one. Evidently someone had failed to batten down the fanlights over the Admiral's quarters. Blast from the 6-inch guns firing right astern at low elevation had shattered the glass and swept through the compartments below. In the main dining cabin, set for lunch, one of the large overhead fans was hanging by a single electric lead; the other had crashed into the middle of the table which had collapsed bringing all the glass and cutlery into a mangled heap on the deck. A small electric fire had started in the other fan motor and the aroma of burning rubber mingled with residual cordite fumes. As a scene depicting the true meaning of the word 'devastation' it was impressive. The Sultan was now due in 10 minutes' time. In the circumstances I felt that reporting to my Captain the highly successful results of the bombardment could best wait.

The Sultan arrived. Short, quiet and slightly overawed by events, he was held in conversation and introductions to gain a few more valuable minutes. A miracle of restoration had been achieved and by the time the VIP Party went below the cuddy had been squared off. Only the absence of the overhead fans and the consequent increase in ambient temperature betrayed the morning's activities.

'As you know, Your Royal Highness,' boomed the Captain, 'we have been bombarding the terrorists in the jungle all forenoon but now we have temporarily ceased fire so as not to disturb your luncheon.'

The Sultan gave a thin smile.

'After lunch,' went on the Captain, 'we shall restart the bombardment and I have arranged for you to be in the firing turret to see what goes on.'

It was a nice idea but could hardly have fallen on less receptive ears. The Sultan paled visibly and in a rather quavering voice attempted to expostulate.

'Not at all, sir, absolutely no trouble and I'm sure you'll thoroughly enjoy it,' cut in the Captain before the little man totally lost his nerve. 'Shall we have lunch?'

At 1430 the Sultan entered 'A' Turret. Five minutes and three rounds later he was out of it and proceeding aft to his waiting barge. He had had enough. But a finale had still to be played out. As his Royal Highness went over the side we gave him a 19-gun salute from the 4-inch secondary armament. Throughout he kept his hand at the salute. It was seen to be quivering slightly, no doubt with gratitude . . . or emotion?

Arrived in Rangoon with C-in-C embarked, we secured to special buoys in the middle of the river, opposite the centre of the town. The huge yellow waterway rushing past made a slightly sinister impression, enhanced by the local advice that we should not be disturbed by human bodies being swept away at the rate of about one every hour.

At that time there were two main political parties in Burma. One formed the Government, the other the Opposition. The latter were generally referred to as the Bandits and behaved (and were treated) as such. From time to time there would be a coup, the two parties would change round and life would be resumed much as before. When in opposition the Bandits were often armed and would give a spirited account of themselves in any scrap. The surging river would do the rest.

A certain Englishman had lived and worked in Rangoon for many years. Now retired, unmarried and something of a recluse, his single joy in life was wildfowling. Across the river to the west lay the huge estuary with its myriad mudflats, the haunt of many wild birds and especially duck. It was there that he was to be found on most days during the season.

One day, while standing at his hide waiting for the evening flight, he was jumped by a small party of Bandits. They were a rough lot. Two of them pinioned his arms while a third took away his twelve-bore and another removed his cartridge belt. Jabbering excitedly, they made it clear that their interest lay not in him but in his gun and ammunition. Laughing and shouting, they pushed him into the swamp and started to move off.

Mr Simpson was not a rich man. By leading a very simple, almost frugal, life he was just able to eke out his pitiful pension and indulge in his love of shooting. If his gun was taken there was no way in which he could possibly afford to replace it. Pulling himself to his feet he shouted at them in their own tongue. This checked the departing Bandits. Surprised, they returned to their victim.

'Do anything,' he pleaded, 'anything at all. Take my money (I've hardly got any). Take my cartridges. But leave me my gun. Without my gun I have nothing to live for. Take it and you might as well also take my life. I implore you to give me back my gun.'

He could do no more. But it was not enough. After a brief pause the Bandits started chattering again. One waved his gun in derision and a second, laughing, pushed him back into the swamp. They disappeared into the tall grass. A wet, tired, utterly dejected Simpson slowly made his way back to his tiny bungalow.

A week later, just as daylight was breaking, Mr Simpson awoke. A rustling noise on his verandah had roused him and as he sat up on his bed he heard it again. Suspecting an intruder he thrust aside his mosquito net and tiptoed out.

There was nobody about, only a rather dirty, ill-fastened brown paper parcel. He picked it up and opened it; there was no message.

Inside was his shotgun.

During our stay in Rangoon we were treated to a rare event called Kissing the Cobra. The Resident said that in the 17 years he had been there he had only seen it once before. This ceremony took place in the tennis court within the lovely grounds of a well-known local film star. Fortunately for their peace of mind the audience sat on a grassy bank outside the wire netting.

A young girl walked gracefully on to the court and addressed us in slow careful English. She explained that the King Cobra which was about to be released was in its full natural state; its fangs and poison sacks were untouched and its lethal deadliness unimpaired. Nor had it been trained or familiarized with human beings in any way. Indeed it had been taken from one part of a certain forest, owned by priests, and on completion of the ceremony would be returned to another, quite different, part some miles away.

She then adjured us to keep absolute silence throughout the whole of her act. No gasps of surprise, no sharp intake of breath, no applause, no noise of any kind. Failure to comply with this could break the spell she would cast on the snake and lead to her agonizing death. To emphasize this she briefly recounted the last performance of her late father from whom she had learned her skill. When nearing the climax he had experienced an overpowering feeling that someone in the crowd was willing the snake to bite him and that the strength of this person's will was greater than his own. So acute was his perception that for a time he had contemplated cancelling his act and withdrawing from the arena. Then pride and his reputation had regained ascendancy and he had continued. At the critical moment his mastery over the snake had failed. The snake had struck him in the face and he had died cursing his unknown enemy.

Against this background of tension and expectancy the girl began her act.

She herself took up a position on the service line at one end of the court. Two assistants entered at the opposite end carrying a large wicker basket. This they placed in the centre of the court where the net would normally have been. One of them undid the fastenings, the other whipped off the lid; both then ran quickly from the court. Up from the basket rose a huge King Cobra, its hood spread and its forked tongue darting in and out at great speed. To the onlookers it was the epitome of malicious evil and they watched frozen in a horrible fascination.

The girl was now humming a lilting tune, her whole body swaying gracefully from side to side, her hands clasped in front of her breast as if in prayer. Slowly, very slowly, she shuffled forwards, always swaying, always humming. It took some time for her to reach the service court and by then a change was noticeable in the behaviour of the snake: the speed of its flicking tongue had lessened considerably. Slower and slower it flicked until finally it stopped altogether.

By now the girl was only some ten feet away from the dreadful creature. Gradually she sank to her knees still swaying, still gently inching forward. When she got within touching distance she paused and gradually extended her arms until she could place her hands on top of the brute's head. Slowly she drew it down until it was on a level with her own. Then she gently drew it towards her and stuffed as much as she could of its hideous snout into her open mouth.

For a few moments time stood still. Then she very slowly withdrew the creature's mouth from her own, released her hands from its head and gently repeated the whole process in reverse. When she reached the edge of the service court she quietly rose to her feet again. Her two assistants ran swiftly up to the snake, clapped another basket over its head and carried it off.

The performance was over and a stunned, thoughtful audience repaired to the house for a badly needed drink.

★

At about 1700 one evening while on passage from Singapore to Hong Kong I was tidying up a few outstanding things in the Gunnery Office. The telephone rang.

'Gunnery Officer.'

'Oh, Guns, Captain here.'

'Good evening, sir.'

'What are you doing in the office now?'

'Just squaring off a few thiings sir.'

'I see. Well you can leave your Gunnery Office. You won't be doing any more shooting.'

There was a pregnant pause. I couldn't think what on earth the man was talking about. But clearly the ball was at my feet.

'Sorry sir, I'm not quite with you.'

'No, no more gunnery now,' chuckled the Captain. 'You've finished with all that sort of thing now. You're a Commander. You've been promoted. Hearty congratulations.'

I sat stunned and delighted. I had not even remembered it was the day for announcing the half-yearly promotions and to have been selected at the first shot enhanced the surprise. Also selected were Peter Mitchell, the Navigating Officer, and Michael Pollock, the Commander. It was quite a party.

Some days later Peter Mitchell and I discussed our prospects. We agreed that it seemed certain we would both be sent to The Admiralty and we would do well to plan accordingly. As bachelors and friends we decided to share a flat in London. Already in our thirties, we gave ourselves the two years or so of our next appointments in which to catch the eye of some lovely girl, failing which we would regard ourselves as finally on the shelf.

Neither of us went to the Admiralty.

Three years later in November, 1957, the 'phone rang again in my office. It was Peter Mitchell. Both of us had since been re-appointed and to my delight only that morning I had read in the paper of his engagement.

'Congratulations,' I said. 'What super news. I'm so glad.'

'Well, it's about that that I'm ringing,' he replied. 'I was wondering if you'd be prepared to be my Best Man?'

'Of course, I'd be delighted but . . . there is just one thing: roughly when do you have in mind to get married? The fact is I'm rather broody myself but I haven't popped the question yet.'

'About February,' he said. 'Does that suit you?'

'Fine – I think. That's about the same time as I hope to be thinking about it. I'll be in touch.'

At that it was left.

A few weeks later I decided the time had come to chance my arm. A good dinner was planned in a cosy little night club in London. All seemed to go well. Towards midnight when the lights were low, the music soft and the general atmosphere fairly smoochy, I popped the question. Hardly were the words out of my mouth when there came a crash of drums, a blare of trumpets and a clash of cymbals from the band – whose leader was about to announce some rubbish. The cacophony blotted out everything, including my hoped-for's reply. Desperately I waited for the racket to subside; she was half smiling so I had grounds for optimism. But it really rather mattered. I had to *know*. Leaning closer, my heart in my mouth, I took the plunge again.

'What did you say?'

'Yes,' said Mary McCall. 'Of course.'

That was the best moment of my life. Tall, graceful, fresh-faced and with a lovely peaches-and-cream complexion, Mary proved to be the most wonderful wife any man could ever wish for. We were married in Holy Trinity, Brompton, two months later, spent a blissful honeymoon in Majorca and returned to a tiny top-floor flat in Pont Street where Henrietta was born a year later. So began a devoted partnership which was to withstand periodical separation and frequent Service buffeting for 33 marvellous years. Throughout them, whether by my side or far away, Mary gave me wisdom, intelligent advice and loving support through thick and thin – and there was some of each. Of her many attributes perhaps the two most outstanding were her absolute calmness in any crisis and her quiet, bubbling sense of humour. We had such happy times together. When she died of cancer when not yet 60 I loved her just as much as when we were first married. The bottom dropped out of my world but this cheerful book is not the place for my private grief. That was the worst moment of my life.

10

OBEY TELEGRAPHS

'Think in oceans and shoot at sight'
Admiral of the Fleet Lord Fisher

In the autumn of 1959, following two gruelling but fascinating years in the Officer Planning Section at the Admiralty, I was appointed to my first command: the Battle class Destroyer *Dunkirk*. She was a powerful ship of 2,500 tons whose main armament consisted of two twin 4.5 inch turrets and ten torpedo tubes. Laid down in 1943 and completed towards the end of the war, these ships were the last destroyers built in that era which really *looked* like destroyers in the traditional sense. Their principal shortcoming was that, despite the great power of their propulsion machinery, they were fitted with only a single rudder and were consequently cumbersome to turn in the tight manoeuvring demanded by the rapidly developing anti-submarine warfare techniques. But with thirteen officers and 240 ship's company they made a fine command and I was very proud.

There were five ships in the Squadron, three Battle class and two Weapon class, led by Captain (D) in *Trafalgar*. George Crowley was a splendid, short, stocky man whose appearance resembled a cock robin. Bright of eye, sound of sense and shrewd in judgement, he understood sailors and had the knack of seeing things as they really were, not just as they seemed to be. He had a very good Squadron Staff and we were a happy and effective team. Of the rest of us (all Commanders) three were identically the same seniority, separated in the Navy List by two or three places. It was the Appointers' joke of the year and it worked 'in spite of' rather than 'because of'.

Three weeks before I took over command I was involved in a serious car accident. It occurred at a roundabout in Battersea where a Tate & Lyle long-distance tanker towing a trailer was too much for my little Austin A40. Evidently I was pushed off the road, through a plate glass window and ended up inside a shoe shop. The car was a write-off and the next thing I knew was when I recovered consciousness on a trolley in the casualty ward of St Thomas's Hospital with people stitching up my head and strapping my ribs and collarbone. They did a good job and the human form is resilient. Within ten days the bandages were off, the stitches out and a dynamic physiotherapist had done her worst to my collarbone. Though still rather shaken and easily tired, I was mending fast. Except for my eyes. The blow on my head had resulted in acute double vision. 'It will come all right in time,' advised my very good eye consultant at St Thomas's, 'but you must take care not to get tired and drink no alcohol for three months.' The drink part was easy, if unpalatable. But tiredness. How could you possibly take a newly commissioned Fleet Destroyer through seven weeks of concentrated operational training, in the middle of winter, at the toughest operational naval work-up base in the world, without getting tired? *My* problem, I thought, and we parted on those terms.

On the morning I was due to take over command I dressed myself unaided for the first time since my accident. It was a painful, tortuous process and took over an hour. At the end of it I was white and shaking and feeling none too good. It did not augur well. My wife drove me to Devonport and at 1100 I stepped on board. One short stroll round the upperdeck with my predecessor was enough to exhaust me and gratefully I sank back into an armchair in what was now *my* cabin. It was time for some realistic stocktaking.

We were due to recommission with an almost totally new Ship's Company in two days' time. Then after a week's shakedown in harbour we were to go to Portland to work up. Portland's reputation was 'make or break' and at that time the emphasis was on 'break'. I was now responsible for the lives and wellbeing of 250 officers and men. It was my first command and I too would in any case be on a steep learning curve. At that time I was not fit to drive a motor car, let alone a Fleet Destroyer. By any objective reasoning I should admit now that in the circumstances it was all too much and ask to be relieved. Indeed no other course of action would be fair to the ship or her company.

There was, however, another side to the dilemma. Without having commanded at sea there was no hope of reaching the highest ranks – and rightly so. Such commands did not grow on trees and if I relinquished this one I might not get another. The Portland myth might be exaggerated. In another week I might be in much better shape. Recently one or two Commanders had foregone their sea commands albeit on flimsier pretexts and had been justifiably despised for it. It was, in short, the easy way out and recognized as such.

Next day I called on my Commander-in-Chief (Plymouth). Backed by his own extensive command experience, Admiral Sir Richard Onslow heard my predicament with sympathy and understanding. It was agreed that I should inform my Appointer and invite him to earmark a possible relief, and that I should report on my fitness to C-in-C 48 hours before we were due to sail. Though this arrangement bought little enough time it was at least a breathing space. With a patch over my damaged eye for the commissioning ceremony I set about my tasks.

Dunkirk was not in a good state. Her machinery spaces were dirty, her gunnery system out of alignment and her general appearance inside and out was unkempt. I had lower deck cleared and pointed this out to All Hands, though they needed little reminding of the obvious. 'It won't do,' I exhorted them: 'we will work until she's clean.' There were many safety and other drills to be checked through and there was not much time; but the ship's company responded well. Going all through the ship getting to know and encouraging everyone was difficult and tiring because of seeing double. Previously I had not realized how often in a ship it is necessary to look down and looking down produced the maximum duplicating effect. Nor was it possible to apply any systematic logic to the problem, such as putting your head on one side or learning that the left hand hatchway was the real one. The phantom hatchway appeared with random confusion. And to see his Captain struggling to climb through a hatch that wasn't there was a hoot to any watching sailor!

For my criterion as to fitness I selected my eyesight. Overcoming physical fatigue was simply a combination of stamina and resolve and could be handled. But double vision was another matter. Unless I could use a pair of binoculars efficiently by night I judged I could not responsibly take the ship to sea. Out of the blue came a temporary reprieve. The Fleet Engineer Officer persuaded the Commander-in-Chief Western Fleet that all ships in the 7th Destroyer Squadron remain alongside in their base ports for the next five weeks and apply extra maintenance to their machinery – otherwise they would simply break down on arrival at Portland and waste everyone's time. Hope revived. Surely in five weeks I could make it?

Each night after dark I went up to my open bridge with my binoculars and peered through them anxiously. I looked along the line of the jetty (but there were two jetties) and imagined whether I could bring the ship alongside (but there were two ships). Everywhere there were lights; for every real one there was a phantom duplicate. The prospect was not encouraging.

With inexorable rapidity the days slipped past. The moment of truth came on the final Friday night. We were due to sail at 0900 on Monday and in accordance with my pledge I had to report to C-in-C Plymouth on the Saturday morning. Short of a radical overnight improvement in my wobbly eyesight it seemed barely conceivable that my report would be other than 'unfit to drive'. With leaden feet I climbed the ladders to the bridge – a pointless charade really but I had to go through with it just to make sure. No change. There were the two ships (for which I had already acquired considerable affection) secured to the two jetties and everywhere double lights. It was hopeless. With a heavy heart I started to lower my binoculars.

In doing so I must have tilted them momentarily and suddenly everything came good. Was it a miracle or a chance fluke? Again I tried and again – and again. Each time the tilting worked and I achieved a clear view of single objects. My relief knew no bounds. Hurrying down to my cabin I ordered a taxi and sped up to Admiralty House. The C-in-C had just finished dinner and was playing snooker with his guests. Bursting in on them unannounced created some surprise but I could not wait.

'Sir,' I said, 'I am *fit.*'

'Are you really?' he asked doubtfully.

'Yes sir, absolutely. I can use binoculars by night with complete normal efficiency.'

'Mmm,' said the C-in-C with a great twinkle in his eye as he lined up a red ball with the centre pocket and handed me a cue, 'pot the red.'

Bending low so as to look up and reduce the number of red balls to one I took careful aim and made my shot. Down went the red with a satisfying clunk. I straightened up with a smile.

'Pass,' said the C-in-C with a broad grin.

Portland is a remarkable place. At any time of the year on a still, sunny day it can be beautiful. A few hours later it can be clamped in impenetrable fog. Yet another few hours and it can be blowing a full gale. The direction of the wind outside the harbour can be radically different from that inside and many of the jetties experience considerable individual wind variations. For the inexperienced Commanding officer bringing his ship alongside this presents interesting problems in which the unexpected features prominently. For the sailor Portland holds a love-hate relationship. The love element stems from a sense of achievement, of winning through despite being pushed to the limit or slightly beyond, rather than any feeling of affection. The hate part? Well, when it's freezing cold, you are soaked to the skin, the horizontal sleet is driving down your neck and there's still another hour to complete a replenishment in the middle of the night, there are cosier places than a destroyer's fo'c'sle. But for every naval officer or man Portland holds professional attraction tempered by challenge. The variety is extensive: from all forms of air, surface and submarine attack with their associated weapon training to full ceremonial; from disaster relief to underwater sabotage; from defence against nuclear or chemical attack to children's parties. It is tough, non-stop training; so it should be. Those who don't like it shouldn't have joined.

We arrived at Portland, 250 individuals, after dark, in winds of near gale force and visibility down to half a mile. Seven weeks later we left, a 250-strong team. In that time I had lost 2½ stone in weight.

★

The Mediterranean in spring presented a cheering prospect. We relieved a squadron of *Daring* Class in which each ship (they are only large destroyers) was commanded by a Captain. On the night of the turnover we were 'dined in' by our Admiral – Desmond Dreyer, Flag Officer Flotillas (Med) – on board his flagship the cruiser *Tiger* and our predecessors were 'wined out' immediately following dinner. When the latter was well under way Dreyer turned to the departing Captains and asked,

'Well, you've now done your last Sliema. I don't suppose any of you will ever do it again. How do you feel about that?'

Sliema Creek was the normal berth for destroyers in Malta. It was a narrow inlet in which there was just room to berth ships of this size two abreast. Entering it through a gap in the rocks it was necessary to turn sharply through some 135 degrees, placing the bow very close to the shore (where there was still deep water) and then drive the ship stern first up the creek and position her between the assigned head and stern buoys. If there were many other ships already berthed or if a strong wind was blowing across the creek there was little scope for error. Ships do not steer well when going astern and reliance had to be placed principally on use of the engines and their considerable power. The manoeuvre was always interesting and often exhilarating – or worse.

The first Captain spoke up. 'Dreadful, sir. I shall miss it greatly. Wonderful experience.'

'Yes,' agreed the second, 'don't know how I'm going to get it out of my system.'

'Quite awful,' twittered the third, 'a real gap in my life.'

'Irreplaceable, irreplaceable – nothing to quite touch it,' echoed the fourth and fifth.

The sixth remained silent.

'Come on, Geoffrey,' prompted the Admiral, 'you haven't spoken.'

'You're a rotten lot,' growled Geoffrey Carew-Hunt. 'I'm the only really honest man among you. I had f – ing kittens every time I did it!'

A few weeks later *Dunkirk* was tasked to be planeguard (Rescue Destroyer) to the *Ark Royal* while carrying out night flying west of Malta. We joined at sunset and were immediately stationed in the usual position on the carrier's port beam. The first launch proceeded without incident and on completion the ships turned out of wind again. Thinking that such a big ship would have a large turning circle I ordered initially only a small amount of wheel. In fact *Ark* whipped round like a top and to tighten the turn I ended up with 35 degrees of wheel (the maximum). When I came to take it off the rudder appeared to be jammed. Thus the planeguard was left circling at 30 knots while the carrier disappeared over the horizon. By progressive reductions in speed, steering control was eventually regained and we clawed our way back to *Ark* just in time for the next launch and recovery. Both these completed, we turned back to the previous course and, now wise to events, this time I put on only 15 degrees of wheel. Yet again the rudder stuck, causing the same embarrassing situation. And yet again we rejoined in time for the final launch. Turning back this time, only 5 degrees of wheel was used but the now familiar jam still resulted. In catching up we were stationed half a mile dead ahead of the carrier for the rest of the night. This was an uncomfortably close position with no tactical relevance and I took the earliest excuse of a doubtful submarine contact many miles distant to get the hell out of it. Which brought me back to Gibraltar for a two-month refit. Apart from the obviously defective steering gear the ship was in good shape and we all grudged the inevitable mess and disruption of being in dockyard hands in Gibraltar.

Eight weeks on, with the ship now looking really smart, we put to sea for trials. Despite all efforts the wheel was so stiff as to be barely capable of being turned by hand at all. Though reported at once the dockyard would have none of it. 'You must give the system a chance to work itself in,' they said airily; 'it will take time.' This was patently nonsense and I knew it. I sent a sharp signal to my Captain (D) and copied it to the C-in-C. The local Flag Officer at Gibraltar was furious and his reaction was predictable – though his Staff still found themselves unable to do anything. Thirty-six hours later our own Squadron Marine Engineer Officer flew in from Malta. He knew exactly what he was doing and within a few hours had completely cured the fault.

By now we were overdue for sailing and the local Flag Officer was still angrier at the incompetence of his own people having been so swiftly and ignominiously exposed. He sent for me. I took the Squadron MEO with me but the Admiral refused to see him. I went in alone.

The Admiral was striding up and down with steam coming out of his ears.

'I am not disposed to let this matter drop,' he spluttered.

I waited in silence for the next salvo.

'I am giving serious consideration to court-martialling your Engineer Officer for incompetence.'

Silence. He appeared to have run out of ammunition.

'Sir,' I said quietly, 'whether or not you court martial my Engineer Officer is your prerogative. But if you elect to do so (on what grounds I cannot conceive) I shall appear in court as his defence and your Dockyard Chief Engineer will be a primary witness facing some very embarrassing questions.'

We then sailed and I never heard any more on the subject.

★

Soon after our return to Malta we took part in a major NATO exercise, a much needed sharpener after these weeks in the torpor of Gibraltar. When it was over and we had all reassembled for the post-exercise discussion, our Admiral gave a splendid lunch party to all the participating Flag and Commanding Officers. I found myself seated between an Italian Admiral (Commander Allied Naval Forces South) and a very senior Turkish Captain. The former spoke English and was an exceptionally nice man, devoid of pomp and stuffiness. He was, however, stunningly good-looking, he exuded old world charm and he was devoted to my own Admiral's wife on whose left he was sitting. After an initial exchange of courtesies I could expect little conversation from him. I turned to the Turk.

'Do you know Malta well, sir?' I asked brightly.

He was a big man with a square jaw, thin lips, huge bushy black eyebrows and a general expression of unrelieved gloom.

'Uhhh?' he grunted.

'Do you speak English?' I tried again.

'No.'

'Parlez-vous Français?'

Silence, then a grudging, growled, *'Non.'*

In growing desperation I turned to the Flag Lieutenant, sitting at the head of the table on the Turk's other side.

'The Captain speaks neither English nor French,' I told him with a naughty gleam in my eye, 'so it's up to you to entertain him with your best Turkish.' He was a very nice person and this was unfair but he was more than a match for me.

'Naturally, sir,' he replied with a smile of total non-co-operation and promptly attended to his other neighbour.

This was it. A senior officer from a friendly foreign navy could hardly be left in stony silence throughout the whole of lunch. I concluded that since he wouldn't be 'talked with' he must be 'talked at' – and that presentationally this would be better achieved in my schoolboy French than in English.

Racking my memory for vocabulary and striving to recall some syntax, I set to. Gazing intently into my neighbour's rather bloodshot eyes I said pointedly in my best Franglais.

'Is it not amazing that the earth is round?'

'Comment?' he mumbled.

'Or that the oceans are full of water?' I continued.

'Comprends pas,' was the grating response.

'And when the sun descends into . . . into . . .' I struggled for whatever the sun does descend into and settled for 'the sea . . . the sky turns red?'

The reaction was an incredulous growl.

Nevertheless I persisted and by half way through the main course I had worked up quite a head of steam. In an unceasing flow of verbal rubbish I bombarded my neighbour into tacit and uncomprehending submission.

Suddenly I became aware that everyone else had finished eating whereas I in my enthusiasm was only half way through. Worse, all other conversation had ceased and my Admiral (and others) was looking anxiously at me.

And I? I was outpointing Brigadier Gerard, I was in mid-sentence in full flood in a quality of the French vernacular that had seldom been equalled and never surpassed.

'Is it not marvellous,' I thundered at the hapless Turk, 'that from time to time the moon is blue . . . or, of course it may be pink?'

Not only the poor Turk, the entire company was spellbound. My Admiral's eyes temporarily glazed, then focused more sharply on me. The forefinger of his right hand was already on route to his forehead in that well known sign aptly described by the continentals as 'toc toc'.

It was enough. Common prudence dictated that I should abandon my self-imposed policy of '*toujours la politesse*' and lie low for a bit. Hastily putting my knife and fork together I did so.

In these bureaucratic times it is tempting to say that there is no need for paper at sea. But even a ship needs some paper to promulgate certain daily orders and we were down to buying or borrowing the last few sheets from local sources. Frequent routine demands through 'normal channels' had resulted in courteous acknowledgement and absolutely no action. Irritated, I sent for the Leading Writer in charge of the Ship's Office.

He was a pleasant and effective young man in his mid-twenties behind whose thick spectacles and diffident manner lay great industry, loyalty and some humour. But he had been brought up to go strictly by the book and any departure from this philosophy put him in a twitter of nerves.

'Take down the following letter,' I said, 'addressed to The Secretary of the Admiralty:

"Be pleased to inform Their Lordships that continued failure to meet my repeated stationary demands will shortly render HMS *Dunkirk* unable to forward reports and returns except on media not normally considered suitable for such purposes."

Now go down to the Heads,' I went on, 'tear off a couple of sheets of bumph from the nearest roll, make sure that the perforations and the wording "Government Property" at top and bottom are intact, and type the letter on that for my signature.'

With a feeble giggle and a rather patronizing acknowledgment of my instructions, as Nanny might respond to a wayward child, the Leading Writer left my cabin.

Half an hour later he returned with my letter impeccably typed on

14. HMS *Albion* — Commando Carrier. In fact a "three-in-one": the
Ship's Company, the Air Group, and the embarked Commando Group
— each of about 800 souls. The forward two "sticks" here shown are
Royal Netherlands Marines.

15. Happiness is beach-shaped. The most delightful photograph of the
South African visit and the one that seemed to cause the most political
trouble in Britain.

The Argus, Cape T

16. HMS *Blake* — Although I had eight different Flagships during
my first two months as Flag Officer First Flotilla, "*Snakey Blakey*" as
she was affectionately called flew my flag most. Apart from HMS
Britannia she was the oldest ship in the fleet.

17. HM Submarine *Warspite* — a nuclear-powered Attack Submarine and effectively the "Battleship" of my Task Group.

'FOR outstanding resistance in the face of severe hospitality during manoeuvres at Simonstown....'

The Argus, Cape Town

18. Another take-off in South Africa following the ridiculous furore in Whitehall.

19. Buccaneer Strike Aircraft — me about to be catapulted from the deck of the previous *Ark Royal*, last of the Royal Navy's Fixed Wing Carriers.

ordinary ship's writing paper. 'This won't do at all,' I complained. 'You've missed the whole point. Sending this normally won't make any impact at all. Now go down to the Heads, get some bumph and do as I said.'

The game was up. Ashen-faced and miserable, the Leading Writer departed, loyally muttering, 'On your own head be it, sir.' He thought that letters addressed to the Secretary of the Admiralty actually *went* to the Secretary of the Admiralty; I knew they seldom did – and would have been only too delighted if they had! He was sure that such action would lead to my instant dismissal with disgrace; I was more sanguine.

The letter – unmistakably on the prescibed bumph – was duly typed, signed and dispatched. Within one week I had an acknowledgment by signal. Within two my stationary demand had been fully met.

One of our more memorable port visits was to Heraklion in Crete. We arrived, on our own, at 0700 on a lovely, still summer's morning with the sun beginning to warm up and the sea like glass. My morning was occupied with the usual round of courtesy calls followed by an official lunch. The latter, on board, was rather heavy going since I spoke no Greek and my guests spoke no English. However, an understanding British Ambassador in Athens had kindly sent his First Secretary to help out and Ralph Stockbridge performed miracles of conversational sleight of hand.

The main event of the visit was to be a large reception on board at 1800 that evening. Preparations for this to be held on the fo'castle were progressed throughout the day; the awning was spread, side curtains rigged and signal flags distributed to lend festive colour. But two hours before, the weather suddenly deteriorated. The sky darkened with great banks of inky clouds and the wind rose sharply. There was only just enough time to dismantle our party preparations before it was blowing a gale. There was no option but to hold the reception in the Ward Room and accept the resultant overcrowding. Meantime I shortened the notice for steam.

Despite the worsening weather (which had now become really rather unpleasant) the party was an evident success. Apart from a few semi-VIPs the majority of guests were drawn from the farming communities in the area: marvellous people with walnut-like faces from constant exposure to the elements and varying in age from 40 to 60 upwards. Few wore collars or ties; instead they sported their last remaining bauble – a 'gold' front stud in the neckband of their shirt. They epitomized the expression 'salt of the earth', and such was their personality that their complete inability to speak a word of English seemed not to detract at all from the happy and unusually genuine conviviality of the occasion. They were drawn to Ralph Stockbridge as to a magnet and treated him as if he were a much loved God. They had all been in the Resistance Movement together after the fall of

Crete in 1941 and Stockbridge had helped to organize and lead them. It was one of the most remarkable and moving reunions I have ever been privileged to attend.

By the time the party ended at about 2000 we were at 30 minutes' notice for steam (which, in emergency, could probably have been reduced to 10) and my concern over the weather was growing. During the evening I had discussed with the Harbour Master the practicability of leaving the tiny harbour under these conditions (our bows were pointing inwards and it would have meant making a sternboard) but he was categoric in advising that it was impossible. Accordingly as soon as the last guest had left we put out every berthing wire we possessed, including hurricane hawsers for'ard and aft, and settled down to 'await the day' as St Paul put it. I decided not to leave the ship and despatched my First Lieutenant to accompany Ralph Stockbridge and some other officers for dinner ashore.

An hour or so later, having had a quick supper, I went up to the bridge to take stock of the situation. Within no time I was drenched to the skin by a green sea which had struck the other side of the breakwater to which we were secured and come right over at bridge level. This was too much. After giving orders for a boat to be lowered to bring off returning libertymen and for a patrol to be positioned at the root of the breakwater to stop anyone attempting to get back to the ship along the jetty (from which they would have been swept off and drowned), I put on my seagoing, foul weather clothes and returned to the bridge resolved to spend the rest of the night there.

It was an eerie vigil. The wind had risen to storm force 10 or worse, the tiny harbour was boiling like a cauldron and was crowded with local fishing boats which had anchored randomly wherever they could find a space. We were at immediate notice for steam and every so often another wire would part. By midnight (when leave expired) all but two of those who had gone ashore had returned safely by boat, which was then hoisted. During the next two hours all the remaining berthing wires parted, leaving only a single hurricane hawser at each end of the ship; and the stern hawser was already fraying ominously. The moment of truth had arrived: we had either to attempt an exit through the foaming narrows at the harbour entrance or risk being driven aground. I decided to put to sea.

The stern rope was severed with an axe and immediately the ship swung round into wind with her bow held by the headrope. A further 90 degrees beyond the eye of the wind was needed to point ship for the exit and with such limited space available every degree gained was of value. The fo'c'sle was cleared and with revolutions for 26 knots rung on the ship was 'screwed' on the headrope until it parted. After gaining a few more degrees there was no alternative to making a dash for the hole in the desperate hope that full power and full rudder would be enough to combat the elements. They were – just – and we shot through into the open sea.

It had been a very hairy manoeuvre but it worked and the ship and her company were safe.

Our Mediterranean deployment passed quickly and all too soon the time came for us to return to home waters. As a finale we visited Alicante in the fashionable Costa del Sol of Southern Spain. The visit was unremarkable save in one respect. Shortly after our arrival we learned that three distinguished local dignitaries – the Provincial Governor, the Mayor and an unidentified Hotelier – were in competition over which of them could provide the most spectacular feast at lunch during the next three days.

1230 on Day 1 saw the Commanding Officers and some others gathered at the Town Hall. The Mayor, a genial soul, bustled round welcoming us, and various other officials, most of whom spoke some English, helped to look after us. We drank sherry for about half an hour then seated ourselves at a single long table. From the number and variety of the knives, forks and spoons at each place it was clear that the competition had started. Soon after 1600 the rather heavy 'love thy neighbour' speeches ground to a close, presents were exchanged and the overfed guests transported their groaning stomachs outside to fresh air and a brisk walk. It had been a pleasant occasion with good food, good wine, good service and a friendly atmosphere. True the number of courses had been considerable and their content distinctly over-generous but we had weathered the first heat without undue difficulty or dyspepsia.

For lunch next day we travelled some miles east to Benidorm where we were entertained in a smallish, delightfully situated hotel under German management. The Home Team was rather smaller and the single knife and fork at each place on the snowy tablecloth gave little clue to the gastronomic future. However, the large, ornate menu card told a different tale as our charming host was at pains to point out. Each of the first ten courses was a different sort of fish cooked in its own distinctive way. The eleventh was a paella with the rice softened by the juices of all ten previous courses. Pudding followed by fruit and cheese rounded off the meal which was then stabilized by coffee and brandy. Not many 'small eats' were consumed at that evening's reception. Two down; one to go.

Later an interim opinion poll indicated that Benidorm had been the apex and all would now be downhill. So it was with stoic resilience that we mustered our remaining reserves of stamina and entered the ring for the final round at 1300 next afternoon. The venue was a hideous concrete building on the foreshore of a tiny, circular fishing harbour a few miles along the coast to the west. By now such was our experience in what the sea had to offer that we felt few further surprises could await us. It was therefore with a certain quiet optimism that we arranged ourselves as directed beside a long chain of trestle tables in tandem, covered by cloths and set for lunch. Placed on the tables at frequent intervals were bowls of olives, almonds and other small delicacies. The steel-framed canvas canteen chairs were all pushed in; nobody sat down. An acute language problem developed immediately, not greatly eased by a fifteen-minute wait before sherry was served in very small glasses. By 1330 the almonds and olives were exhausted and so were our smiles and gestures of warm friendship. By 1400 some shrimps and more sherry had come and gone, provoking en passant an exchange of excruciatingly silent toasts. By 1500 most of the king prawns had been eaten, enough sherry had been drunk, eyes were turning longingly to the long cool bottles of beer distributed along the tables (but which remained unopened) and everyone was dying to sit down. Nobody did. At 1530 our host, the Provinicial Governor, equipped at last with an interpreter, suggested that we might descend to the restaurant for lunch. By now any pangs of hunger had long since passed. Nor did the placing of a large oblong dish piled mountainously with chicken and heavily saffroned paella stimulate the palate. The event terminated with a brief stroll round the public gardens of the local cemetery as the clock in the church tower tolled 1700.

Next morning we sailed – and never found who claimed he had won the competition.

There were other vicissitudes in our return from Malta to UK.

My wife, Mary, flew back, taking with her our two-year-old daughter, Henrietta. At Rome Airport she had to change flights. The concourse at the time at this airport was huge and dominated by a striking centrepiece of massive glass cases in which were a variety of life-sized bears, tigers and other stuffed animals. As at any international air terminal there was a milling throng of people hurrying to and fro. In the middle of all this my wife put down her hand luggage and briefly let go of Henrietta's hand while opening her bag to find her ticket. It took but a moment, but in that moment Henrietta had gone. Slippery as an eel she had nipped off into the crowd and there was no sign of her. Hideous visions of child-stealing and crowds trampling to death flashed through Mary's mind as she set off in search of the Information Desk to get a broadcast made. Her route took her close to the centrepiece and as she passed the enormous picture windows her eye was caught by movement within the tigers' cage. There, inside, having the time of her life, was Henrietta.

My problem was different; it was a cat. Some months earlier we had acquired a tiny kitten from the local Lost Animals' Home. Its rateable value was one shilling and sixpence (15 p today). Black with a white sock on each paw he was christened Bantu and quickly became an important member of the family.

At the time it was recognized that cats were potential carriers of rabies although they were not themselves susceptible to the disease. However, Bantu having been very much a house cat for many months, it seemed reasonable to take him back in *Dunkirk* and get him straight home on arrival. Preparations were made accordingly. Extra buckets were filled with earth and stowed on board and a corner of my bathroom was suitably prepared for the passenger.

The Squadron sailed from Malta for the last time in the teeth of a Gregale, each ship flying its contribution to the signal 'East or West Home is Best'. Admiral Sir Guy Grantham, the Governor-General, came down to Sliema to see us off. A brief gleam of sunshine brightened our ceremonial exit and it made a brave sight.

As soon as we cleared the harbour we butted into heavy seas. It was before the days of stabilisers and the ship began to move quite vigorously. I nipped below to change into seagoing rig – just in time to see the miserable, heaving form of Bantu. Having, from personal experience, considerable sympathy for those who are seasick I immediately sought the best solution (fresh air) and, unthinkingly, grabbed the victim and rushed him to the bridge. It was an open bridge and the sight of the now huge waves sweeping past on either hand was too much for the unfortunate animal. He was terrified and it was all I could do to hold onto him. Back we went to the bathroom.

In due course the gale blew itself out. Bantu got his sea legs and quickly developed a sense of fun and great affection. By day he sat curled up on my desk on top of any paper on which I was working. By night his basket was progressively shifted from bathroom to day cabin to sleeping cabin. None of it would do. He was allotted an area at the foot of my bunk; that wouldn't do either. The only position he would settle for was with the top of his head wedged firmly under my chin.

At sea I always slept fully dressed so as to be instantly available. Often in the course of the night I would be called to the bridge for approaching shipping. Frequent calls become tiring and on returning to my bunk I would quickly fall asleep again. Not so Bantu. The effect on him was a stimulus and a game. When I came down from the bridge he would go berserk around the cabin with a wicked kink in his tail. Waiting till I had dropped off he would then spring at me and softly land on my face. My startled expletives caused him great amusement and off he would go again after another non-existent mouse before repeating the facial. It was an exhausting passage home.

In due course we berthed at Devonport. In a moment of mental aberration Petty Officer Steward Farrugia left my cabin door open. Quick as a flash

Bantu was over the side and half way up the nearest dockside crane. Poor, wretched Farrugia.

'You have three hours,' I told him coldly, 'in which to retrieve that animal in good order. Then I am going ashore – with the cat.'

Mary brought Henrietta on board for lunch and Farrugia achieved a miracle of persuasion with a dockyard workman over recovering the cat. At 1530 we set off in our car, Mary driving and Bantu in a pusser's grip at my feet. Henrietta sat perched on my knee, my fingers poised over her posterior ready to give it a sharp nip and cause her to bellow if Bantu spoke out of turn as we passed through the officials at the dockyard gate. In the event the pinching was not necessary as Bantu remained discreetly silent. He lived to a great age.

11

EBONY AND IVORY

'Like other amphibious animals we must come occasionally on
shore; but the water is more properly our element, and in it . . .
as we find our greatest security, so we exert our greatest force'

Lord Bolingbroke

The early 1960's saw Singapore in its heyday for the British Services. This
small island, only 17 miles across and lying some three degrees north of the
Equator, at the tip of the Malay Peninsula and linked to it by the Johore
causeway, was a focal point for East-West traffic by sea or air. It occupied a
commanding position strategically and commercially and had been developed
accordingly.

The busy, noisy, bustling activity of Singapore City with its important
entrepot port contrasted starkly with the quiet peace of the kampongs and
up-country Malaya. This contrast largely reflected the differing characteristics between the clever, resourceful and often ruthless expatriate Chinese
of the town and the gentle, easy-going, dreamy Malays of the country.

The suburbs of the town were extensive and very well-to-do. Spacious
areas of immaculately chopped bamboo grass were protected from the
burning glare of the tropical sun by tall, graceful trees. The houses were
large, well proportioned and airy for as yet air-conditioning was still
rudimentary. In places a more European style of urban development
intruded; high-rise blocks of flats had been constructed to house the
increasing number of city-dwelling locals. It was not a success. A typical
four-roomed flat might have been adequate for a two-generation family if the
practice of birth control had been more diligently observed. But by the time
both sets of grandparents and a range of uncles, aunts and cousins had been
squeezed in the result was crowded squalor.

Out in the kampongs there was space. To combat ants and flooding the
wooden houses with their shady verandas were built on stilts. The steps
leading up to these were often flanked by pots of brilliant geraniums, while
naked children, stray dogs and scrawny chickens made full use of the
communal ground between.

To Europeans the climate had become the whipping-boy for all that was wrong. True it was hot but the temperature seldom averaged much more than 80° F. It was the similarity of the climate throughout the year, the lack of seasonal change and the very high humidity, often approaching 100%, which generated lassitude in some and laziness in most. The solution to this problem lay in taking a bit of healthy exercise in the early morning or late evening and those who did not advertised it by their irritability. Often it rained but seldom for long. When it did the roads and streets quickly became awash and the monsoon drains running beside them turned into raging torrents of water stained yellow by the laterite. An hour or two later the sky would clear, the sun blazed once more and all was fresh and clean.

Perhaps the most striking thing to the newcomer was the rich greenness of everything, which made a perfect backcloth to the vivid colours of the flame of the forest, jacarandas, bougainvillaea, hibiscus and cannas. That and the inimitable smell of the East, a mixture of warmth, damp and spices tempered by an infinite variety of more specific local additives.

Each of the three Services had established a main base on Singapore Island: the Royal Navy towards the head of the main channel on the north-eastern side, not far from the causeway; the Army at Tanglin in the outskirts of the city; and the Royal Air Force at Changi and Tengah where there was ample flat space for full-length modern runways. Over the years a consider-able panoply of amenities had been built up at each base: married quarters, social and sports clubs, swimming pools, playing fields, golf courses, sailing marinas and such like. Indeed so good were these facilities and so self-contained that the inhabitants of one had little inclination to move outside their own patch to visit another. Despite this (or perhaps because of it) the social life was brisk with a cocktail or dinner party every three or four nights. On a weekend many families would cross the causeway and drive up the east coast beyond Mersing to relax and picnic on one of the many unspoilt beaches. Fine white sand, safe warm sea abounded – as did sunblistered shoulders and sandflies. This contrasted with the waters of the Johore Straits where sandflies were replaced by sea snakes. The newly arrived water-skiing enthusiast was offered encouraging advice on these: 'When (not if) you are bitten by a watersnake do not attempt to pull it off. On the contrary, tighten your grip (advancing rigor may assist this) so that when later you are carried into the British Military Hospital it will facilitate the doctor in identifying the snake and enable him to give you one, effective serum injection instead of 43 experimental ones – towards the end of which you may be running out of time anyway.' For longer spells of seasonal leave the west coast (Penang or Port Dickson) or up in the hills (Cameron Highlands or Fraser's Hill) were popular. The latter made a particularly welcome change; crisp air by day and by night sweaters and log fires; even porridge for breakfast.

*

The work load for those in the Services varied considerably. The RAF operated generally at about 65% capacity, the Army at around 75% and the Navy at seldom less than 90%. If anyone had got it wrong it was the Navy, for it meant that in a crisis there was little reserve to draw on and the additional stretch generated substantial fatigue. Often since then I have noticed similar operating patterns among the Staffs at the Ministry of Defence in Whitehall.

Admiral Sir Gerald Gladstone (a former Commander-in-Chief Far East) had perceived his main role as that of roving ambassador throughout the vast area, which mainly involved travel by sea. To this end he had established an organization at the Fleet Headquarters whereby in his absence the Chief of Staff (a Rear Admiral) acted as de facto C-in-C and four Chief Staff Officers of Captain's rank acted as mini-Chiefs of Staff in their respective fields of Plans and Operations, Intelligence, Technical, and Administration. As 'P & O' I also dealt with weaponry, communications, logistics, aviation and meteorology; it was enough to prevent time hanging heavily on my hands.

On the planning side I was the naval member of the Joint Planning Committee, which also included the Head of Chancery. Sometimes a meeting would be convened at very short notice, too short to study the relevant papers which were highly classified and often had only just been received. The half-hour's drive from the Naval Base to Phoenix Park in the outskirts of the town did little to ease this problem for at that time I suffered acutely from sickness if I attempted to read in a moving car. Thus I was continually facing the dilemma of whether to arrive at the meeting white and shaking but fully conversant with the subject or robust and sparkling but aware only in outline of the purpose of the meeting. It was my RAF colleague who provided a way out of this impasse. He was only too delighted to express his views at length on any matter that was put to him. Immediately on arrival, therefore, I would put a topical (but not necessarily relevant) question to him at the same time drawing the Chairman (a soldier) into the discussion. Usually it was good for ten minutes or so during which I hastily grasped the main points of the papers.

At the higher level was the British Defence Co-ordinating Committee, the three Service's C's-in-C with the High Commissioner (or in his absence the C-in-C longest in post) in the chair. But in the course of 1962 Unified Command was established. A single C-in-C, appointed separately and rotated between the Services, became the top man. The High Commissioner was replaced by a Political Adviser and the Head of the three Services became respectively the Naval, Army and Air Commanders. This gave rise to a domestic problem. By longstanding rules tediously negotiated with the Treasury and Civil Service Department only a C-in-C was entitled to a Residence and only a Residence was complemented with a Chief Steward or equivalent and a full retinue of domestic staff. The difficulty was neatly sidestepped by adopting the nomenclature of 'Flag, General or Air Officer Commanding in Chief'. However, in the naval case this resulted in the signal abbreviation 'FOCINFEF' (Flag Officer Commanding-in-Chief Far East Fleet) and in turn raised the daunting question of whether the 'C' should be pronounced soft (when 'FOSSING' sounded rather simpering) or hard (when 'FOCKING' came very close to a more basic interpretation). Such matters occupied an inordinate amount of time and involved a number of exchanges with Whitehall. Eventually the die was cast in favour of the hard 'C' and surprisingly the sailor, who is usually game for a bit of good natured jocularity towards authority any day of the week, made very little of it.

The most vociferous in the opposition to setting up Unified Command had been Admiral Sir David Luce. After relief by Admiral Sir Desmond Dreyer and a spell of leave in UK he was posted back to Singapore as the first Unified Commander. In Whitehall this was conceived as a shrewd 'poacher turned gamekeeper' gambit, but in practice that other metaphor about 'taking a horse to the water but not being able to make him drink' was more relevant. David Luce continued to conduct business as he had when acting as Chairman of the British Defence Co-ordinating Committee. In this he had developed considerable adroitness, a necessary attribute, for some of his Commanders were none too easy when it came to decision-taking. The Army Commander (General Sir Nigel Poett) was a charming person but inclined to pontificate at length on any subject under discussion. The Air Commander (Air Chief Marshal MacGregor), a dour New Zealander, tended to be brusque and intransigent and often seemed completely disinterested in the affairs of the meeting. David Luce would listen patiently to all the views expressed, only occasionally putting in a question or gently hauling the discussion back onto the rails; then he would sum up. 'Well then,' he would say, 'I think we're all agreed that we should do so and so.' Almost always he was right and seldom was there any dissent. But it was intriguing to note that often 'so and so' bore no relation whatsoever to the preceding views expressed.

Because of my involvement in the Joint Planning Committee and thence the top level BDCC it was appropriate that I should call on the High Commissioner. Accordingly one afternoon I drove to Government House to write my name in The Book. As I was leaving a rather grubby, totally disreputable-looking woman rose from her knees in the flower bed by the front door and we exchanged a few words – in the course of which it was not difficult to deduce that I was talking to the High Commissioner's wife. Three weeks later Mary and I were invited to dinner.

Of the dozen and a half or so present we were by far the youngest and found that we did not know any of the other guests. A good dinner followed the conventional pattern though the men hung interminably over their port. Being very much 'boots' of the rather distinguished party I re-entered the drawing room last.

'Ah Captain Leach,' said my charming hostess, peering rather distractedly at her crib, 'let me see now, who haven't you seen sitting next to? Have you talked to this delightful lady?' and she pointed to a small twosome sofa on which Mary was sitting.

'No,' I replied quite honestly, 'I haven't had that privilege,' and quickly sat down beside my wife.

'Tell me, Mrs Leach,' I began, 'I have got the name right, it is "Leach" isn't it?' Mary's containment of her mirth started to crack. 'Have you been out here long?'

'No only a few months.'

'And do you find the climate very trying?'

We quickly developed a useless dialogue, question and answer becoming more and more ridiculous and our composure collapsing into open laughter. Time passed quickly. Suddenly we became aware that everyone else was on their feet and saying goodbye. Last out were the Leach's, murmuring genuinely grateful things to our kind hosts. Neither batted an eyelid and to this day I do not know if they realized what had happened.

Second in Command of the Far East Fleet (FO2FEF) was Vice Admiral Jack Scatchard, flying his flag at sea. I had known him as Commandant of the Joint Services Staff College at Latimer where he was famous for his hospitality to visiting lecturers and students alike – salty sailor of the old school, who called a spade a spade and told political lecturers in unequivocal terms what he thought of their views. At sea technological and professional progress had rather overtaken him; nevertheless he injected a substantial element of uncertainly into the exercises he conducted. He was more concerned with the speed of reaction to a signal when executed than with the correctness or tactical sense of the action taken; thus the immediate emergence of a puff of black smoke from the funnel of a destroyer (indicating that more fuel-sprayers had been opened up to increase speed) tended to score good points on the Flagship's bridge even if the screening ship concerned was hastening in quite the wrong direction. Sadly he had forgotten some of his naval signal flags and their meaning.

Came the day of Jack Scatchard's relief and subsequent retirement. The Commanding Officers of the two Australian destroyers which were operating with the Far East Fleet at the time combined to give him a slap-up lunch in the senior ship of the two by way of farewell to their departing Admiral. I was invited also. After a few drinks we sat down at a small highly polished table, glistening with silver and glass, in the centre of which stood a slender silver mast mounted on an inscribed plinth flying a silk Flag Echo. This flag when hoisted singly at the Flagship's yardarm at sea means 'Flag and Commanding Officers have time for the next meal'; when it is subsequently hauled down anything is fair game but while it is flying its meaning is strictly observed and those in command know they can enjoy a short break. Throughout Jack Scatchard's 18 months as FO2FEF never had Flag Echo been used.

Once seated our hosts worked hard to keep the conversation going but the Admiral's attention kept wandering to the centrepiece Flag Echo. There was something faintly familiar about it but for the life of him he couldn't remember what. After some time he leant forward and picked up the centrepiece so as to examine it more closely. He started to read the inscription on the plinth which began 'Presented to Vice Admiral J. P. Scatchard . . .'; then he quickly returned it to the centre of the table. Throughout the rest of the meal he remained evidently distracted by this wretched little flag and what it might mean, but enlightenment never dawned until the moment came for the presentation when our host found it necessary to 'translate'. It was a shrewd memento.

On the occasion of a South East Asia Treaty Organisation (SEATO) Planning Conference taking place at Singapore, representatives at senior staff level from UK, US, France, Thailand, Australia and New Zealand gathered for a working week of discussions and meetings lightened by social events. I was the senior UK naval representative and in view of the numbers involved and the limited size of our quarter my wife and I decided to split the naval visitors into two halves and invite one party to dinner and the film in the Naval Base Club on Tuesday and the others to a final lunch on Friday. Such an arrangement also eased the problem for our domestic staff which consisted of Fong Hing, ancient Cantonese cook of around three score years and ten and mainly opium habits; and Rose, the young ahmah who helped look after our daughter.

The week got off to a bad start. A very senior Thai Captain arrived by air at Paya Lebar airport and having failed to read his brief went to the wrong place where there was no one to meet him and no transport. Being a little man of unparalleled pomposity and no sense of humour, he was upset and was quick to indulge in a frenzy of complaint.

40 minutes *before* the scheduled start time on Tuesday evening I was standing naked under a shower. It had been a long hot day and I was just beginning to cool off in the tepid water when the front door bell rang. Cursing, I wrapped a towel round my waist and went down to deal with the visitor. It was one of the Americans and at once I knew that he had got it all wrong: wrong day, wrong time, wrong meal. He had been invited to lunch on Friday, not dinner on Tuesday! I should have told him so straight out

but in the interests of international relations I did not do so. Secretly I hoped (without much confidence) that it would all turn out all right and we should find that he had exchanged his invitation with that of his colleague. Forty minutes *after* the scheduled start time as we were about to move in to dinner, it became clear that this had not happened; the second American arrived.

Hastily we grabbed a canvas-back canteen chair from under the stilts, re-arranged the table places and sat down. Immediately two further complications arose. The Frenchman, although placed next to my wife, started a prima donna act over the canvas chair. Only when asked if he would prefer to stand (there were no other chairs) did he grudgingly condescend to sit. At the other end of the table I was between the Thai Captain (the better to keep him under control) and the young wife of our Air Engineer Officer who was within a couple of months of having a baby. Hardly had we sat down when the girl gave a tremendous heave.

'Oh Lord!' I thought, 'surely she can't be starting already, she must have known and would never have come out if it were so.'

As if to answer my thoughts she gave another convulsive heave, which set all the glasses jangling, and by now looked distinctly uncomfortable. It did not augur well and the frequency and violence of the heaving increased. The conversation petered out and was replaced by an awkward silence.

It was broken by the Australian Captain, a brash officer to whom the word crude meant normal. 'Did I tell you the one about how I spent last night?' he thundered down the table. No answer was needed and painfully agog we awaited the inevitable unfunny follow-up. It came with a rush: 'I spent last night between two thighs, I mean Thais, I mean . . .' His voice died away in the stunned silence and with a desperate finale of 'it was dinkum' he gave up. The girl beside me heaved again vigorously. The Thai Captain's face was a mask of outraged rectitude. He was uncertain whether to treat the affair as a personal insult or just porn. Either way it merited complaint and he opened his mouth to indulge in his favourite pastime. But before he could utter I seized the initiative and questioned him closely on whether he understood the meaning of 'dinkum' and whether there was a direct equivalent in his language.

There came a great shout from the Australian. 'Eureka,' he cried and, leaping to his feet, held up a half-dead Chit Chat (one of those friendly chameleon-like lizards which dart about the walls and ceilings in the Far East and occasionally drop off). Having fallen, this one had been pursued by our sporting Siamese cat Ching until we sat down to dinner when, as cats will, it instantly sensed that the girl on my right was allergic to cats. Here was sport indeed: a grounded Chit Chat to tease to death and a shapely pair of bare, allergic ankles against which to brush. Every time a caress was

127

planted the donor was rewarded by a shuddering heave from the ankles' owner.

It only remained to drag through the rest of a very good dinner and arrive late at the Officer's Club for the film. As we slunk into our reserved front row seats everyone hissed genially. 'An old English custom,' I explained to the by now amazed Thai Captain. The film was *Tea and Sympathy* in which an adolescent schoolboy falls in love with the headmaster's wife. It could hardly have been more inappropriate or embarrassing.

Towards the end of 1962 the Brunei Revolt occurred, quickly leading to the Indonesian Confrontation which spread throughout North Borneo and Sarawak. In plain terms this was an invasion by Indonesia and one way or another the resulting jungle war embraced the whole of what is now Eastern Malaysia.

At the outset the Commander-in-Chief and nearly all the Service Chiefs were away in Hong Kong. A Company Group was deployed in reaction to the incursion but it quickly became apparent that this was a case of too little too late. Consequently the force level was raised to brigade strength. Next, the Army Commander returned from Hong Kong and changed the Brigadier in the forward area. Thereafter further units were deployed on the ground and frigates patrolled near the borders at sea. Coastal minesweepers operated up the rivers and RAF and Naval Commando helicopters operated with increasing intensity in support of the ground forces.

In retrospect it seemed an untidy beginning to what turned out to be a protracted campaign lasting nearly four years. Against this there had been poor intelligence giving very little warning of events despite some hindsight claims to the contrary. Moreover the terrain over the majority of the area of operations was deep jungle in which reconnaissance and movement were extremely difficult. Helicopters were crucial in providing mobility but even they were limited to locally cleared landing sites which quickly became obvious targets to the lurking enemy. Acclimatization and experience in jungle warfare were essentials which could not be acquired overnight. Most of the British troops and perhaps especially the Royal Marine Commandos were well trained for this type of warfare but replacement units fresh out from UK took time to adapt. Surprisingly the Malay troops were initially disappointing. Hardly had the first regiment been deployed to North Borneo when it suffered a sharp (and deserved) blooding. Shortly before sundown one evening the sentries were withdrawn and the entire unit settled to evening prayer. While in this posture it was jumped by an Indonesian patrol which inflicted a number of casualties. It was all very well for the Tunku subsequently to proclaim that 'God would avenge this dastardly act'. The realities of the situation were that war was no longer a game, the regiment had been unprofessional and The Almighty's attention was not noticeably concentrated on the Far East at the time.

Because of the impending arrival of our second daughter (Philippa) Mary flew back to England a couple of months before me. While out East we had decided that the time had come to set up a home of our own and to this end we had been on the books of most of the Estate Agents to be found in the early pages of the glossy magazines – but with little effective result. It was an educative exercise and one quickly grasped the realities of the Estate Agents' jargon. At the time one of the most fashionable phrases was 'low flush suite', which simply meant that you pushed instead of pulled. 'Ripe for development' meant the the whole structure was shaky and the roof was about to fall in. 'Suitable for domestic or business purposes' was shorthand for a great barrack of a place. And so on. By the time Mary flew home only one rather remote possibility not far from Weymouth remained on our short list and the travel problems from Dorset to London or Portsmouth seemed to rule that out.

For me those last two months were both lonely and busy and it was several weeks before I got around to thinking about house-hunting again. The time was fast approaching when Mary would have to stop dashing about the country looking at possibilities and concentrate on the safe and timely arrival of No. 2. One Sunday afternoon after a particularly good and well-laced curry lunch with friends I wrote a long and carefully worded letter home putting all the pros and cons and recommending raising our tentative bid for the Weymouth house so as to prevent its going to auction. All this I summarized in a brief cable next morning and sent them off. Though I knew my proposition contained sizable drawbacks I was getting rather desperate. Two days later I received a reply cable which read: 'Hold hard offer for Wonston Lodge accepted'. That was all. I had never heard of Wonston Lodge and did not even know which county it was in; but clearly my beloved wife had used her natural initiative and done a brave thing; now what she needed was support. So at once I whipped off a further cable saying 'Well done Wonston Lodge fully supported.' *What* I was supporting I had no idea.

The days passed. Of course I wrote home at once congratulating Mary on her good work and gently asking such fundamental questions as 'Where *is* Wonston Lodge? How far to the nearest station? Any garden? What about drains? Cost?' Later I got a rather curt reply enclosing the Agents' particulars. Clearly my wife was irritated by my persistent queries when she had (as she thought) told me full details already; why did I have to keep on keeping on? 'Impending motherhood,' I muttered darkly to myself and shut up. Two more weeks went by, then one day a large packet of tapes arrived. We had given each other a cheap Japanese tape-recorder the previous

Christmas thinking that this would help bridge our temporary separation. Unfortunately Mary had put insufficient stamps on the package for air mail and it had taken its time by sea. That night I played back the tapes and all was revealed; she *had* evidently done a very good thing.

In due course I flew back home, saw the house and garden each with great potential and was delighted with the prospect. When the time came to move our furniture in Mary was in hospital, busy. While hurrying to and fro supervising the removal men I put my foot in a rabbit hole in the rough grass outside the back door and severely twisted my ankle. It seized up quickly and by midday it was all I could do to hobble about with the aid of one of those Victorian poles with a crook on the end for pulling down sash windows, as a crutch. But at last everything was moved in and more or less placed in the right rooms and I returned to my In Laws, who lived half an hour's drive away, for the night. A few mornings later I woke up with a tearing pain in my chest. At the time I smoked cigarettes despite the initial scare about lung cancer being at its height. I was in no doubt that I had got it. Equally that in view of the suddenness and violence of its onslaught there was nothing to be done about it and little point in even consulting a doctor. It being the height of the hay fever season, each time I sneezed or blew my nose this red-hot pain seared my chest. 'Oh well,' I ruminated, 'what a pity, it would have been such fun to have worked up Wonston Lodge together but still . . . at least I have provided Mary and the family with a nice house to live in.'

A couple of weeks later and equally suddenly I awoke one morning to find the pain completely gone. By this time Mary had returned with a super second daughter accompanied by a Maternity Nurse. That night, following a day without a single twinge in my chest, my confidence in survival was restored and I told my silly story against myself. The nice Nurse gave me a withering look. 'Why on earth didn't you tell me?' she said. 'You must have pulled one of your intercostal muscles, I could have strapped you up and you'd have had no problem.' I experienced a strong feeling of all's well that ends well.

12

GALLOPING GALATEA

'We few, we happy few, we band of brothers.'
William Shakespeare

In November, 1965, I took over command of *Galatea* and as Captain (D) 27th Escort Squadron. She was one of the earlier Frigates of the highly successful *Leander* Class. Being then about halfway through her first commission everything was new but all the bugs had been got out of the systems. At the time she was undergoing a maintenance period in Portsmouth.

It was Saturday and the whole of the South of England was gripped by one of those freak cold spells which sometimes occur for a few days at the start of winter. Outside the weather was bitter and even between decks it was bleak, for the air-conditioning had been shut down for maintenance and only a handful of electric radiators could be using owing to a defect in the dockyard power supply. Having seen my predecessor over the side I settled down to work in my icy cabin.

By supper time my fingers were so cold that they could hardly grip a pen. With difficulty I curbed my natural instinct to summon the Electrical Officer and demand at least some heat in my quarters. 'Don't be irresponsible,' my conscience told me; 'you have a very comfortable cabin even if it is a bit chilly. Think of your sailors on their much colder messdecks and remember that power supplies are strictly limited. And start as you mean to go on – which should not be by creating scenes over domestic trivia.' Of course my conscience won (it usually does) and around 2200 after forlornly checking that the hot tap in my bathroom predictably ran only cold water, I sought comfort in my bunk. The night was not a success: I never got warm and achieved very little sleep.

Next day, Remembrance Sunday, dawned with two inches of snow on the ground. Ships in harbour without their own Chaplain were expected to send a strong contingent to the lovely St Anne's Church in the dockyard. Having no reason to suppose that my sailors were much less miserable than I was, I declined to send them stumping through the snow and told my First Lieutenant that I would conduct a short service in the hangar instead.

During the course of it I stood with my ankles only about six inches in front of a black radiator and by the end of the service began to feel my feet again. It was enough. Flinging my shivering conscience over the side I sent for the Electrical Officer and slithered my way for'ard to my cabin.

'Unless,' I said, 'you wish to have a useless and very cross Captain (D) by start of play tomorrow morning I *must* have some heat. I'm not asking for much and I don't care how you manage it but I will not endure another 24 hours in a deep freeze.'

'No problem, sir,' he replied brightly. 'They finished the air-conditioning this morning and in another hour or so it should be operating again.'

'Very good. Make sure that it does.'

Throughout the afternoon and evening the temperature rose steadily. By after supper I was warm again. Still no hot water but as the previous night had been such a disaster I turned in early and immediately fell asleep. I woke at midnight feeling hot. I sensed that the temperature was now in the high 70's F. – and still rising. I stripped off one blanket, then a second, then the sheet, then my pyjama top. Still it grew hotter. It was like being back in Singapore. Sweating like a June Bride I fell once more into a fitful slumber for the rest of the night.

When the Squadron Staff assembled in my cabin next morning they were met by a Captain (D) who had been fully 'conditioned'.

Galatea was a lovely ship. She derived her name from ancient mythology of which there were two principal versions. The first was that she was the beautiful Sicilian daughter of the sea-god Nereus and the nymph Doris, famous for her white coloured skin. She was courted by the one-eyed Cyclop Polyphemus but she fell in love with a young shepherd named Acis. Tradition states that when Polyphemus caught them together inside a cave he threw a rock which killed Acis. Galatea's sorrow for the loss of her lover was so touching that the Gods pitied her and made Acis into a river. Thereafter Galatea spent endless time near the shore mourning him. The waves of the sea and the water of the river together are perhaps a symbol of her weeping.

In the second myth of Galatea she became the wife of Pygmalion, King of Cyprus and famous sculptor. He created the statue of a young girl out of pure white marble and named it Galatea (which means the colour of milk). Then a strange metaphysical event occurred; Pygmalion fell in love with his creation and his behaviour towards the statue Galatea was so pathetic that the Goddess of Love, Aphrodite, took pity on him and breathed life into the cold marble (the kiss of life). Thereafter Pygmalion married her and had a son with her named Paphos.

Galatea the ship handled beautifully and you could manoeuvre to an inch.

The Operations Room was well laid out and contained the latest equipment. The Type 177M Sonar was a 'good' set (some were better than others) and produced excellent results at better ranges than most. And the Wasp helicopter provided a new dimension in anti-submarine warfare flexibility.

The Squadron Staff were an exceptionally good lot and we had a fine Ship's Company. In short, *Galatea* was a happy and efficient Leader.

Out in the Mediterranean we became extensively involved in NATO exercises. In these it soon became apparent that we could give a lead. Due partly to our superior equipment, partly to the increased range in weapon delivery accorded by our helicopter, and partly to a rather deeper appreciation of anti-submarine tactics, we established something of a reputation with the US, French, Italian, Greek and Turkish naval forces with which we operated. Many of the Flag and Commanding Officers of these other navies quickly became close friends and excellent rapport was maintained. But there were some awkward moments too.

The senior seagoing Greek Flag Officer was in fact their C-in-C Aegean Sea. Vice Admiral Athanassiu was an elderly man, short in stature and round of figure but possessed of great charm and genuine friendliness, with a good command of English. He was perhaps a trifle out of date in his anti-submarine warfare thinking. He flew his flag in an elderly ex-United States destroyer with no flight deck and no helicopter. Often in exercises I had offered to collect him in my helicopter and bring him over to *Galatea* to see our equipment in operation and stay for lunch; but when it came to the point he had always declined. At the briefing meeting before our last exercise together I renewed my invitation and he promised to accept when the time came. On this occasion I got a clear impression that he really meant it and accordingly I gently warned him that before being winched up by my helicopter he would need to put on a Mae West (lifejacket) and Bone Dome (flying helmet). Here a language problem arose. My friend got the message about the lifejacket but stumbled over the flying helmet; I finally got through to him with the explanation 'metal hat', adding that my Aircrewman would lower the necessary items together with the strop on the end of the winchwire. With much handshaking and warm smiles we parted and shortly afterwards put to sea.

A few days later there came a convenient lull in the exercise and, having obtained the Greek Admiral's confirmation that it was a good moment for his visit, I duly sent my Wasp over to collect him. Since the Greek Flagship was only a couple of miles away the transfer should be completed in a few minutes. I returned my attention to the exercise and quickly became absorbed in its tactics.

Half an hour later we became involved in a major submarine incident which required my full attention. It also required my helicopter which had still not returned. A signal was sent instructing the pilot to expedite the manoeuvre. Not long afterwards the Wasp returned and landed on safely. Since we were still deeply involved in hunting the submarine I remained in the Operations Room and left the Greek Admiral to be dealt with by my Flight Deck Officer.

The door of the Operations Room burst open and in staggered Admiral Athanassiu. White to the lips, dripping with sweat and shaking like a jelly, he looked on the verge of collapse; certainly he was too far gone to speak. Gently he was eased into a chair and a stiff glass of cognac summoned. In came the pilot. He too was ashen and less composed than I had ever known him. Clearly some dreadful thing had happened. Tony Pawsey was a quiet, highly competent young pilot, not readily perturbed by the unexpected.

'Well, sir,' he said 'it was all a bit awkward. I went into the hover over the fantail of the Greek destroyer and then I saw what I took to be the Admiral waiting on deck with a steel helmet on his head and his Mae West fully inflated. Of course I couldn't winch him up like that. He'd never have got through the rear door, so I tried to get his Ops Room to pass the word aft. They didn't seem to understand and after some time, during which it was getting rather turbulent because they weren't on a very good flying course, I moved over to the quarter and got my Aircrewman to write the message on a board and show it to them through the doorway. Have you ever tried to deflate a Greek Admiral who's already approaching a nervous breakdown, sir? It takes time. Throughout it all I was hovering, my Aircrewman was gesticulating like mad and . . . well eventually we did it but now I'm knackered, sir.'

So was the Greek Admiral. It took a second cognac and some lunch before he regained his equanimity. He spent a happy afternoon in my Operations Room and in due course was returned without further incident.

Relations with the French were particularly good and Contre Amiral Bouillot as Admiral in charge of their Mediterranean Flotilla (ALFLOMED) became a close personal friend. Yet among the more junior French officers there was sometimes a rather stiffer attitude, a kind of assertiveness stemming from misplaced national sensitivity or uncertain pride.

For one of the phases of a major exercise the main briefing fell to me. I spoke very slowly and expressed relief that I could do so in English because it was the NATO language. Hardly were the words out of my mouth when an agitated voice called out in French,

'Ce n'est pas vrai. Français est la language de NATO.'

'We are both right,' I replied. 'English *and* French are the official languages of NATO. I am conducting my briefing in English.'

There was no more trouble.

The ensuing exercise contained little real activity until towards the end of my time in Tactical Command when it started to hot up. No sooner had I handed over to the French Admiral than we were 'attacked' in all three elements: air, surface and submarine. I rapped out orders to the force to counter these simultaneous threats and over the next hour or so directed a series of spirited actions involving every ship present. When things quietened down I suddenly realized that the Frenchman, not me, should have been in tactical command and I had completely ignored him! This was inexcusable and at one stroke could undo all the good that our previous close relationship had achieved.

'*Je regrette infiniment . . .*' I signalled (and a good deal else besides).

'I agreed with your actions,' he courteously replied.

So I asked him over for lunch and he stayed on board for our return to harbour at the end of the exercise later that afternoon. Some weeks afterwards he kindly invited me to lunch with his charming family outside Toulon.

A big man in every sense, but . . . phew!

After a major NATO exercise in the Atlantic ships taking part assembled at Gibraltar for the washup. *Galatea* berthed on the South Mole, just ahead of the Dutch Submarine *Zeelieu* which had been part of the 'enemy' forces and which we had engaged in a number of actions. These actions had been spirited and her Commanding Officer, Lieutenant Commander John Leflang, was clearly a man of mettle; in due course he became the head of the Netherlands Submarine Service. Throughout the exercise the weather had been dreadful and the level of activity high so that everyone was tired and glad of a break ashore.

Gibraltar is not large and its facilities for eating and drinking other than in the limited number of highly expensive hotels are readily swamped by a visiting fleet – albeit such visits are a major source of livelihood. And so it was on that warm spring evening. Main Street was crowded with NATO naval officers and men exuberantly searching for worthwhile knick-knacks to take home; the bars and restaurants were crammed and there was much merriment. Many international relationships were sealed over a friendly glass.

One such was experienced by my First Lieutenant, Lieutenant Commander Julian Howard, with his opposite number in the Dutch Submarine. The former was a short, stocky, powerfully built man; the latter very tall and lanky. They met in a restaurant, in the course of several drinks became firm friends and dined together. By midnight everything ashore was closing and the kindly Dutchman invited Howard back to the *Zeelieu* for a nightcap.

There they were soon joined by the rest of the Submarine's officers (and one or two others) and an active session of drinking and party games ensued. By about 0400 exhaustion began to take hold and the final competition was enacted. Its rules were basic and considerably tempered by wine, the principal element being the forceful removal of the trousers of all present. With fond farewells and exaggerated expressions of goodwill the party broke up and the visitors returned to their own ships. It was a lovely, balmy dawn and any minor cooling of the air without was more than compensated by the warmth from the Bols within. Faced with a walk of less than a hundred yards Howard did not bother to put his trousers on again, returned to *Galatea* in good shape and immediately turned in to snatch a couple of hours' rest before the Hands turned to at 0630. It had been a very good evening and sleep came quickly.

It also came deeply; called at 0615 he dropped off and was finally roused by the ominous report '5 minutes to Hands Fall In, sir'. Scrambling out of his bunk he flung on shirt, scarf, trousers, monkey jacket and shoes and went on deck. Too late he realized that there was something rather odd about his trousers; they seemed to hang in endless folds about his ankles and their extreme bagginess impeded his every movement. But by now he was facing all the Seamen, waiting for him to detail them off for work. Oh why had he cut it so fine in turning out and how would he ever live it down?

Meantime on board the *Zeelieu* with throbbing head and leaden limbs, their First Lieutenant had climbed up onto the casing to give orders to *his* sailors. The vertical ladder had seemed unusually steep and difficult that morning but it was not until he was confronted by his men that the reason became clear. His trousers, which were extremely tight-fitting, came to just below his knees leaving the rest of his hairy legs naked.

The final curtain was rung down on this international incident by a signal from the Dutch Submarine. It read

'*From*: H.M.NL.S *Zeelieu* – Wardroom
To: HMS *Galatea* – for the Executive Officer

An inquiry among the wardroom members resulted in finding some-body who had experienced great difficulty to get in his trousers each morning. As he refused to reveal where he got his trousers from we are not quite sure these trousers enclosed are the ones you are missing. The person in fact was not interested in the considerable large trousers you received. So an exchange will not be necessary.

A good advice may be useful for the next time: never put off your trousers in Gibraltar.'

Towards the middle of 1966 *Galatea*, wearing the flag of the Commander-in-Chief Mediterranean, Admiral Sir John Hamilton, with *Troubridge* (Commander Nick Hunt) and *Carysfort* (Commander Martin Sands) in company, paid a visit to Venice. We were allocated fine berths just opposite St Mark's and secured to buoys in the middle of the fairway.

Although as Flag Captain I was involved in the fairly heavy programme of official entertainment, there was also plenty of time for sightseeing. Mary joined me and we stayed in one of those splendid Italian Naval Officers' Clubs which Mussolini had so thoughtfully instituted. Prior to leaving Malta I had arranged for the ship's dghaisa to be hoisted inboard and together with the owner and his son took it with us to Venice. Formerly this had been common practice but in recent years it had been largely given up. Thus we were able to explore the fascinating network of canals at our leisure and were spared the exorbitant charges of the local gondoliere. The latter gathered in small groups and peered down on us from the quaint little bridges that so frequently span the canals. Their reaction was generally one of amazement, sometimes of merriment, occasionally of glumness; but with the White Ensign fluttering proudly from the sternsheets there was little they could do about it.

Each morning we awoke to fog which got more dense and took longer to clear as the days passed. Twenty-four hours before we were due to sail I discussed our exit plan with my Squadron Navigating Officer, Lieutenant Commander Derek Wallis. He was a very good officer – professionally expert, a strong personality, calm in a crisis and an excellent leader. In particular we assessed the practicability and risks involved in a 'blind' exit (i.e. totally dependent on radar) in the event of fog and concluded that it was a feasible and seamanlike undertaking. This view was strengthened by the fact that, under the port's regulations, outgoing traffic had right of way. We recalled that during a previous visit (before our time) the squadron had run into fog on departure. One ship had anchored and soon afterwards was run into by an inbound merchant ship; having relinquished her manoeuvrability there was nothing she could do to avoid the collision. The balance of advantage seemed to lie clearly with remaining under way and manoeuvring with caution. The departure plan was framed accordingly.

Next morning dawned bright and clear. There was no trace of mist and at 0900 as planned we slipped from our buoys, formed up and made our way down harbour. It had been an enjoyable visit and it was with some nostalgia, and certainly a keen desire to return one day, that we cast a final fond look at the mellow stonework of St Mark's. Hardly had we completed our 90 degree turn to starboard into the main channel when we ran into a blanket wall of fog. The usual precuations were taken, speed reduced to 3 knots (the minimum to give steerage way against the $2\frac{1}{2}$ knot tidal stream which was flooding) and the Squadron instructed to act independently while loosely maintaining the present formation.

It soon became clear that despite our ceremonial exit (and outgoing right of way) the port regulations were not being complied with. Radar showed that while several ships were properly waiting off the seaward end of the channel, three were ignoring the local rules and, having entered the channel, were coming up at a steady speed. The nature of the land on both sides of the channel was very low-lying and not conducive to accurate navigation by radar close inshore. It therefore behoved the prudent mariner to keep well to the centre of the channel – and this is what everyone was doing.

The first ship held steadily on with no apparent deviation of course. Having edged as far to starboard as seemed prudent, a last-minute steadying of her bearing (indicating that collision was imminent) was avoided by the emergency order 'full ahead', accepting the risk of damage to machinery. We crept past a small coaster without mishap and concentrated on the next ship, now approaching faster than I could have wished. Manoeuvring to clear her again involved 'full ahead' and use of full rudder to swing the stern clear; a medium-sized freighter lumbered past and in doing so clipped a communications aerial off our yardarm and brushed the upper platform of the accommodation ladder which had been triced up but not swung inboard. This slight jar was felt throughout the ship and brought C-in-C to the bridge just in time to hear me order 'full ahead' for the third time in half an hour (and the only times in my entire naval career).

'Very unpleasant,' he commented cryptically and immediately returned below to my cabin to continue writing his 'thank you' letters.

The third defaulter was successfully negotiated. Not long afterwards we were in the open sea and the fog lifted. All in all I thought we had come through a difficult situation with credit. This view was reinforced at the subsequent Board of Inquiry at Malta although there were some indications from the tartness of his questions that its President, a Commodore whose personal seagoing experience was dated, was going out of his way to find fault. What was my surprise, therefore, when some weeks later while again acting as Flagship the C-in-C sent for me late one evening and informed me that he intended to court martial me.

It was an interesting if somewhat harrowing business and one which I would not commend to others as a desirable experience. The wheels of bureaucracy grind slow and exceeding small and it was some weeks before the whole long-drawn-out affair was over. This imposed some strain, largely emotional because one's personal professional reputation was at stake, and not helped by the fact that my wife was taken very seriously ill at the height of things, leaving me to care for our two small daughters. But with the help of some wonderful friends we struggled by.

Two Courts were convened, one for my Navigating Officer, the other for myself. We were acquitted on the serious charge of 'hazarding the ship' and on two lesser ones, but convicted on a third minor one which amounted in plain terms to 'going too fast for the prevailing conditions' – and sentenced to be 'reprimanded'. Since *Galatea* had been steaming at about half a knot above the minimum speed to permit steerage way against the opposing current, neither of us felt much chastened by this verdict.

The children were sent back to England to the care of my sister-in-law. Mary quickly recovered and after a period of convalescence herself returned home. *Galatea* resumed her operational duties with her customary vigour. A few months later her time in the Mediterranean came to an end and we too returned to the UK. We berthed at Portsmouth on a lovely sunny day in the early autumn. As soon as we were secured alongside the Chief of Staff to the Commander-in-Chief Portsmouth came on board. Broady Hoare was an old friend and a very experienced naval officer. After exchanging initial greetings he handed me two official blue envelopes, one addressed to my Navigating Officer and the other to myself. Their contents stated that the Court Martial convictions had been quashed by the Admiralty Board.

It was a happy return. Mary, now fully fit again, and the two girls came on board for lunch and soon afterwards we drove to our home a few miles north of Winchester. But not for long. The rest of the Squadron were still out in the Mediterranean and there was only one opportunity to catch them and say goodbye before they split up to their base ports in UK and their Ship's Companies dispersed. So two hours later found me on the road for London Airport en route back to Malta for this very important round of farewells. Such a quick in-and-out at home together with a night flight left me feeling slightly disorientated and light-headed. But the warmth of the welcome I received in the other ships soon put that right. That evening the other Commanding Officers dined me out in the Dragonara Palace, by then a Casino with an excellent restaurant. We had a delicious dinner and talked far into the night. Next morning I flew back to England.

Galatea now recommissioned with all the officers and the majority of the Ship's Company changing. The new team were unusually young; out of 250, more than eighty were under the age of 21. But they were a splendid lot and quickly started to pull together. Almost at once we went to Portland to work up.

The Working Up Base had long been a centre of excellence and controversy. It had been variously described as 'seven weeks' hard labour' and 'Borstal at Sea'. Certainly the going was tough, the routine intensive and the weather usually foul. The work-up produced a co-ordinated team, tempered in the fire of hard training, safe to operate at sea, and with sufficient competance and cohesive spirit to give a good account of themselves at most things.

There was, however, one serious shortcoming to this admirable set-up. Efficiency was achieved mainly by stereotyped methods (the 'sausage machine') and scant attention was paid to tactics. In consequence the advantages of technological progress in sensors, in weaponry and in the presentation of data to the Command were inadequately exploited. Thus there tended to be an over-concentration on the Action State (the 'First Eleven').

I had long been aware of this and regarded it as not in the best interests of efficiency. It seemed to me that in war such a philosophy would hand an enormous advantage to the enemy. Most fit people can do without sleep for about 48 hours (and indeed I used regularly to train myself – and others – to do so) and can then operate effectively with two or three hours' sleep in 24 for about 10 days before having to rest more fully. The enemy would know this and by posing a major threat for, say, 48 hours without actually engaging, would then have to deal only with the 'Second Eleven' with consequently improved chances of success. To reduce this problem to a minimum I had implemented the 'Long Watch System' whereby at any time in the 24 hours a fully balanced team was closed up and only in exceptional circumstances was it necessary to go to Action Stations. This maintained an acceptably high level of expertise indefinitely, at the same time providing adequate rest for those off watch. It was not a new idea nor one originated by me; indeed it had for some time been practised in the Carriers when conducting round-the-clock operations. But it was new to Portland.

They did not like it. Despite two months' warning of my intentions, they tried hard to make me conform to their norm. But although I knew I would be handing over command soon after the work-up was completed, I was determined to train the Ship's Company in peace as they would have to operate in war. The result was that they flung the book at us in an attempt to break the system – and we had a rattling good work-up!

It culminated in a Sea Inspection lasting nearly five days (and nights). Tired but well pleased with our performance we berthed alongside in Portland at about 1300, there to await the Admiral's return an hour later to tell us how we had done and to say goodbye. 1400 came with no sign of him. Nor yet at 1500. By close on 1600, it being but a few days to Christmas, it was beginning to get dark and I did not relish a night passage to Portsmouth which I was determined to reach that evening; we really were very tired. At last he arrived. He spent some minutes alone with me in my cabin, the rest of the Ship's Company waited in the gathering gloom on the Flight Deck. He had some quite nice things to say before criticizing the ship's anti-submarine efficiency – of which I was rather proud.

'Your trouble is your TAS Officer (Torpedo/Anti-Submarine Officer),' he said. 'He always lets you down.'

I was amazed since I regarded my TASO as being one of the best in the Fleet (he has since been promoted to Flag Rank) and said so.

I thought hard and quickly through my fatigue.

'What is the name of the officer to whom you refer, sir?' I asked.

'Johnston.'

'There is no officer of that name in this ship,' I replied.

Further discussion being pointless, I escorted the Admiral to the Flight Deck. There he talked *at* the Ship's Company for 10 minutes. In the circumstances it seemed too long, the more so as its tenor was vague and at times barely relevant. As an example of leadership by encouragement it left a lot to be desired. We said goodbye and sailed for Portsmouth.

As the culmination of long weeks of constant endeavour and hard work it had been an uninspiring finale. Irritated, I decided to sleep on it, before taking any further action. Next morning a signal from Flag Officer Sea Training to C-in-C Western Fleet, copied to us, was received. It read:

'*Galatea* completed a satisfactory work-up but has yet to develop her full potential.'

That clinched it. Summoning my First Lieutenant I told him to Clear Lower Deck (a muster of all Hands except those actually on watch) at midday so that I could speak to the Ship's Company and give them something to bite on. Then I signalled Flag Officer Flotillas (Home) who was now my Administrative Authority (Rear Admiral Michael Pollock, later to be First Sea Lord) asking if I could call on him at 1230.

When the Ship's Company had assembled they looked their usual cheerful, expectant young selves, none the worse for a good night's sleep. In talking to them I had to draw a fine balance between loyalty to my Senior Officer and honesty.

'Yesterday afternoon at Portland,' I said, 'when the Flag officer Sea Training addressed us we were all very tired. At the time I was not too clear what message he was delivering and from the look on your faces you weren't either. Having slept on it I'm still not clear so I've sent for you to give you a message you *will* understand.

'Over the past weeks I have watched you grow from a collection of 250 individuals into a single Ship's Company, a *team*, which is *Galatea*. We have all made mistakes and we have all learnt a lot together. But we have now established a very firm base from which to develop further experience and full efficiency. I tell you straight, I would happily take you – this ship – anywhere at any time to tackle anything and know that you'd do it well. This I will tell my successor when I hand over command in a few days' time and I'm only sorry I shall not be with you for longer.'

Over in the flagship Michael Pollock looked at me quizzically.

'You're very angry aren't you?' he said.

'A bit cross, yes sir,' I admitted and recounted our departure from Portland saga.

'Knowing you wanted to see me I got my Staff to ring up Portland,' he went on, 'to find out what their signal really meant. I wasn't sure I understood it myself. "Oh," they replied, "it means Henry Leach didn't agree with our ideas."'

13

INTO WIND

'In sea affairs nothing is impossible and nothing is improbable.'
Admiral Lord Nelson

In the spring of 1970 in Portsmouth I took over command of the Commando Carrier *Albion*. I had not much looked forward to the prospect for three reasons. First, as I viewed it, at 23,500 tons displacement she would be too big and too impersonal for pleasure. Second, because of her size and ungainliness, berthing and manoeuvring in harbour would always involve being pushed around by tugs and the professional fun of shiphandling would be minimal. And finally, I was convinced that I should find conning a Carrier from a bridge necessarily offset from the familiar centreline a difficult thing to which to adapt. I was to find out quickly that I was dead wrong on all counts.

Three distinct elements, each about 800 strong, composed my new team: the ship and her Company, who formed the secure base from which to operate; the embarked Commando Group, who were the main armament; and the helicopter squadron of 18 Wessex 5's who provided flexibility and tactical mobility. Each element had a different background, expertise and outlook; to weld them into a single, cohesive whole was an interesting challenge.

The Captain's harbour quarters in a Carrier are situated right aft in the stern. They are relatively remote from the sights, noises and smells of the main hurly-burly of life about the ship and it is easy to lose touch. To avoid this and to pick up an initial feel of my new command I had turned up the volume control of my ship's main broadcast loudspeaker. My first day had been a long one – taking over, meeting the Heads of Departments and others, talking to a number of people, finding my way about the ship, checking and revising standing orders. By 2300 I was tired and turned in.

In the middle of the night I was rudely awakened by that well-known but awesome broadcast 'Fire, fire, fire. Fire in 4 L 7. Fire and Emergency Party muster at the scene of the fire', followed by a rapid ringing of the ship's bell.

(For ease and precision of identification a warship's decks are numbered sequentially upwards and downwards from the upper deck and the ship's length is divided by letters corresponding to the main transverse bulkheads, starting from for'ard) Reacting automatically I was out of my bunk slipping on shoes and trousers over my pyjamas and grabbing my monkey jacket. Then a thought struck me: 'Steady on, what d'you think you're doing? You're the *Captain* of this great ship; it's not your job to go mucking around with fires; there are plenty of others to do that; if you're wanted the Commander or the Officer of the Watch or the Engineer Officer or a score of others will come and tell you. And anyway you haven't the foggiest idea where 4 L 7 is and you'll only make an ass of yourself. Stop being over-exuberant and get back into bed.' It was all so true. Sheepishly I undressed and turned in. But not to sleep.

My conscience, always an energetic and irritating encumbrance, started to prick. 'You haven't got it right, have you?' it said. 'You know you're just taking the easy way out. It's not responsible. Get up top and behave properly.' My wretched conscience won again and, flinging my clothes back on, I stepped out onto the quarterdeck. But where to go? At that moment one of the Emergency Party carrying a portable fire extinquisher rushed past.

'Where is the fire?' I asked hopefully.

'4 L 7 sir,' he panted and disappeared for'ard. No help there.

I sauntered for'ard to the gangway and with a knowing air addressed the Quartermaster.

'Where exactly is the fire?'

'4 L 7 sir,' he replied.

'Ah yes,' I acknowledged and continued my stroll.

At last, blessed relief, I spotted a thin trickle of smoke rising from a hatchway. I was at the scene of the fire. It was minor and had already been dealt with. I returned to bed and slept with a quiet mind.

But my teething troubles were not yet over. Later, on being called, I got up to shave. Nowhere was there a point for my electric razor, nor did I have a plug adaptor. Summoning my Chinese valet, a young Leading Steward, I told him to get hold of the Duty Electrician.

'Yes Sah. Me understand sah,' he beamed and disappeared. Ten minutes later the Chief Yeoman arrived with my signals!

Few things are more personally demoralizing that starting the day unshaven for no good reason. You feel scruffy and dirty and cannot escape the impression that everyone you meet feels the same about you. But now the day had started and I was beginning to run out of time.

Just after breakfast the Midshipman of the Watch reported routinely that it was five minutes to colours. Picking up my cap and telescope I made to go up to the flight deck for this little daily ceremony. Desperately I tried to remember the route: up the ladder, turn for'ard, first left, through the door facing . . .

'Morning sah, velly nice day,' and broad grins all round. I was in the Chinese Bathroom (all the Cooks, Stewards, Laundry Crew and 'Unofficials' – numbering nearly 200 – were Chinese).

Hasty retreat. Quicken pace. Try another door. This time it was the Chinese Messdeck. I gave up.

The bigger the ship the more remote is the Captain and the bigger the problem of learning names. As an essential minimum I set my target at knowing the name, Christian name and principal job of every officer in the Ship, Squadron and Commando Group. Apart from the Heads of Departments (HODS) the frequency of personal contact was not great and this presented quite a challenge – perhaps especially with the Commando and Squadron who were continually changing. I discovered that Commander (Air) ('Wings') kept a 'rogues' gallery' of photographs of the aircrew and from him I demanded a copy. This I studied assiduously and matched the names to the faces in my mind. It is not a new trick nor a clever one but it takes time and application. By the day the Squadron embarked I was fairly confident I had the problem hacked.

In they came and from the Bridge or Flying Control I watched them land on. Not long afterwards a young Lieutenant in flying overalls walked through Flyco to the Bridge. Clearly a newcomer but his face was unfamiliar to me. Twice more during the next half hour he passed by and I was about to summon Wings and reprove him for not having his set of photographs up to date when he pre-empted me by reporting that all the Pilots were assembled to meet me. It was too late. As I looked down the line I knew them all except one – *this* one, about three from the far end. When I came to him I stood back and we stared at each other for a few moments without a glimmer of recognition. Irritated to have my masterly homework tarnished by this one stranger I asked sharply,

'Who the hell are you?'

'Ellerbeck, sir,' he replied.

Instantly I knew him. The wretched fellow had shaved his beard off! In the months to come we often flew together and once from Culdrose he took me up in a Tiger Moth (all open cockpits and bits of three-ply and wires) and afterwards his charming young wife Janie gave me supper at his tiny cottage. Tony Ellerbeck had been in the Merchant Navy and was not too clear in his mind how to plan his life ahead. In fact, twelve years later, he was to become famous as the pilot of *Endurance*'s Wasp when he was a major participant in the sinking of the Argentine submarine *Santa Fe*, in the early stages of Operation PARAQUET, the recovery of South Georgia, during the Falklands War. For this he was awarded a very well deserved DSC.

I soon overcame my initial reservations about a big ship being too impersonal and found that in reality quite the reverse was the case. The same held good for my earlier qualms about conning the ship from off-centreline. It only remained to eliminate my repugnance of being handled by tugs when berthing and unberthing in harbour. Within three weeks there was a national tug strike. Next day we sailed for Liverpool to act as Flag Officer Plymouth's (Vice Admiral Sir Anthony Griffin) flagship for the annual Battle of the Atlantic Anniversary celebrations and service in the Cathedral.

We reached the mouth of the Mersey at 0200. A fresh Westerly was blowing and the visibility was down to half a mile. Ships of all sizes were milling around waiting for pilots; some were at anchor, most were underway. For 45 minutes or so we milled around too. It was an unhealthy situation. Then we got our pilot – a tall elderly man of great natural courtesy and charm. For all I know he was a good pilot but on this occasion he was drunk and his contribution going up river was both minimal and imprecise. He left us on anchoring at 0530, there to await slack water before proceeding across river to Prince's pier and berth without tugs two hours later. Before he went I ascertained that he would be sailing with us a few days later. Since the tide dictated a departure time of 1330 it would have been inhospitable not to invite him to lunch with me first. That was the good reason. The real reason was that I wanted to keep him under my wing for an hour or so before we slipped so as to control his intake of alcohol. It worked a treat and I don't think he ever suspected an ulterior motive.

A couple of months later we left Portsmouth for the Mediterranean to take part in various amphibious exercises. By now I had become deeply interested in flying helicopters and set my sights at completing a satisfactory deck landing, unaided, from the left-hand seat. I also stipulated that I must fly with every pilot in the Squadron so as to get to know them; there was no better or quicker way.

When we reached Cyprus it fell to me to go ashore to call on the Brigadier. Since the latter had his own helipad at his Headquarters I decided to do so by Wessex 5 (any opportunity to get in a few more flying hours was welcome). The First Pilot was a young Lieutenant, Hugh Malim, a competent pilot and a great one on a party or with the girls. We had not flown together before so perhaps it was excusable that he should take it for granted that the Second Pilot should have briefed himself on the navigational aspects. I had not done so (indeed I never did); nor had he.

It was a hot day and very humid, but, despite this, because we were

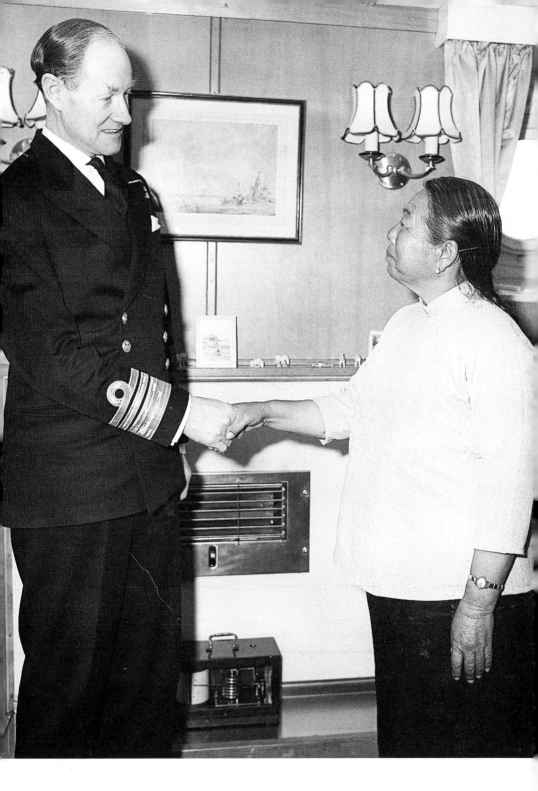

20. With "Jenny Side Party" in my day cabin in *Blake* at Hong Kong.

21. HMS *Norfolk* — Flagship for my Gothenburg visit.

22. Beat Retreat in the main square of Gothenburg after presenting HM King Carl XVI Gustav with his Honorary Admiral's Flag (made of silk and encased in a casket of *Victory* oak).

23. Hauled ashore by my splendid small Staff, Portsmouth, November, 1975. Final sad moments as Flag Officer First Flotilla.

24. NATO Top Brass — seated right to left: Admiral Ike Kidd (Supreme Allied Commander Atlantic), General Al Haig (Supreme Allied Commander Europe), Dr Joseph Luns (Secretary General), General Zeiner Gundersen (Chairman Military Committee), the Author (Allied Commander in Chief Channel).

25. Silver Jubilee – Her Majesty The Queen, Lord High Admiral, reviews her Fleet at Spithead 28 June 1977. HMY *Britannia* passing through the lines.

26. One of JAK's best cartoons at the time of the Spithead Jubilee Review.

"Tell the C-in-C! I am the C-in-C!"

initially flying over water, I was required to wear a dinghy pack as well as a Mae West. Even before take off we were both sweating streams. As we approached the coast Hugh enquired,

'Whereabouts is the HQ landing site, sir?'

Of course I hadn't the remotest idea and said so.

'Oh well, we'll just cruise around until we find it – it shouldn't be too difficult to spot.'

But it was. For ten minutes we searched the area before finally identifying the likely pad, a small gravelly circle more suited to a tiny Sioux than a Wessex 5, and already almost directly underneath us. Pulling up short I started to descend but at much too fast a rate for my equanimity. When only 100 ft up I had full power pulled but we were sinking fast and bits of light gravel were being sucked up and rattling the rotor blades. It was all too clear to me that a very heavy landing resulting in rather a nasty accident was imminent. But with my extremely limited experience I knew of no appropriate action to recover the situation and said so.

'This is beyond my vocabulary,' I said to the First Pilot, controlling my voice with an enforced calm which I did not feel.

'Me too, sir,' he replied cheerfully. 'Shall we try a little forward speed? I have control.'

It worked. He extricated us, did a tight circuit and landed on without further incident. By this time the entire staff of the HQ had left their desks and were out on the balconies watching the extraordinary antics of a naval learner-pilot. Slipping my dinghy pack I climbed out of the cab to be greeted by Brigadier Windsor-Clive. The sweat was pouring off me and on reaching his office he kindly offered me a fresh limejuice which I gratefully accepted. We sat and talked at a mahogany table covered with a smart green baize cloth. The drink arrived, in a tall slender glass so full that it had a meniscus. Eagerly I made to grasp it, only to find that my hand was shaking so much that it would have been quite impossible to have raised the glass from the table to my lips without spilling half the contents and making an unseemly mess. 'Never do to display agitation in front of a soldier,' I thought and with great reluctance withdrew my hand and went on sweating.

The half-hour's call neared its completion and still I hadn't touched my drink. 'Must be steady enough now,' I thought and cautiously lifted the glass off the table with my right hand. It was *very* full. Instantly the shakes returned. Too late I clapped my left hand on and with an ugly jerk managed to get a good gulp of the delicious lime. But a shaming, dark pool of liquid disfigured the immaculate green baize in front of me.

There was only one thing to be done; come clean. I did so and we had a good laugh.

★

One evening at sea we were steaming quietly along in the warm stillness of the Mediterranean at its best. Not another ship was in sight. I was walking up and down the flight deck with Bruce Thomas, my Second-in-Command.

All at once the peace was shattered by the boisterous eruption at the after end of what appeared to be the entire Chinese element of the Ship's Company, numbering around 200. Evidently they were in an ugly mood, arguing noisily and vehemently and jostling each other with a viciousness only just short of exchanging blows. The whole atmosphere was vindictive and nasty; what on earth did it mean? Was it mutiny or worse? The Commander and I continued our walk but with a weather eye cocked for the next move.

It came unexpectedly. Suddenly there was complete silence. Two Chinese detached themselves from the rest and at a word sprinted up to the bow and back. The noise broke out again but now it was happy, contented stuff with much hand-shaking and laughter. As quickly as they had arrived they disappeared below. All was again peace.

The Chinese are great ones for gambling.

While anchored off the east coast of Corsica and in the middle of an amphibious exercise involving the French as 'enemy', President de Gaulle reluctantly relinquished his immortality and died. Accordingly a 'truce' was declared for 24 hours, the exercise stopped and those of us concerned returned on board to change into smarter uniform before attending a memorial service in the local church.

The nearby town was quite small but headed by the Mayor and Corporation it turned out in strength for the occasion. The Mayor's party occupied the whole of the front pew and, as an act of courtesy, being the senior visitor, I and my team were ushered into the one behind. The service was, of course, in Latin but although this was beyond my schoolboy recollection I was able to follow it without much difficulty for about the first third. Then I got hopelessly lost. In an attempt to get back on track I leant forward to peer over the Mayor's shoulder to read the number of the page of his prayer book which he was obliginaly holding well up in front of his face.

It was of little help. He was holding it upside down.

Being a big ship we carried a Physical Training officer, a splendid man of great enthusiasm who inspired a number of officers and men to take up fitness exercises. As Captain I felt duty bound to lend support to this activity even though I would never normally think about it. One day at sea I summoned the PT officer and demanded a copy of the Canadian pamphlet on personal physical exercise which was fashionable at the time – known in the trade as '5BX'.

Next morning, in the narrow confines of my sea cabin, I selected a series of exercises described as 'suitable' for the Under 7's and Over 70's (which seemed a reasonably harmless start to my venture) and set to. Space precluded following the complete list but touching my toes 20 times presented no problem. Until about the fifteenth time when something seemed to go 'click' in my chest and it became acutely painful to raise my right arm. I stopped, showered, had breakfast and went out onto the Bridge to read my signals and meet my Heads of Department. The latter were required to make contact with me individually each day between 0800 and 0830.

Half an hour later the Officer of the Watch reported a ship he had just detected some miles distant. From my Bridge chair I automatically leant forward and grasped my binoculars which were on a shelf just in front. Then I nearly screamed because of the tearing pain in my chest. The rest of that day passed quietly though without undue enjoyment.

Next morning when I went on the Bridge I was surprised to find *all* my Heads of Department already there. We chatted about this and that until the Officer of the Watch again reported a ship. Again I reached automatically for my binoculars, only to gasp with pain. At which point Mike Jackson, my splendid Principal Medical Officer, tapped me authoritatively on the shoulder and said:

'I think we'd better come along to your sea cabin sir and let me have a look at you.'

The ship reported did not exist. The whole affair had been a put-up job. I had pulled a muscle and soon recovered.

In the autumn of 1970 the Admiralty Board at last got around to abolishing the tot – the daily rum issue for which all ratings over the age of 20 serving in HM Ships in commission were eligible. The tot consisted of a generous measure of rum blended from sources as far apart as the Caribbean and Mauritius. Leaving aside schnapps and possibly certain vodka, Pusser's Rum was about the strongest drink in the world and quite the finest rum. The practice had been initiated in the navy early in the 18th century owing to the limited storage for beer. It was a time when conditions at sea were really hard and any alleviation of the harshness of a seaman's lot was highly desirable. Contrary to popular belief it was seldom used as an anaesthetic – for which a metal skull cap and a stout mallet applied smartly to the appropriate part of the cranium had proved more effective. Nevertheless one third of a tumblerfull of the fiery spirit, taken neat, was not without effect on the imbiber. So it came about that in 1740 Admiral Vernon decreed that in future while senior rates could continue to draw their rum ration neat, that for junior rates was to be diluted by two parts' water. The mixture came to be known as grog since Vernon himself was nicknamed 'Old Grog' because of his habit of wearing grogram.

Grog 'went off' and became unpalatable after being kept for a short time but the neat spirit, if re-bottled, could be kept indefinitely. Though strictly illegal such harbouring was sometimes perpetrated against a future birthday or other occasion for celebration. The subsequent additional consumption often led to excesses and acts of indiscipline.

Rum is something of an acquired taste and not every eligible youngster cared for it. Those who elected not to draw their tot were compensated to the tune of threepence per day – which had been of little significance to a sailor's budget for the past 50 years. Of far greater influence was the implied stigma of lack of manliness by not drawing. Many young sailors got round this by drawing their tot then surreptitiously passing it to one or more older men. 'Sippers' as it came to be called again resulted in occasional excesses and associated trouble.

The rum issue was made at noon, immediately preceding the main meal of the day. It was a traditional routine but lacked wisdom and had become increasingly out of tune with the demands of operational life in a modern warship. By the time of the Korean War in the early 1950's, Carrier Captains had found it necessary to defer the issue to Afternoon Watchmen (1230–1600) until they had come off watch. The degradation of efficiency in a man required to scrutinize a radar display in a darkened operations room after his tot needs little imagination.

In 1968 when taking up my appointment as Director of Naval Plans my courtesy call on Michael Carey, the head Civil Servant in the Navy Department, had been cut short.

'Frightfully sorry,' he said, 'but I have to see the Minister over the vexed question of the tot.'

'Why vexed?' I enquired.

'Well,' he answered, 'no First Sea Lord would like to go down in history as being the one who abolished the tot would he?'

'I think you have got this absolutely wrong,' I replied. 'Any First Sea Lord worth his salt should welcome being the one who had the nerve to grip an issue which everyone else had ducked.'

'Oh!' he said, 'That's an interesting new line which I had not heard. You had better walk along the corridor with me.'

I did and told him the facts of life at sea in respect of rum and efficiency. He seemed impressed but it took another two years of prevarication.

Now at last the plunge had been taken. The news was not ill received in the Fleet and many sailors welcomed it. But, like the young 20-year old not drawing his tot, it did not do to say so publicly. The subject was an emotional one and it needed careful handling in suitably low key. What was my dismay, therefore, to receive a signal from my Commander-in-Chief informing me that eight members of the media plus the editor of *Jane's Fighting Ships* would descend on me to witness the final rum issue. I remonstrated by exclusive signal, emphasizing the importance of playing down the event and pointing out that all our careful conditioning to this end would be prejudiced by such publicity. But it was no good. Back came a shrewdly worded reply saying that importance was attached to it being handled by a very senior and experienced Captain. There could be no further argument.

They came. I had them all in my cabin for a drink and the editor of *Jane's* asked for a rum. It was the one beverage I didn't stock! A junior Supply officer took them for'ard to watch the issue, after which they left. Next day the *Daily Telegraph* printed an obviously touched-up photograph of the ullage (remains) being ditched over the side. It all fizzled out very quietly and was a good riddance.

Our return to the UK from the Mediterranean was not without incident. We had to make a fast passage at 22 knots and to avoid the main southbound shipping route we stood well out into the Atlantic before turning north. In the middle of one night I was alerted by the Officer of the Watch to a ship he had just detected fine on the starboard bow, 10 miles distant. It was on an opposite course, doing 24 knots and was assessed to pass 2 miles clear. Derek Wilmot was an experienced and reliable Special Duties List Lieutenant and I knew I could depend on his professional judgement. The situation reported was normal and gave no cause for anxiety. He told me he was entirely happy. I switched off the Bridge Intercom and sank back on my pillow. Yet I was *not* entirely happy; I decided to go to the bridge. Since I invariably slept fully dressed when at sea this took but a moment and on checking the situation I found it exactly as reported. It was a fine night with a thin haze and the visibility was about 3 miles. The two ships approached each other on parallel courses at a relative speed of some 45 knots. Sure enough at 3 miles the other ship's main steaming lights were sighted as expected. It only remained to check her green side light when it came within range and all would be well. The range closed rapidly and soon a coloured light became visible. But to my consternation it was red (port), not the expected green. The wretched ship had deliberately altered course 135 degrees at the last minute so as to put me in the position of 'overtaking ship' with the onus of giving way. She was now cutting across my bow.

'Port 35. I have the ship,' I ordered, thus taking over all responsibility from the Officer of the Watch.

We went round in a circle and by the time we had completed it the other ship had resumed her original course. Her performance had been the height of unprofessional irresponsibility but unfortunately, despite putting a searchlight on to her, we failed to establish her name and of course she did not reply to my signals.

It had been a curious case of, largely, intuition. Left to himself, no doubt the Officer of the Watch would have taken the correct action but there had been no time for niceties. I think both of us had pumped a bit of adrenalin that night.

During my final months in *Albion* I was appointed ADC to the Queen, selected for promotion to Rear Admiral and assigned to the key post of Assistant Chief of Naval Staff (Policy) in the Ministry of Defence. The future was thus one to which to look forward but it was tempered by the extreme sadness of leaving such a fine team and happy ship. The parting was fragmented: first the Commando Group was landed in Cyprus; then the helicopter squadron disembarked off Culdrose (near Helston in Cornwall); finally I brought the ship into Portsmouth for the last time and said goodbye to my Ship's Company. Impending promotion to Flag Rank was fine but the realization that never again would I handle my own ship was a sobering reflection. Years later when, as a full Admiral, I was the Fleet Commander, people would often ask me,

'How are you enjoying the finest job in the Navy?' and I would reply,

'I am of course enjoying this super job enormously, but you are wrong to describe it as the finest! It is in fact the third finest.'

'How so?'

'Because the finest is to command your own ship, whatever her size or shape. Then everybody and everything is *yours* and every action, for good or ill, is ultimately *your* fault. It is a very personal business. The second finest is to command a Flotilla, that is a number of squadrons and ships. There you are necessarily rather more remote and the 'ownership' is a good deal looser. But you are still living in ships and among sailors and spending most of your time at sea. When you become C-in-C you move ashore and, while you have the delight of commanding the entire Fleet, that command is inevitably still more remote and less personal.'

Back home among my family I soon lost my sadness and looked forward to my first ever skiing holiday. Mary had done if off and on for most of her life and was a reasonably experienced, safe downhill skier. I had never skiied.

My dear old mother spent Christmas with us as usual. She was a marvellous person, in her late '70's, whose vitality and sense of fun could not be curtailed by her crippling arthritis.

When not travelling abroad with my father she had spent all her life in the country and, like me, had never skiied. Not surprisingly, perhaps, she now displayed a certain lack of enthusiasm over my taking it up. Picking her moment with care and waiting till my wife was out of the room so that the two of us were alone she suddenly rounded on me and in her inimitable, direct way said:

'You *are* a fool.'

'Why?' I asked innocently. I knew exactly what she meant but didn't see why I deserved such an assault.

'You know perfectly well what I mean.'

'I do not. You had better explain.' I saw no reason why I should give in too easily.

'Well, fancy taking up skiing at *your* age!'

This irritated me. 'What's so odd about my age?' I retorted. 'Dammit I'm only 46. Brabazon didn't start until he was 50.'

My mother gave me a withering, 'I-know-I'm right' look. '*You* are *not* Lord Brabazon.'

Of course she was absolutely right. She usually was.

14

THE ROLLING DEEP

'Who controls the sea controls all'
Themistocles

In the Navy there is an old Appointer's saying that rather than sending a chap to purgatory (in which there is thought to be no specific naval establishment) you send him to be Resident Naval Officer Pembroke Dock. I must confess to never having personally been to Pembroke Dock nor to being conversant with the range of duties of its RNO. But it is widely accepted that the former holds little appeal and the latter are somewhat short of stimulating. In brief the combination carries a kind of negative cachet and in naval appointment terms is generally recognized as being the end of the road.

Towards the end of my time as Assistant Chief of Naval Staff (Policy) a rather elderly Commander from the Naval Staff (who had done quite a lot of work for me over the years) was kind enough to call on me before leaving the Ministry of Defence to take up another appointment. Though nice enough as a person he would perhaps have been categorized by the ruthless Clausewitz as 'stupid but industrious'. He was also a very serious officer.

We chatted for twenty minutes or so. Then,

'How much leave are you getting?' I enquired.

'Only one week, sir.'

'Hmm,' I replied. 'That doesn't seem much after two long years in Whitehall.'

Conversation was beginning to wear a bit thin and to keep it going a little longer I told him my Appointer's story.

'Of course,' I said jocularly, 'you've probably heard that yarn about how the Appointers go on. You go in and see your man on a Thursday afternoon to find out your next job. You are greeted with friendly openness tinged with admiration. "Marvellous job," your Appointer enthuses, "congratulations, specially asked for by the Commander-in-Chief himself – must be set for stardom eh?" Later, bursting with pride and gratitude, you take your leave. Just as you reach the door, "Oh, by the way," the Appointing Commander calls after you, "there is just one thing I didn't mention: C-in-C wants you to start next Monday." Your face falls. You turn back to gain time and think this through further. After all, you *had* promised your wife to redecorate the drawing room *and* take the whole family to a Cornish beach for 10 days. You reach the Appointer's desk and in a subdued voice with an expression of deepest gloom you explain this.

'Quite understand,' booms the Appointer cheerfully. 'Of course if you really *must* have leave I can give you three weeks and then send you off as Resident Naval Officer Pembroke Dock. But . . .' his voice trails off into inevitability.

'I'll take the Staff Job,' you mutter and, choking back your anguish, leave the room.

'Silly story really,' I ended up, 'but curiously close to real life sometimes.'

My visitor evinced no reaction at all. His face remained completely impassive, unrelieved by even the glimmer of a smile. Time was up and I rose from my chair to indicate it. Walking slowly to the door I opened it, shook my caller by the hand and thanked him for his work. Then a final thought struck me:

'By the way,' I said, 'you never actually told me where you *are* going next?'

The blank, expresionless face was slowly turned towards me for the last time. 'Resident Naval Officer Pembroke Dock, sir.'

The door closed.

Midsummer 1974. My three long hard years as ACNS (P) in 'The Zoo' as I affectionately called the Ministry of Defence were over. They had been fascinating if exacting. Not for more than half a century had anyone been kept in that post for so long. But the work had been highly classified and has no place in this narrative. Now, after a welcome spell of leave, I was at sea again – Flag Officer First Flotilla.

As Tactical Commander of rather more than one third of the surface Fleet I was almost always at sea though I had a small house-cum-office in Portsmouth Dockyard. In my first two months I had eight different flagships. To support me I had a very small operational staff and relied for technical advice on the Heads of Departments in the flagship.

On taking over I hoisted my flag in the Cruiser *Blake* in Portsmouth. Two hours and a snack lunch later I was in my car en route to Portland accompanied by the Staff. There I shifted my flag to the Guided Missile Destroyer *Devonshire* (who did not even belong to my Flotilla) and we immediately sailed for an exercise off the coast of Scotland.

I have always felt it important to extract every ounce of value from exercises and to this end was prepared to drive myself – and others – hard. For the next 10 days I virtually lived in the Operations Room, often going without sleep for 48 hours, and then relying on 2 or 3 hours in the 24 to keep me going. By the end of it, when we entered Rosyth, I was tired but satisfied that I had washed Whitehall out of my system and was back in tune with real flesh and blood. When I left the ship it was with acute sadness for even in that short time my first flagship and her people had generated in me considerable affection. Subsequently whenever I met *Devonshire* I always felt we had a mutual affinity.

Back in *Blake* we soon sailed for another exercise. At sea things can happen quickly, especially at night, and I had long made a practice of sleeping fully dressed so as to be available immediately. In the middle of the first night out the Officer of the Watch had occasion to call his Captain on Bridge Intercom to report a nearby ship. The loudspeaker in my sea cabin had been inadvertently left on and in an instant I was out of my bunk and half way up the ladder to the Bridge. The reaction had been intuitive. Then I suddenly remembered that I was *not* the Captain, I was the Admiral; it was no longer any of my business. Feeling rather sheepish I turned round and crept back to my cabin, hoping nobody had noticed. Next day I owned up to Peter Herbert, my Flag Captain, and we had a good laugh.

When at sea *Blake* produced a daily Ship's Newspaper. It was short and very much to the point. Known as *The Oily Rag* it was crude but never obscene, and never subversive. Not a thing could go on in that ship without it being brought to the notice of the Editor, a Leading Marine Engineering Mechanic in the Engineers' Office. The Flag Captain and I were depicted as cockroaches on whose transparent wings were displayed our badges of rank – so that nobody was left in any doubt as to the personalities involved. Indeed nobody was left in any doubt about *anything* in that paper.

I soon found that *The Oily Rag* was of great assistance when writing home to my two daughters, then of school age: often I would cut out the latest series of Cockroach Cartoons or racy anecdotes and enclose them with my letters. But there was a difficulty here. While the front of a page might contain reasonably suitable material, often on the reverse side was a story or drawing of quite stupendous vulgarity. I got round the problem by blanking out the offending bits with a thick black felt pen. Months later my girls told me that whenever they received one of these cuttings with bits blanked out they knew they were something worthwhile. They immediately took it to the nearest desk lamp, held it up to the light and disclosed the tit-bits! It was probably a valuable part of their education.

From time to time attempts were made to start up a rival ship's paper on lines less earthy than *The Oily Rag*. They all foundered on the rocks of dull conformity. *The Rag* kept going and for years after I had ceased being FOF 1 I would get a personal message from it on my birthday, promotion or new appointment. Despite its basic nature, or perhaps because of it, it was a marvellous example of successful human communication and the finest ship's magazine I ever experienced.

At about 2100 one evening *Blake*, my flagship, was quietly steaming down channel south of Lyme Bay en route to the deeper water of the Western Approaches for a night exercise. I was holding a short briefing meeting with my Staff. In the middle of this the young Bridge Messenger arrived and reported that the Starboard Lookout had just sighted a green grenade (the standard signal used in exercises to indicate the firing of torpedoes by a submarine). Since the exercise itself was not due to start for another 12 hours I acknowledged the report and sent him back to the Bridge. A few minutes later the Midshipman of the Watch came down to report that this time the Officer of the Watch had seen a green grenade.

'Right,' I thought, 'this is a classic example of an unexpected and unplanned incident from which we should be able to extract some value.' And so I put it to the Staff. The 'war' had not yet started. We were still in a state of low tension, constrained by tight Rules of Engagement. If we did nothing the 'enemy' might sink a valuable unit (e.g. my flagship), indeed he might already have done so. If we overreacted and 'destroyed' the threatening submarine it could start a major war which might otherwise have been averted by diplomatic negotiation. From the background setting it was reasonable to deduce that the 'enemy' had little wish to provoke a war but was indulging in vigorous brinkmanship in an attempt to gain his ends by threat. On the other hand we might be dealing with a nut-case, some over-exuberant loner who was prepared to perpetrate a suicidal act for the sake of notoriety. If this was so it was important to neutralize him quickly or he might survive to repeat his assault – and, once again, start the war by misadventure. The problem then was how to communicate with the submarine. Flashing at him by light would give away our precise position and give him an easy target at which to aim his next salvo of torpedoes. In any case he would probably not be able to read English. The only way seemed to be via Fleet Headquarters: an urgent signal reporting that two attacks had already been carried out and requesting that the 'enemy' be informed by fastest possible means that any further attack would be met with ruthless counter-attack was duly transmitted.

For once the Fleet Headquarters was not its usual helpful self. In due course we got a rather stuffy reply saying that 'checks had been made, the incident was not part of the exercise and we should continue down Channel to our assigned rendezvous. No further action was intended. Probably it was a fisherman in Lyme Bay.'

I expect it was but *we* learned quite a lot from him even if Headquarters did not.

★

In the autumn of that year I took a group of ships, including a nuclear-powered Fleet Submarine and a Helicopter Cruiser, around the Cape of Good Hope (the Suez Canal being still closed) and out to the Far East, exercising with the Navies of other countries on the way. We reached Table Bay during the first week in October, the Submarine, Frigates and Royal Fleet Auxiliaries berthing in Simonstown and my Flagship in Cape Town. As was customary for such a visit, before entering harbour I fired a national salute of 21 guns. Though no longer a member of the Commonwealth the status of South Africa then, as now, was that of a friendly foreign state. There was nothing provocative or mischievous or in any way unusual about this piece of ceremonial – and so it was sensibly regarded in South Africa.

But in London the reaction was different. A newly elected Labour Government had been in office for just one week. Election fever had evaporated, the Cabinet had been selected and announced, there was no other national news and there was nothing momentous internationally. In short there was no news at all and the Press were hungry for food. So the *Daily Mail*, with nothing better to print hung out, like a carrot on a string before a donkey, an exaggerated version of my national salute to South Africa. And sure enough there was a donkey in the form of a left wing Labour MP only too eager to nibble it. He was outraged.

'What right had FOF 1 to pay such a mark of respect to a dreadful country like South Africa?' he demanded; 'Who had authorized him to do so? Should he not be recalled? Or court-martialled? Or keelhauled? He (the Member) knew only too much about that awful country' (though expert, he had never actually been there and hence did not know how delightfully awful it was). Fleet Street was tickled pink. Its wildest dreams were exceeded as more and more political donkeys cantered up to have a bite of the juicy carrot before it dried up. Then the South African Press took it up (the other way round of course) and magnified each aspect of what was, by any standard, a highly successful visit. The cartoonist of the *Cape Argus* portrayed British sailors cavorting with glamorous bikini-clad girls on South African beaches. This fuelled further efforts by Fleet Street; reporters went out to interview naval wives. Were they not frightfully upset by the thought of their husbands being lured into compromising situations by these South African hussies? Was it not seduction on a grand scale under the hot South African sun? When had their husbands last written to them? The wives, bless them, though a little uneasy, kept their cool.

Late one morning *my* wife came up from the garden to put the potatoes on for lunch. She had been dunging the roses and was fairly covered in muck. It was the day the local laundry van called and, finding a couple of men hanging round the back door, she assumed that they were from it. Thrusting the laundry box into their reluctant hands she disappeared indoors promising to return at once with the monthly cheque. When she did she discovered that the visitors were reporters from the *Daily Mail*.

'What can I do for you?' she asked.

'Well, um we wondered how you felt about your husband having such a riotous time in Cape Town?' asked one snidely.

'What are you getting at?' my wife replied tartly. 'When did *you* last spend $3\frac{1}{2}$ weeks at sea – or even a weekend away from home? Don't answer, I know you haven't. I think my husband and his sailors deserve that and more.'

'Oh! Well what about letters? Is the mail regular?'

'What a silly question. How do you expect letters to be collected from ships at sea? And as I've just told you, they've been at sea now for more than 3 weeks. Of course mail isn't regular.'

'Are you worried about all that entertainment ashore?'

'There is always hospitality when ships go into port. It is the tradition for navies all over the world. The local people put on concerts and dances and invite sailors out. Would they be expected to refuse because it offended the politicians?'

That was enough. The reporters left rather sheepishly, looking as discomforted as they deserved.

Out in the Far East my flagship *Blake* was about to replenish with fuel from a United States Fleet Tanker, the *Caloosa Hachi*.

Blake was the oldest ship in the British Fleet. Her main machinery and hull were of wartime construction and her hull plating had not been 'pickled' against corrosion. Consequently after a prolonged spell at sea, especially in bad weather, rust seeped through everywhere. She looked her age. This was in spite of valiant efforts by her splendid Ship's Company who worked extremely long hours to try to keep her efficient and smart. Painted in black on her side was her identifying Pennant Number: 99.

Caloosa Hachi on the other hand was brand new. She was the pride of the American Fleet Auxiliaries and had only recently entered service. She looked big and immaculate and was lavishly equipped with all the latest technology for replenishment at sea. Her Pennant Number, in gleaming white, was 01.

During the closing stages of the approach a huge board on the side of the tanker's superstructure became noticeable. On it, in bold lettering was the arrogant caption:

'We are Number One and proud of it'.

The flagship steadied in station, the lines were passed and the fuel hose connected. Just as pumping was about to start there came a ripple of laughter amongst those working on the upper decks of both ships. They all looked upwards towards *Blake*'s Gun Defence Position, abaft the bridge. There were four sailors holding a long strip of rough canvas on which had been hurriedly painted 'We are Ninety-Nine and feeling it'.

Following a major SEATO exercise off the Philippines the participating ships anchored in Manila Bay for the usual analysis and discussion. Throughout the exercise a vigorous US 'civic assistance' programme had been conducted ashore. It took the form of constructing a small Drug Rehabilitation Centre – for which there was considerable local need. The Centre was to be opened with a ceremonial open-air concert performed by young addicts at various stages of rehabilitation and attended by the senior officers of all the nations taking part in the exercise.

The local naval authorities had kindly provided me with a car and driver for use during my time in harbour. The evening before the opening ceremony my Flag Lieutenant checked that the driver knew the venue and agreed a departure time. No problem.

Next morning dawned bright and very hot. There was no sign of the car. For over half an hour we searched vainly for a taxi and eventually nobbled an elderly ramshackle vehicle whose grinning driver assured us in broken English that he knew exactly where to go. Sweating profusely in our white ceremonial uniform we set off at speed for what we supposed was a fifteen-minute journey. Forty minutes later in the middle of a large deserted cemetery we called the driver's bluff and persuaded him to stop. Clearly the wretched man had no more idea of our destination than we had.

By now we were very late indeed. Jehu had nothing on our driver in his attempt to recover the situation. Foot hard down on the floorboards, he raced about this way and that and eventually we found it. Careering down the dirt approach-road he clapped on his squealing brakes beside a temporary stand full of spectators dressed in their best and we skidded to a halt. Shakily we clambered out to negotiate the fare. At that moment a stifling cloud of dust, stirred up by our frenzied passage down the dirt road, overtook us. Like a cowboy movie we were enveloped in dirty sand which penetrated eyes, ears, nostrils and smothered our once-white uniforms.

The spectators looked on agog. Here was an unprogrammed extra and they enjoyed the light relief. An elderly WAVE (US Women's Naval Service) of almost incredible unattractiveness advanced towards me as if stalking her prey. In her arms she carried a large lei (necklet) of orchids. Having been to Hawaii several times I reckoned I knew the drill for this: bend the head to facilitate the lei being placed round your neck, extend each cheek in turn to be kissed, reciprocate the kisses on the donor's cheeks. By now we were in a close quarters situation. The lei was slipped over my head without difficulty. I offered my left cheek nothing happened. I tried my right cheek; still no reaction. Perhaps my memory was playing me tricks and the kissing procedure should be the other way round. I leant forward to try it out. Immediately the ugly WAVE recoiled to avoid my approaching lips. I had had enough. Confident that I was right and with all the other spectators riveted by the side show I determined to do it properly. Further and further forward I leant, further and further back went the WAVE. Then suddenly she lost her balance, broke from the scene and disappeared into the crowd. I never planted my kiss and for once I was not too disappointed.

By now the concert was at its half-way point. Each act was performed by a different group of young people (usually in their late 'teens but ranging from 12–25) who sang – quite beautifully – a topical or popular song with a haunting tune, occasionally punctured by a solo. The concert had started with people who had been completely cured of their addiction. It progressed through other groups who were only partially 'unhooked' (and whose appearance and manner indicated this). It ended with a tragic little group of three youngsters in the very early stages of treatment. They looked what they were: drugged. Their singing was only just tuneful and co-ordinated and they had difficulty in standing steadily. They were still in chains. It was a most moving finale.

At the subsequent reception I had a long talk with the man in charge of the Centre, an American missionary aged about 35 who had been working on this for five years. He was a very impressive young man whose make-up combined quiet, unassuming dedication with delightfully cheerful realism. He explained how the majority of his clients were young teenagers from well-to-do families suffering from acute boredom. Drugs offered the limited excitement of the unlawful and the unknown and in the initial stages added a tiny zest to an otherwise excruciatingly dull existence – or so the afflicted thought. By the time they came to grips with the degrading and seamier side of this fallacy it was too late and they were hooked. In the early days the missionary had managed to partly cure a very small number of young addicts and had immediately sent them out into the town to recruit more. It was a long, tedious, uncertain business with more frustration than success and demanding infinite patience. But little by little he had established a basis of communication and trust and his 'practice' was steadily growing. It was a remarkable performance by a remarkable man.

Whenever a British warship entered Hong Kong she would be descended on by a local Chinese 'Side Party' who quickly and expertly repaired the ravages of the sea on the ship's side and touched up the 'boot topping' (the black waterline) using paint and brushes or rollers supplied by the ship. In return they enjoyed the privilege of removing the gash (rubbish) and its disposal after meticulous scrutiny for possible further use. Two 'firms' operated in this way, each led by a woman – Jenny and Susie – and each composed entirely of women of varying ages known as 'the girls'. Though they lived modestly it was a profitable business and even by Hong Kong standards Jenny and Susie were passing rich.

My links were with Jenny, a plump lady of uncertain years and great cheerfulness. She worked her girls hard and ruled them with a rod of iron. She was also an arch snob and revelled in photographs and letters from past Admirals. Her favoured ones were usually confined to the Executive Officers of big ships and the Commanding Officers of all. Once on her list you were there for life and every Christmas a handsome card liberally embellished with gilt and dragons would arrive.

I carried out my inspection of *Blake* in Hong Kong. This involved looking at every compartment in the ship as well as her boats, the upper deck and her general external appearance. The ship was alongside and the final serial in a long and intensive programme was to walk along the jetty and then embark in the whaler to view the other side. This was timed for 1600 in the afternoon.

I had completed my inspection, including the ship's side nearest to the jetty when I was approached by a rather worried looking Executive Officer.

'Sir,' said Harry Mucklow, 'you've had a very long and exhausting day. We thought you might like a bit of a break now, have a cup of tea and go round the ship in the whaler at 1700.'

This sounded rather fishy. Going round the ship in the boat would take less than five minutes and involved no physical effort at all. Much better to get it over and done with. I said so.

'Thank you but I'd rather finish the job now.' His face fell and he looked distinctly unhappy. Clearly there was more to the proposition than met the eye. I probed further.

'Is there any *other* reason for this change in programme, Commander?' By now he was looking really miserable.

'Well, sir, the fact is that Jenny and her girls need another hour to finish the boot topping on the other side.'

'Ah,' I replied, 'I quite understand. We'll make it 1700 then.' The Commander beamed and we parted.

Promptly at 1700 (never keep boats waiting) I stepped on to the jetty and walked to the whaler under the port quarter. Jumping down into the sternsheets I turned to the saluting Coxswain, who I knew quite well, and said, 'Good evening'.

'Good evening, sir. Nice to have you back with us.' (I had, in fairness, been out of the ship the previous week to give her a better chance to prepare for my inspection.) 'What was it like in UK, sir? Are they having a good summer? Did you manage to get some leave, sir?' And he prattled on.

Soon it occurred to me that this was deliberate prevarication. Further, that the Bowman was standing on the jetty several yards away evidently awaiting some signal. No, it simply didn't run. I was on the brink of cutting the voluble Cox'n short and telling him to get on with it when the Bowman ran back, jumped into the boat and we cast off.

It took time to manoeuvre the boat clear of the jetty and the ship's berthing wires. Then slowly (a rather overdone seamanlike precaution in case of passing boat traffic on the blind side) we crept round the stern and stood off with engine almost stopped so that I could look at the ship. As we did so I just caught a glimpse of Jenny's workboat slipping out of sight around the bow. No 'face' had been lost.

A few years later when I again visited Hong Kong as C-in-C Fleet I presented Jenny with a well-merited MBE. It would be hard to say who derived the greatest pleasure from that occasion.

When I left Whitehall in 1974 the relations between the RN and RAF within the Ministry of Defence were at an all-time low. Though futile, this situation was not new. Apart from the obvious ingredient of a personality clash at the top, fuel was provided by almost every one of the seven deadly sins, of which 'seeking after riches' and 'coveting thy neighbour's goods' predominated. I was determined to do something positive to alleviate this unhealthy state of affairs and to this end I resolved to fly an operational sortie in every one of the RAF's front line aircraft. There was, as I knew from my limited experience in naval helicopters, no better or quicker way of getting to terms with another human being (regardless of rank) than to fly with him under conditions of some stress. My first move was to call on the C-in-C Strike Command without whose backing I should never be able to penetrate the system.

Air Chief Marshal Sir Denis Smallwood had recently been Vice Chief of the Air Staff and I had got to kow him reasonably well. 'Splinters' as he was affectionately termed by both Services was an essentially human person with a breadth of mind and a rationality of thought well beyond the mental make-up of most senior RAF officers of his day who tended to be out for 'grabs for crabs'. He readily accepted my proposition and gave me the most marvellous backing – without which it would not have been possible. It had been previously, if tentatively, arranged that I should fly back to Portsmouth from High Wycombe in a RAF helicopter. For this purpose I had taken my flying gear with me. Casually I asked the C-in-C if the aircraft was available and, more particularly, whether I could fly it.

'Yes,' he said, 'the chopper *is* laid on and you *will* be allowed to fly it.'

By this time my spirits were soaring. Quickly I changed into flying rig. Splinters accompanied me down to the pad and there was a gleaming Whirlwind helicopter. Too late I realized that this was the C-in-C's personal aircraft and that my co-pilot was his ADC. Further that a Whirlwind 9 was not equipped with Auto Stabilization, i.e. it had to be flown entirely 'manually' – which was well beyond my limited capability in those early days. But there could be no turning back now. Steeling myself for the ordeal I said a grateful goodbye, settled into the left-hand seat and lifted off. As we lurched rather unsteadily into the afternoon sky I blessed my luck and thought what a funny life it was. Guthrie Young, the co-pilot, had nerves of iron and was very tolerant of my amateur performance. Subsequently we flew together several times and became good friends. Rapport between the two shades of blue had started.

My general concept was first to call on the appropriate Group Commander to get his blessing and then through his staff to organize visits to selected Air Stations from which operated the various types of aircraft. I would normally arrive in the afternoon, look around and get the Station Briefing, have supper informally with the CO and a few others and next day after a full pre-flight briefing fly my operational sortie. These visits were necessarily intermittent as they had to be fitted in to my higher priority commitments in running my Flotilla. It was quite an exacting programme.

Sorties varying from 4 to 8½ hours in a Shackleton (Airborne Early Warning), Nimrod (maritime surveillance and anti-submariine), Vulcan (maritime radar reconnaissance) and Victor K1 (tanker) were interesting if unremarkable. My next visit took me to Leuchars where I hoped to fly a Phantom. On arrival I discovered that they wouldn't let me do this as I had not been through the air medical checks at North Luffenham. However, they kindly laid on their aerobatics ace from 43 Squadron to give me a 15-minute demonstration watched from the tarmac. In the final act the aircraft emerged suddenly from behind a hangar, flew upside down along the runway at a height of less than 100 feet and when just opposite us turned vertically upwards. A split second error of 'pull' instead of 'push' on the stick and the pilot would have been into the ground and certain death. It was an awe-inspiring performance. We then strolled across to the Squadron Mess for tea, shortly to be joined by the aircrew of the demonstration. The pilot was a young Flight Lieutenant; he sauntered in nonchalantly, helped himself to a cup of tea with his hand steady as a rock, lit a cigarette and was clearly bright-eyed and bushy-tailed. Brushing aside my suggestion that he must need his tea after his recent performance he merely muttered that it was 'SOP' (standard operating procedure); he wouldn't give an inch. A few moments later in tottered the Tac Nav; his face was the colour of chalk, his hands were shaking and he was bathed in sweat: moving unsteadily to the nearest wall he leant against it for support and for several minutes was reluctant to speak. Being in the back seat the circumstances of the aerobatic demonstration had given him little to do. For the first time I realized something of what I had let *myself* in for.

But how to overcome the hurdle of North Luffenham? Determined to fly all the fast jets, I reckoned if that was what the RAF stipulated (and why not?) that was what I had to do. The most formidable aspect of the medical check took the form of Explosive Decompression. For this they put you in a decompression chamber, simulated taking you up to 70,000 feet and blowing off the canopy, then brought you back down in very quick time. It put quite a strain on the human system and a prerequisite for the test was a 'blood chit' from your own Service Doctor certifying that you were physically capable of undergoing it. Having made a date with North Luffenham I arranged to fly there from Lee on Solent in a naval aircraft having called in at the Royal Naval Hospital Haslar for my overdue routine medical (PUL-HEEMS) and my blood chit.

At Haslar I was greeted with consternation by the Surgeon Rear Admiral who, after a few warning remarks, handed me over to a Surgeon Captain. Peter Preston was a brilliant doctor and an old friend. Chatting incessantly about our wives and families he took me through my PULHEEMS, failed to spot my developing hernia and so to the question of the blood chit.

'I cannot possibly give you that certificate,' he said. 'To do so would require your having extensive electrocardiograph tests over three days and you have only given me 10 minutes. And anyway you would be mad to do such a thing at your age.'

'This was an unexpected blow which shattered my plans. I thought very quickly and resolved to rely on a mixture of inter-Service courtesy and bureaucracy.

'Very well,' I said, 'in that case please give me a chit saying just that, namely that I am fully fit for sea service but that under no circumstances should I be put through Explosive Decompression.'

He did and away I flew to North Luffenham where I made a rather untidy landing in a cross wind with an unfamiliar Heron – much to my Flag Lieutenant's discomfort. There I was shown round the Establishment, given a very good lunch and taken along to the decompression chamber. This was the moment of truth.

'Have you a blood chit, Sir?'

I handed it over.

After a moment's pause: 'That's fine, Sir. We'll take you up to 70,000 feet but let you down quite gently. Then we'll show you a film of the real thing.'

Watching the film alone made me feel faintly sick but I left amid broad grins and with full clearance to fly RAF fast jets!

My first opportunity to do so came a few weeks later. After a NATO exercise in which I had flown my flag in the Cruiser *Blake* the latter made an informal visit to Malta. This had long been planned and I had arranged to get my wife and family out for a week's fun in the sun. We were to borrow a friend's house and were all much looking forward to an enjoyable break. Shortly before the usual reception on board on the evening of our arrival my RAF Staff Officer approached me bubbling over with cheerfulness.

'Great news, sir. Treble One Squadron [Lightnings] is at Luqa on a training deployment and they're all set to take you up for a supersonic sortie tomorrow afternoon.'

I suppose my dilemma showed in my face. Tomorrow was Saturday and I had promised to start my inevitably fragmented leave with an expedition and picnic. My wife didn't care much for my flying activities anyway, regarding them as my sticking my neck out unnecessarily. However, being a game girl she suffered in silence and only occasionally registered mild disapproval. But to rot up at the outset the first major family outing in years would be asking too much. 'No way,' I replied. 'That would spell instant and justifiable grounds for divorce.' Not in the least set back by my reaction, RAFSO left still grinning knowingly.

The party started, filling quickly and soon gathering momentum. In due course the Station Commander at Luqa was introduced to me. 'Awfully glad to hear you're so keen to fly with us, sir,' he boomed enthusiastically. 'Have you heard? By an amazing piece of luck we've got Treble One with us on a training mission and they've jacked up a special programme for you tomorrow. I hope to see you then.' I groaned inwardly; the situation was rapidly getting out of hand. Muttering some grateful, non-committal platitude I turned away – to come face to face with 'Wing Commander Tony Parks, sir, CO of Treble One.'

I shook hands dully.

'Marvellous that you're coming out with us tomorrow afternoon, sir. We've got a pretty intensive programme but can just fit you in then (we fly back to UK on Monday). What a stroke of luck that you've caught us in the nick of time. You'll meet the boys over lunch, then we'll get you kitted out and I will take you up.'

It is important to face up realistically to can't-win situations. I did so: 'Thank you,' I said, 'I shall greatly look forward to it.' Later, out of the corner of my eye I saw an exuberant RAFSO introducing Parks to my wife. Mary, bless her, as ever took it on the chin and clearly regarded my bad behaviour as typical. What a wonderful girl.

Next afternoon went as planned. Despite the intense heat on the ground I went through the sound barrier for the first time and revelled in the finger-tip delicacy of poling a Lightning. It was an exhilarating experience. My family did not quite understand but were tolerant.

My next sortie, some time later, was in a Buccaneer of 12 Squadron from Honnington. After extensive type and safety drills the pre-flight briefing was coming to an end. The plan was for two aircraft to fly out to Tain Range off the east coast and there I would watch (from my aircraft) the other carrying out medium toss bombing runs.

'Should I not be doing some bombing runs in *my* aircraft to see what it's like?' I enquired.

'Well, er, perhaps, but there is not much point in doing it if you black out,' was the reply. 'And anyway the visibility is dicey and there's not a lot of time on this range.'

'I agree. But would I black out?'

There followed a quick conference in which it was evident that opinions differed. Then, 'Yes, sir, we think you would.'

Soon afterwards we took off as a pair. Skimming over the huge cornfields of Lincolnshire at a height of little more than 50 feet was exhilarating, if initially slightly tense-making. As we reached the coast the clouds rolled back and we found ourselves in brilliant sunshine. While the other aircraft carried out its bombing runs we 'ghosted' in parallel a little distance off until the moment of weapon-release and pull-up when we did a more gentle turn away. Within 20 minutes the bombing practice had been completed (and very impressively too). My pilot spoke enthusiastically over the intercom:

'Well, sir, he's finished early and we've still got a bit of time in our range slot. Would you like to try a few medium toss manoeuvres?'

Of course I had to say 'yes' and did so.

He talked me through the manoeuvre in his gentle, confident voice: steady low level approach – just coming up to the release point – now, pull up, release – back down to low level for disengagement . . .' Slowly, very slowly, my stomach returned to its normal position from somewhere around my tonsils and a little blood started to flow back to my head. I felt deathly faint. After two more runs in quick succession my entire frame seemed to be liquid, or at least jelly.

'All right, sir?' came the cheerful enquiry from the front seat.

'Fine,' I croaked, thankful that further conversation was not called for.

As we started our return harvesting act over the cornfields I pondered miserably on my fate. My old friend Air Marshal David Evans, Air Officer Commanding 1 Group, was coming specially to Honnington to have lunch with me. All thought of food or drink was anathema. Indeed I seriously doubted my ability even to climb out of the cockpit and the ignominy of having to be lifted out did not bear contemplating. But the human body is a remarkably resilient mechanism and as each minute passed my condition improved. By the time we landed, though every stitch of my clothing was soaked in sweat, I had recovered sufficiently to clamber to the ground and greet my host without making an ass of myself.

They understood about these things at Honnington. After a long shower my recovery was complete and I was able to enjoy an excellent lunch, albeit in a slightly disembodied way.

Air-to-air refuelling in a Phantom from Coningsby was surprisingly easy but rolling a Canberra by night over Plymouth I found disorientating. My problem was to distinguish the stars from the city lights when upside down and all the time my instructor was urging me to do it more quickly. It was only after we had landed back at St Mawgan that I learned there was a strict embargo on rolling Canberras at all. My flight in a Hunter was unremarkable but two sorties in Jaguars from Lossiemouth provided a lot more edge. The first consisted of general flying to get the feel of the aircraft but ended up with 15 minutes' aerobatics which reduced me to pulp. My subsequent half hour on the ground was insufficient for complete recovery and it was still with a rather unhappy stomach that I took off again, this time with a charming but lunatic Flight Lieutenant who boasted that he was expert on the stately homes of the Highlands. We followed terrain at a height of about 100 ft. out to the west coast and back again, manoeuvring violently to avoid overflying each castle and pulling a lot of 'g'. On return my Instructor tucked voraciously into his chicken-in-the-basket in the Squadron Mess; I rinsed out my mouth with cold water.

Most traumatic of all was my second sortie in a Harrier GR3. The first had been fun and I had enjoyed handling this highly versatile aircraft whose vertical landing was not unlike that of a helicopter. But it had not been representative of a fully operational sortie and when I gently pointed this out to West Wittering they determined to give me the full works. I went up with a Section of four; each pair took it in turns to be 'cops' and 'robbers'. For $1\frac{1}{4}$ hours they did everything in the book and one or two things outside it. After 20 minutes I reached the limit of my endurance; after 40 I was beyond caring; after 60 I would have welcomed a quick death as a merciful release from suffering; the final 20 minutes were beyond description. I had got what I had asked for and appreciated it. But it was 48 hours before I could again enjoy food.

I was only just in time with all this flying. Not long afterwards (when I was Vice Chief of the Defence Staff) there was a witch-hunt in the RAF about safety standards and an embargo on anyone flying who was not fully qualified and in date. David Evans, now Vice Chief of the Air Staff, came to my office one day and with great reluctance told me that I could no longer fly any of their aircraft, even helicopters. He was very nice about it and I think genuinely sorry to have to pass on the Air Force Board's ruling. Of course I had to accept it, but sadly.

A few weeks later I had occasion to fly down to Portsmouth from Northolt in a Whirlwind 10 of 32 Squadron. I was allowed to occupy the left-hand seat up front (the co-pilot's) but not by the new rules to take the controls.

The pilot was a promising looking young Flight Lieutenant (Peter Thomson) who I had not previously met. Timing my approach with care so as not to push my luck I waited until he had lifted off and settled on course and at height. Then very casually I enquired,

'Are you going to let me fly it?'

'Have you ever done it before, sir?'

'Well, yes I have actually. I'd love to have a go and of course I'll do all you tell me to.'

'OK, sir, she's yours – I'll monitor you.'

This was beyond my wildest dreams, but I could only suppose the pilot hadn't yet heard about the embargo. I had no wish to get him into trouble.

'You do realize don't you,' I asked, 'that this is strictly forbidden in your Service now and that if anyone gets to hear of it you will be crucified?'

'That's all right, sir,' he replied. 'No one need know.'

I took control and he soon realized that I had done it before and relaxed totally. We approached Portsmouth, where we were due to land at HMS *Vernon*, near the Harbour Station.

'Are you going to let me put it down?' I asked in my most offhand, innocent voice.

'Have you done it at *Vernon* before?'

'Oh yes, several times.'

'All right, I'll follow you through.' And down we went without a problem.

That evening I flew back to Northolt. Suddenly with no warning from Air Traffic Control, as we approached London a light aircraft appeared out of the blue, crossing from left to right about 200 yards away. I slammed the collective down and we dropped to safety.

'That,' said my pilot, cross that Air Traffic Control had given no warning, 'was a near-miss and I shall have to report it as such. The other fellow almost certainly will.'

The following week I had occasion to be flown in a HS125 (executive jet) by the Squadron Commander who I had got to know quite well and who had become a friend.

'I hear you had quite an episode on your way back from Portsmouth last week.'

'Mmm,' I replied. 'I gather there was some other aircraft which had not been notified by Air Traffic Control. But of course,' I added, 'you can't really see much out of the cabin.'

To this day I do not know if he knew that I knew a bit more.

All good things come to an end. Too soon the time came for me to hand over the First Flotilla to Tony Morton and, after a spell of leave, take up my new appointment as Vice Chief of the Defence Staff – then a 'non-job' to which I was not looking forward. The change of command was to take place at Portsmouth on board *Blake*. Although she had often been my flagship and I had got to know a number of her Company quite well, my relationship as 'the Admiral' had inevitably been less personal than as Captain of one's own ship. While being extremely sorry to leave such a super job, therefore, I did not expect much emotional problem over leaving. I was wrong.

When I stepped out of the front door at 3, The Parade (my small shoreside Headquarters) on that final morning the approach was lined as for a wedding by my Staff Instructors – a very stalwart team of Fleet Chief or Chief Petty Officers. Each was wearing the recently acquired 1st Flotilla Staff tie and all were armed with cutlasses with which they gave me a farewell salute. Evidently they had put in some practice for the drill was good. Suddenly I realized what a wrench it was going to be to leave these fine men, possibly never to see them again. Their send-off set the tone for a surprisingly wretched morning of farewells, reaching a depth with my final departure.

As I watched my successor inspect his Guard of Honour on the Quarter-deck I realized acutely that this was the final curtain on a performance I should never be able to repeat. We were photographed together by the Ship's bell; Tony Morton with a happy grin of anticipation, me trying desperately to hide my misery behind a ghastly forced smile. Then to the brow for final leave-taking with my Flag Captain, over the side and away.

But at the brow was what seemed to be an extraordinarily large Side Party, all armed with Bo'suns' Calls to pipe me over the side for the last time. As I got close to them I saw what had been done. The Side Party was composed of a wide cross-section of those with whom I had had particularly personal dealings. The Navigating Officer, the Operations Officer and the Gunnery Officer (all dressed as sailors), the Petty Officer Marine Engineering Mechanic who had cut my hair, the Flag Captain's Petty Officer Steward, the Leading Marine Engineering Mechanic, Editor of *The Oily Rag*, and many others. It was a very moving gesture.

Rather blindly I went down the brow. On the jetty at the foot of it were my Staff, headed by my Staff Officer Operations (David Morse) and Secretary (Geoff White). They were manning a dockside trolley on which had been secured a chair covered in green baize. I gingerly levered myself into the chair and they 'towed me' the whole length of the ship to my waiting car. The full extent of the send-off then became apparent. Virtually all officers and men not actually on watch had turned out and were manning every available foot of shipside and superstructure space, waving their caps and cheering. The trolley came to a stop, I said goodbye to my Staff and left. My sadness was tempered only by my pride in this splendid, loyal team.

15

THE UNFORGIVING MINUTE

'The true Commander dispenses with the book. If he dispenses
with the book he dispenses with protection. If then things go
wrong he loses his head.'

Anon.

In the spring of 1977 I was promoted to full Admiral and appointed
Commander-in-Chief Fleet with my Headquarters at Northwood. The post
carried five 'hats': nationally the Fleet Commander was also the Polaris
Force Commander – the four Polaris submarines forming the national
independent strategic nuclear deterrent force; and Commander of the
remainder of the submarine force, subsequently assumed by Flag Officer
Submarines when his Headquarters was moved from Gosport to Northwood
and incorporated in the Fleet Headquarters. Two NATO hats were also
included: Allied Commander-in-Chief Channel (CINCHAN) – a Major
NATO Commander (MNC) in his own right; and Commander-in-Chief
Eastern Atlantic Area (CINCEASTLANT) – a Major Subordinate Commander (MSC) to the Supreme Allied Commander Atlantic (SACLANT).

Reduced to the simplest terms the National Command embraced the
whole of the seagoing Royal Navy worldwide and was responsible for its
fighting efficiency (the shoreside coming under the Commander-in-Chief
Naval Home Command (CINCNAVHOME) at Portsmouth. On the NATO
side the Channel Command covered a relatively small area and involved
those ships (mainly Minecountermeasures Vessels from the European
Navies) assigned to it in war. Nine NATO nations were represented at
Northwood, headed by a Rear Admiral as Chief of Allied Staff (COAS) who
was traditionally Dutch. For reasons of economy and efficiency many of the
National Staff also held dual NATO appointments. A British Vice Admiral
was Chief of (National) Staff.

Located within the same Headquarters complex at Northwood was the
Headquarters of No. 18 (Maritime) Group Royal Air Force – erstwhile
Coastal Command – commanded by an Air Marshal. Thirty minutes drive
away was High Wycombe, Headquarters of RAF Strike Command –
effectively all the operational elements of the RAF in the United Kingdom.

I had no preconceived ideas concerning my various responsibilities, but it quickly became apparent that whereas my National tasks were straight-forward, already highly organized and effective, my NATO duties were more nebulous and in some respects even anomalous. I therefore resolved, while maintaining the closest touch with the Fleet, to apply a major effort to improving and establishing my position in NATO. As a MSC to SACLANT, CINCEASTLANT was clearcut and presented no problem but in the case of CINCHAN there was much to be done.

As a MNC CINCHAN (always a British Admiral) was one of the top three Military Commanders in the Alliance. The other two, SACLANT and the Supreme Allied Commander Europe (SACEUR) were invariably a US Admiral and a US General respectively. In terms of size and strength of forces assigned, CINCHAN's command was puny by comparison. Indeed in strategic theory it was an anachronism. In practice it gave the UK a seat at NATO's top strategic military planning table; it was also highly regarded by the European member nations as 'the voice of Europe'.

SACLANT at this time was Ike Kidd. A true professional sailor, as had been his father before him until killed in the Japanese attack on Pearl Harbour in 1941, he was a dominant personality who was disinclined to take anything for granted and spoke his mind to seniors and juniors alike. A former USN boxing Champion and as a Captain a remarkably handsome man, his figure had now lost something of its youth – a great leader, a bit of a bully (as most leaders have to be prepared to be) and much loved by all – not least myself.

As SACEUR Al Haig was different in every way. More of a politician than a soldier, he had jumped from two star rank to four with no military experience in between and not all that much before. Having been President Nixon's Chief of Staff at the time of Watergate he had been considerably in the public eye and he liked it that way very much. Throughout his time at SHAPE he did an excellent job for which he deserves due credit. But his affairs were conducted with an eye to the main chance and when he retired it was to run for President (though predictably as an unsuccessful contender) rather than because of the need for change in the European Command.

Irrespective of Service the MNC's point of contact was with the Chief of Defence Staff (CDS) of each member nation. At NATO Headquarters in Brussels it was with the Chairman of the Military Committee (CMC) and the Secretary General (SecGen). It was also important to know, and be known by, the various Ambassadors to NATO (PERMREPS).

Zeiner Gundersen, CMC, was an experienced Norwegian professional soldier. A sensitive, courteous gentleman of slight build and quiet manner he spoke excellent careful English and invariably remained calm, however rough the going became. His impossible task was to please everyone and in this he achieved a very fair measure of success. During his few off-duty moments he loved to go for long, quiet rides on his horse. By nature he was neither dynamic nor innovative, preferring to maintain the status quo. His family motto could have been 'anything for a quiet life'. He was absolutely straight and genuine. I liked him and apart from the occasional sharp clash over getting something changed we got on well together.

The Secretary General, Joseph Luns, was literally a tower of strength. Well over six feet tall, his huge physique was matched intellectually by his breadth of vision and skill at negotiation. He was probably the most experienced diplomat in the whole of the Alliance and he led NATO in a big way. During World War II he had served in the Dutch Navy, rising to the level of Leading Signalman (a quirk in the system had ruled him out as an officer because he was three days too young); he never lost his love of the sea and ships. He was also an extremely knowledgeable historian and knew a great deal more about past events in the Royal Navy than I did. When conferences were held in the United States during the heat of the summer we all suffered the chill of excessive airconditioning; Joe Luns would stride in wearing a tropical suit and, before sitting down, wrap himself up like a mummy in a huge grey horse blanket. He was a marvellous person and everyone loved and respected him.

As is often the case with top level business, the real work of NATO leading to major decisions was mainly done 'in the margins' of the formal meetings and involved informal bilateral or multilateral discussions leading to formal endorsement at the appropriate main meeting. One of the most influential of such meetings was the Nuclear Planning Group (NPG), chaired by SecGen and with the Defence Secretaries of the NPG member nations, accompanied by their CDSs, participating. SACLANT and SACEUR both attended; hitherto CINCHAN had not. Thus 'the European view' was not directly represented, nor was the UK's, despite being the only European nuclear power (apart from France – whose position in the Alliance was equivocal, having withdrawn from its integrated military structure).

I was determined to correct this paradox. It was not easy: the American MNCs were entirely content with their unique position and were restrained in their welcome to an 'outsider' to the club. For my part I made it clear that either I *was* a MNC in the full sense of that post or I would not be a MNC at all (which the European members would not tolerate); there could be no such thing as a sort of 'second class' MNC. Logic and good sense were on my side and, after a good deal of hard lobbying, so were SecGen, CMC and the CDSs of the NPC member countries. In particular, nobody could find any valid reason why I should *not* participate. The result was that I was voted in; it led to some interesting experiences, some of which are described later in this chapter.

Admiralty House at Northwood was delightful. Set in what had once been a lovely garden but which sadly had been allowed to run down, it was big enough to dine 24 comfortably yet not so big that you rattled round when on your own. It was three minutes' drive from the Headquarters, but a long way from the sea and the Fleet. When the Headquarters was first established ashore in the 1960's insufficient thought had been given to this remoteness. It would not have been difficult to have installed a small flight of helicopters and operated a shuttle service to each of the Base Ports. But at that time an overriding obsession prevailed to avoid disturbing the residents in this well-to-do London suburb and the opportunity was missed. Ten years later the economic constraints were such as to preclude applying such a solution retrospectively. In 1973 the then Fleet Commander (Admiral Sir Edward Ashmore) had the foresight and the nerve to put up a strong recommendation that the entire Headquarters complex, including the RAF's 18 (Maritime) Group element, should be resited at HMS *Vernon*, just inside the entrance to Portsmouth Harbour, where a prime waterfront site with extensive facilities which were shortly to become redundant already existed. The cost would have been £20m – about half that of a small Minecountermeasure Vessel. But the Admiralty Board showed no great enthusiasm for the project and the Air Force Board were stuffily opposed to it. Once again the opportunity was missed, probably for all time because of the subsequent reconstruction on a massive scale of the underground NATO Headquarters at Northwood.

Back at Admiralty House in the early days we were giving our first dinner party. The guests were a cross-section of the more senior members of the National and NATO staffs and their wives: it was too soon to have got to know many of those present at all well and while the evening had gone pleasantly enough there had been a distinct aura of 'best behaviour' and it had not exactly been a riot of fun. Dinner ended and, led by Mary, the wives retired, leaving the men to a final round of port. As the wives made to go upstairs they were warmly greeted by Brumble, our Golden Retriever, grinning and grunting with pride, tail wagging vigorously and trailing from her mouth (and quite obviously so) my pyjama trousers. It broke the ice (never very thick) admirably and from then on things went with a swing.

A few weeks later we gave another dinner party, this time primarily in honour of the new French Naval Attaché in London. Though the Attaché spoke fluent English, his wife was still on the learning curve and preferred to conduct her conversation in her native tongue. My own French was basic and rusty but we got along all right until the main course was finished. Pudding was to be *'une omelette flambée'* for which precision in timing was important – not helped by the long transit from the kitchen at the extreme opposite end of the house. To ensure perfection in the presentation of the sweet there was inevitably a delay and to fill the conversational gap I embarked on a detailed explanation of the '*flambée* drill' – namely that the first person to allow the flame to die had to kiss the most handsome partner on their left or right. This strained my schoolboy French to the limit and whilst I got the general theme across I was less confident about the details. In due course the omelette arrived, flaming splendidly. With due ceremony it was held aloft for all to admire, and then offered to the Attaché's wife. She gave me a look of uncertainty. '*Madame, c'est magnifique, n'est ce pas?*' I murmured. She took a deep breath, turned away and blew out the flame.

Instantly an enthusiastic young Steward switched all the lights out!

A Turkish Lieutenant Commander was appointed to my Staff. He was the only representative of his country at my Headquarters and I was therefore at some pains to ensure that he and his charming wife and young family moved straight into a Married Quarter – which presented no problem. In due course I sought confirmation from my Secretary that they were happily settled in.

'Oh yes, sir, they're fine. And quite happy except – all their ground floor windows have been broken.'

'Who on earth by' I asked.

'Don't really know, sir. Must be the local Greek community I suppose.'

'Local Greek community, in Ruislip? Nonsense. Tell the Security Officer to see me.'

The latter, a Royal Marines Captain, duly reported. 'I want you to send a small patrol out to this Married Quarter at random intervals at dusk over the next few nights with authority to take appropriate action with any baddies they come across. Keep me informed.'

'Very good, sir.'

Two nights later they caught five local yobbos red-handed. Taking them into the adjacent bushes they explained firmly the error of their ways and sent them packing. There was never any more trouble.

Soon afterwards I invited the Turkish couple to lunch, with a number of other people to keep them company. Mary was not up that week and I had paid little attention to the menus. The main course arrived. It was roast pork but fortunately covered with a thick sweet and sour sauce and with the crackling removed. The wife of my Turk was suspicious and looked enquiringly across the table at her husband. 'Oh my God,' I thought, 'what an appalling blunder. All the good I may have done by various little kindnesses will now be more than offset by this thoughtless insult.' The husband turned to the Petty Officer Steward who was handing out the joint.

'What is this?' he enquired gently.

Fortunately the splendid Petty Officer realized something was wrong. Quick as a flash he replied, 'Roast lamb, sir'.

The day was saved. Later they both had second helpings!

As a security measure it was decided to equip the Royal Marines Security Platoon with guard dogs. For this selected men were sent to a Dogs' Centre to learn the techniques of handling and become familiar with their animals. The course was not very arduous and the food was excellent. Three weeks later the plump, smiling newly qualified handlers returned to Northwood together with their lean and hungry dogs, kept that way deliberately. But this policy took no account of the warmhearted kindness of sailors towards animals. As the months passed so did tit-bits from the dining hall. By midsummer the position had been reversed: plump, happy, smiling dogs were to be seen towing their lean and hungry handlers about the Headquarters precincts.

Security was always a problem at Northwood. Being a well-to-do area close to London made it a tempting target for burglars. At Admiralty House at least one of the retinue was always at hand, day and night, as watchman.

One night we were dining out and returned at about midnight to learn that while we were away intruders had broken in. On duty at the time was Leading Steward Stephen Pottage, a delightful, tall young man in his early twenties. He had been watching TV in his sitting room at the back of the house when he thought he heard a noise in the main hall. On entering the hall he was surprised to find that all the lights had been switched out and soon became aware of three shadowy figures closing in on him. Keeping his back to the wall he moved to one side but then they were upon him. Two of them pinioned his arms and the third started punching him. This hurt and annoyed him and though not in the very best physical condition at the time he managed to free his right arm and delivered a powerful blow to his assailant's mouth. Whereupon the gang panicked and fled, leaving a breathless Pottage to dial 999.

While waiting for the police to arrive he experienced a stinging pain in the back of his right hand. By now the lights had been switched on again and on examination he found embedded in his knuckle what appeared to be one of the burglar's front teeth. This he duly handed over to the police. The latter hoped that by contacting all the dentists in the area during the next few weeks the intruder would seek treatment and they might nab him. Two weeks later exactly that happened.

This little tale has a still happier ending. At the time of writing Petty Officer Steward Pottage has just married a Petty Officer Wren. The service was taken by the Chaplain of the Fleet in St Anne's, Portsmouth, and was a fitting climax to the life of a loyal and brave man.

Arthur was a grey squirrel. He was the darling of both Cooks and Stewards at Admiralty House. Daily he would hop up onto the pantry windowsill and sit with a heartrending look of appeal and paws outstretched for goodies. Usually he was successful but occasionally the offerings from within did not match his criteria of quality and quantity. Arthur would then resort to the nearby dustbins where greater variety was usually to be found. Over the months he had developed the technique of prising up the plastic lid with one paw, and extracting the selected tit-bit with the other before making his getaway without himself getting trapped inside the bin.

One afternoon we were treated to a convincing display of Arthur's skill. At lunch the previous day the main course had been roast beef with the usual circular Yorkshire pudding. Today the Staff had been busy, Arthur had missed his breakfast and was hungry. Clearly the dustbin called. He was not disappointed: inside were several uneaten Yorkshires. Selecting the biggest he extricated it without difficulty and shortly afterwards was seen dribbling it down the drive like an expert footballer.

The foreign guests at that day's lunch were fascinated.

In June, 1977, as part of her Silver Jubilee celebrations, The Queen reviewed her Fleet at Spithead. This was a major event for which a great deal of organization and meticulous planning were needed. Spithead had been traditionally (though not invariably) the venue for such occasions. The ships and submarines were moored in long parallel lines and included vessels representing Foreign and Commonwealth Navies as well as our own Merchant Fleet.

I hoisted my flag in *Ark Royal*, the last of our Fixed Wing Carriers, commanded by Captain Ted Anson – himself a brilliant aviator. The programme was brisk: throughout the weekend I received and returned calls from the Flag Officers present and all Foreign and Commonwealth Commanding Officers. Since the weather was cold, windy and at times wet I treated my visitors to a glass of cognac in addition to the traditional cup of coffee. Clearly I could not survive level-pegging so by arrangement with my Chief Steward I was served with a revolting brew of cold tea, in a liqueur glass, the colour being carefully matched to that of the brandy. Each caller was allocated 20 minutes, starting with inspecting the Guard of Honour on the quarterdeck. After eight minutes my Flag Lieutenant (Jamie Miller, now a Commander) was briefed to come in and announce that the visitor's barge was alongside – which allowed just sufficient time for the last of the cognac to be swallowed, the visitors' book signed, presents exchanged and the guest escorted to the gangway with due ceremony. All went well until it was the turn of the Portugese Senior Officer who was late; indeed his barge was nowhere to be seen. The minutes sped by. The next-but-one caller, a Belgian Admiral running ahead of schedule, was already lying off waiting to be beckoned alongside. At last the Portuguese barge appeared under the quarter. The cox'n made a desperate plunge at the gangway, missed it and had to go round again. 13 minutes of the Portuguese slot had now gone. A very embarrassed Portuguese Commander clambered up the starboard ladder. There was time only to inspect the front rank of his guard, exchange a few pleasantries on deck, give him his framed presentation copy of the Review Chart and ease him over the side again.

The day before the Review was to be a full dress rehearsal. Accompanied by a small staff I went up and down the lines in the helicopter training ship *Engadine*, following the precise route and timing to be taken by the Royal Yacht *Britannia* next day and looking out for any shortcomings in appearance or errors in the drill of manning and cheering ship.

Soon after setting off we passed the *California*, the United States Navy's latest nuclear-powered cruiser, wearing the flag of Rear Admiral John Dixon (an old friend). She looked very smart indeed and had manned ship impeccably, but as we steamed past we were treated to a stony silence in the place of the customary three cheers. Instinct told me that this omission was not simply a slip in the drill and the thought occurred that perhaps it was not the practice to cheer ship in the United States Navy. Accordingly I made a personal signal to the American Admiral saying that if this was indeed so it was quite understood and I would see that the Queen was so informed; on the other hand I pointed out that *California* would then be the only ship in the entire Fleet which did not cheer. Dixon replied that they would cheer (though indeed it was not their custom to do so) and all was well on the day.

At the end of the line were the merchant ships, headed by the Shell training tanker *Opalia*. Freshly painted and shipshape she had manned ship smartly, if thinly, with her 35 Cadets and had clearly been at pains to get everything exactly right. Next astern was a BP Tanker, the *British Respect*; her appearance was anything but right. Evidently she had not been painted for some time and rust streaks stained her side throughout its length; she had not manned ship at all and the only sign of life as we passed were half a dozen crew in singlets lounging about the superstructure; there were no cheers. This posed a problem: the merchant ships were under my operational control for accuracy of berthing and ship safety in the event of bad weather, but they were not under my command for administrative matters. On return to my flagship I made a carefully worded signal which was taken across by boat to ensure its timely and accurate reception:

"LET DAD HAVE THEM, ALFIE—HE MISSES HIS OWN FLEET !"

27. More defence cuts impending.

28. A shrewdly perceptive parody on the well-known Players Navy Cut Cigarette Packet, originated by one of the Frigates, and widely circulated in Whitehall without much apparent effect.

29. The Admiralty Board — in session in the Admiralty Board Room, 1981. Keith Speed (Under Secretary of State for the Royal Navy) in the chair, then clockwise Arthur Hockaday (Second Permanent Under Secretary), Alan Pritchard (Deputy Under Secretary (Navy)), Tony Cragge (Head of Defence Secretariat 4, Secretary), John Charnley (Controller Scientific Establishments and Research), Admiral Sir Desmond Cassidi (Second Sea Lord), Vice Admiral Sir John Fieldhouse (Controller of the Navy), Vice Admiral Sir William Pillar (Chief of Fleet Support), Vice Admiral Sir William Staveley (Vice Chief of Naval Staff), the Author (First Sea Lord and Chief of Naval Staff).

'As a token of British respect, when the Queen passes tomorrow I hope you will man ship and give Her Majesty three cheers'.

No reply was received but the following evening over dinner I checked with the Queen that the ship had done her stuff; she had. Unfortunately somebody leaked my signal to the *Daily Express* who printed it in a tiny half-inch column at the foot of their front page. Two days later, back at my Headquarters, I received a vicious letter from the Managing Director of BP; in it he accused me of totally failing to comprehend the manning standards and operating characteristics of commercial tankers, ending with remonstrating for my having made such a signal. I replied briefly stating the facts and making it clear that I was simply trying to uphold the good name of BP and prevent a royal disgrace. Shortly afterwards I received a further letter from the Managing Director, this time full of apology and courteous thanks.

The Review itself went off as planned, marred only by the unseasonably cold and windy weather. That evening the Queen, accompanied by the Duke of Edinburgh and the Prince of Wales, honoured us by dining in *Ark Royal*. She arrived looking magnificent; the assembled Flag Officers were briefly presented and I led Her Majesty into my day cabin for a drink. There stood a selected smart young naval Steward with a carefully prepared dry martini on a silver salver (I had been at pains to find out that this was the Queen's usual choice at this time of day).

'Would you care for a drink, Ma'am?'

As briefed the Steward stepped forward. Her Majesty looked suspiciously at the proffered glass. 'What on earth is that?' she enquired.

'A dry martini, Ma'am, which I understood to be your preference.'

'It doesn't look like it to me.'

'Well would you care to try it, Ma'am, and if it is not to your taste we'll try to do better.'

Very gingerly, as if picking up a snake, the Queen grasped the glass, raised it doubtfully to her lips and took a sip. Then a radiant smile lit up her whole face.

'You're quite right,' she said. 'It is!'

Later we moved into the hangar for dinner. We sat down 250 strong – the full Admiralty Board together with every Flag and Commanding Officer (irrespective of rank) save the few necessarily absent on operational duty; it was a brave gathering.

I sat with the Queen on my right and the Prime Minister (Jim Callaghan) on my left. In the course of conversation with Her Majesty discussion turned to a comparison between *Ark Royal* and *Eagle*, the Navy's two biggest Carriers. I knew that the former had been launched by the Queen Mother but in a moment of mental aberration couldn't recall who had launched

Eagle (recently taken out of service and scrapped). I expounded on how *Eagle*, though much smarter in appearance both inside and out, had never seemed to develop quite the same esprit de corps as *Ark*, nor indeed the same level of efficiency and had suffered from a higher aircraft accident rate. Whereas *Ark*, despite her more careworn appearance, had always enjoyed a wonderful spirit and had a better operational record.

Gently but firmly the Queen remonstrated.

'Steady on, Admiral,' she exclaimed. 'You remember who launched the *Eagle*?'

Too late I realized that the Queen herself had done so. Nevertheless what I had said was factually correct and in guarded terms I said so. Her Majesty looked at me pensively.

'Yes,' she said, 'I suppose so. Mummy has green fingers and everything she touches grows.'

Wasn't that a charming way of putting it?

In 1978 the NATO Nuclear Planning Group met in Denmark. This top-level forum was composed of the Defence Ministers of the relevant countries accompanied by their Chiefs of Defence and political advisers; the NATO Ambassadors (Permanent Representatives) and Major NATO Commanders were in attendance.

On this occasion security was exceptionally tight. This was due in part to anxiety over controlling local anti-nuclear demonstrators who were particularly active at the time and in part to the recent kidnapping of Signor Aldo Moro, Prime Minister of Italy, by the Red Brigade. Armed Police and soldiers were everywhere and scrutiny of personal passes was frequent and strict.

The first morning's session passed uneventfully and we all adjourned for lunch. This was held in a nearby mock-Tudor restaurant where we sat round a huge horseshoe-shaped table. The fare was lavish and ample time had been allowed for its enjoyment. About half-way through the main course there occurred a noticeable reduction in the level of conversation. It was not exactly a hush but most people stopped talking and the few that continued did so in subdued tones. Shortly afterwards a member of the Italian delegation rose from the table and, with a face of abject gloom, left the room. The word was passed in a whisper from place to place: 'They've found Aldo Moro's body'.

One by one the rest of the Italians got up, some with tears trickling down their cheeks, and left. The whole room was charged with emotion and such conversation as was restarted was conducted desultorily and in hushed voices. General Al Haig (SACEUR) went outside to offer his personal aircraft to fly the Italian delegation immediately back to Rome. Shortly afterwards Admiral Ike Kidd (SACLANT), not to be outdone, left to make a similar offer. Admiral Henry Leach (CINCHAN – the third MNC) sat tight; he did not have a personal aircraft to offer.

Somewhat subdued, the delegates (less the Italians) re-assembled for the afternoon session. Last to enter the Conference Room was Secretary General Joe Luns. Settling his huge frame into his throne-like chair he crashed his gavel (also huge and highly ornamental) for silence. In sombre tones he announced the terrible fate of Aldo Moro, declared our shock at this outrage, and the deep sympathy of all nations represented to the Italian people and called for two minutes silence in tribute to the dead leader. We all sat with bowed heads as the leaden seconds dragged by.

Sitting immediately in front of me was Sir John Killick, UK Ambassador to NATO. Clever, highly experienced as a diplomat and with a puckish sense of fun he was one of those rare senior statesmen who had remained entirely devoid of pomposity. We had quickly become good friends. As the silence ended John turned round to me and with a wicked gleam in his eye muttered: 'I do hope they've found the right body'.

They had not. It was another three weeks before the real corpse of the unfortunate Aldo Moro was discovered.

By arrangement with the Danish Chief of Defence a visit to Greenland had been organized. This huge island situated partly in the northernmost part of the Atlantic and partly in the Arctic spans the mid-point between Europe and America and is of considerable strategic importance to sea and air operations in that region. Most maps show it as a deeply indented coastline with a narrow coastal fringe of soil; the whole of the centre is depicted as a white blank. And that is exactly what it is: a huge, impenetrable glacier covering thousands of square miles.

For some six months in the year, apart from the main US all-weather airfield at Sanderstromfjord half way up the West coast, the airstrips are closed to fixed wing traffic and only occasional short range hops by helicopters are possible when the weather permits. For the rest, movement, which is problematic at the best of times, is confined to the coastal strip where dog-drawn sledges can sometimes get through. The weather changes between extremes with great abruptness and often unpredictably. Brilliant sunshine with glassy calm can turn to a howling blizzard in a few hours. Like the land in which they live the inhabitants are charming but rugged; they have to be to survive the endless dark and bitter cold of the long winter months.

The plan was for me to fly from Northolt to Kinloss, pick up Air Vice Marshal Jock Kennedy, the Northern Maritime Air Commander, transfer to a Nimrod Long Range Maritime Patrol Aircraft, drop him off in Iceland and fly on to Narssarssuaq airstrip in the south-west of Greenland. The Nimrod would then return to Sanderstromfjord (where there were base facilities) while I embarked in a Danish frigate which would take me up the west coast to visit the Danish Resident Naval Officer's tiny Headquarters. After two days and a night in that area the frigate would bring me back to pick up the Nimrod for the return home. Timing was critical for two reasons: the availability at Greenland of the frigate; and on the day following my return to the UK the long-planned, first-ever visit to my Channel Command Headquarters of the entire NATO Council (Ambassadors) led by the Secretary General.

Everything went according to plan. I was warmly welcomed on board the Danish frigate, spent a happy night in her going up the coast and had an interesting time visiting the local Headquarters and looking round the neighbouring countryside. The weather was calm and sunny and I was able to make extensive use of the helicopter to get further afield. The Resident Naval Officer and his wife were charming hosts evidently delighted to receive such a visit which was a rare event. When the time came for me to go the little local base gave me a very friendly send off. The weather, which had been continually monitored throughout, remained unchanged and the forecast was good. The frigate sailed.

It had been two fairly long days and, full of fresh air, I turned in early. In the middle of the night I was roused by that familiar nudging shiver which comes from a ship flexing her hull in strong winds and a rising sea. I recognized it for what it was but since there was nothing I could do about it and we were well on our way I soon dropped off to sleep again. By daylight next morning the wind had increased greatly, a heavy sea was running and it was impossible for the frigate to go up the narrow fjord leading to Narssarssuaq.

Immediately my thoughts turned to the visit by the NATO Council to my Headquarters next day. The council is the highest authority in the Alliance. The occasion was unique, for they had never previously visited Northwood; the Ambassadors of all fifteen member nations were coming, led by the Secretary General. What would they think of the courtesy of one of their Major NATO Commanders if they arrived as invited at his Headquarters only to find that their host was away in Greenland 'on a swan' as they would critically interpret it? It took little imagination to realize that my international reputation would be destroyed for ever. Bitterly I cursed myself for not having allowed enough margin for the unforeseen. I *had* to get ashore somewhere. I strode to the bridge to put pressure on the Captain and his helicopter Flight Commander.

The wind, now 70 mph and frequently gusting to well above that, tunnelled down the narrow fjord boiling the sea and creating great turbulence in the air. The Flight Commander reckoned it was too hairy to fly up that fjord (the most direct route to the airstrip) but was prepared to risk it with a wide detour. Thankfully I accepted this and as soon as his helicopter was ready we lifted off. It was a daunting experience: the little Alouette aircraft was buffeted hither and thither and a glance at the icy raging cauldron below indicated a short survival time if we were forced to ditch. And they hadn't even provided us with Mae Wests! But he was a good pilot, clearly experienced in bad-weather flying and we made it. As we stepped out onto the airstrip the wind hit us like a physical blow and it took a real effort to lean hard against it to keep out footing.

The airstrip Manager, a charming Dane, collected us in his van and drove us to his nearby house where his wife had kindly laid on some sandwiches and coffee. They were a delightful couple who spoke good English.

'Cutting it a bit fine, aren't you?' suggested the Manager.

'Afraid so,' I replied, 'but if we can't get out today that's just too bad and we'll have to wait till tomorrow.'

'Some hope,' laughed the Manager. 'These winds normally last for about four days and this is our last operating day this season; tomorrow we close the Airstrip for six months!'

We discussed every conceivable escape route, but there was none until the wind moderated sufficiently for the Nimrod to pick us up; there were no aircraft stationed at the strip. Our hosts kindly lent us a couple of rooms and, still fully dressed in flying kit we lay down on our beds for a couple of hours and slept the sleep of the frustrated.

I awoke at about 1700. If anything the wind was stronger than ever, as indicated by a lone tree bent over at an angle of 45 degrees which I could see out of my window. The airstrip had no night operating facilities and closed at 1800 with the onset of dusk. I lay on my bed mentally drafting explanatory signals to the NATO Council, each beginning with phrases like 'I deeply regret . . .'

At 1730 there came a gleam of hope. A helicopter was approaching for an emergency landing having almost run out of fuel. There was a chance that this might take us to Sanderstromfjord and thus connect with the Nimrod. But the aircraft almost crash-landed and the pilot was adamant that conditions were unsuitable for any further helicopter flying that evening. It seemed the last chance had now gone.

Then, with only 10 minutes to go before the airstrip shut down, a light executive jet en route to Denmark via Iceland from America signalled it was low on fuel; the pilot had expected a tail wind but it turned out to be a strong headwind. Hurriedly I got hold of the Airstrip Manager and tried to persuade him to drive us out to the aircraft when it landed but to refuse fuel unless the pilot would take us on to Iceland. The Manager's nerve cracked at this point and he declined to have anything more to do with us. However, he did allow us to use his van. Quickly my Flag Lieutenant and I jumped in and sped off across the apron to where the incoming HS125 was taxiing to a halt. With a screech of tyres we drew up alongside it, leapt out and stood either side of the aircraft's door. As the three occupants emerged we took each firmly by the arm and ushered him into the waiting van. Then we slammed the door and stated our terms: not a drop of fuel unless they agreed to fly us to Iceland. The crew consisted of the Danish pilot and engineer and their American pilot-instructor; the aircraft was being delivered to a Copenhagen firm. They were three to two and bigger than us so it was fortunate that they readily fell in with our suggestion and no resort to threats or rough stuff was necessary. We fuelled, bid a grateful farewell to the manager and took off for Reykjavik. The aircrew even managed to contrive a bite of supper and we quickly became good friends.

We landed at Reykjavik at 0100, crossed by car to the US Air Force base where the Nimrod was waiting and took off for the UK. By switching our destination from Kinloss to Brize Norton I was able to get back to my Headquarters by 0830 – with just time for either a bath or breakfast but not both – before setting off back to Brize Norton to meet the NATO Council. For once I missed my breakfast.

Later, over lunch, I was able to tease my distinguished guests by expressing doubt that they had ever before sat down at table with a common hijacker. They were rather surprised.

When the Aswan Dam was completed the economic necessity of irrigating the Nile Valley as soon as possible overrode the cultural desirability of re-siting various ancient treasures before flooding up. In consequence the Temple of Caesar Augustus was deliberately submerged. The Egyptian Navy was then tasked with the recovery of this historic building and their divers set to work. The undertaking was a formidable one and it was not long before the Egyptians sought help from the Royal Navy.

The Lieutenant Commander in charge of the RN Diving Team came to see me at Northwood before departure and although the chances seemed negligible at the time I promised to visit them on the job if I could. A few months later I found I could just fit in a flying visit en route to Oman and India, so off I went.

It was not the most comfortable of itineries in that my Flag Lieutenant and I did not land at Cairo until 0400 and we had to be up again one hour later to check in for the local flight to Aswan at 0600. To the evident consternation of the nice Egyptian Commodore who was hosting us, nobody could find the aircraft and the righteous impatience of a strong party of professional American tourists (sixtyish, plump, rimless spectacles and dedicated to putting a tick in the 'I've seen Aswan' box) hardly bolstered his national pride. In desperation we walked out on to the apron and strolled from aircraft to aircraft asking any pilot we could find if he was going to Aswan. Eventually we found one who was; the time was then 0900.

The flight over the desert was interesting and full of stark contrasts. The lushness in the vicinity of the Nile, almost unreal in the richness of its green, faded abruptly to the endless arid waste. And here and there the featureless sea of sand would be pierced by a rocky outcrop as if thrown up by a giant earthworm. Perhaps the most dominating feature was the Temple of Abu-Simbel looking proudly down from its position of splendid isolation.

By comparison Aswan was a delightful oasis. Here were water and flowers and life. We found the divers, British and Egyptian, in the tourist hotel in which they were accommodated and joined them for lunch. All wore track-suits without badges of rank. The language problem was overcome by the totally friendly atmosphere in which they lived and worked and by their shared professionalism. As an example of genuine international co-operation it was unsurpassed.

Afterwards we visited the site and spent some time watching the progress of work. The depth of water was about 30 feet and presented the least of the problems. But the silting and mud, inevitably stirred up by underwater movement, hampered visibility in an operation which quickly became dangerous if not conducted with care and precision. The blocks of stone weighed half a ton and each had to be lifted separately by means of a wire strop passed round its exact centre of gravity and firmly secured so that the block itself did not tilt and slip. Lifting was achieved by a crane lighter, moored alongside which was the headquarters craft – a remarkable museum piece left behind by the Russians when building the dam. Built as a tug in the 1890's it was stoutly constructed, coal-burning, so slow as to be almost unmanoeuvrable, and in defiance of contemporary design belched thick black smoke incessantly from its tall, bell-mouthed funnel. It was hot, filthy and uncomfortable but it worked – just. Anyway nothing else was available. Once lifted, the blocks were taken ashore and laid out in careful numbered sequence in a 14-acre field. Subsequent reconstruction on a nearby site had already been started.

Back in Cairo next day I was given a splendid farewell lunch by my friend the Commodore. It was held in the Meridian Hotel and was one of the most lavish I have ever experienced, ending with woodcocks' thighs. All this took a considerable time and I became increasingly anxious that we would miss our flight and thereby cause a diplomatic discourtesy in Oman where we were due that evening. Cairo airport was in the suburbs at the far side of this busy city where streets were notorious for traffic congestion; the Commodore did not share my anxiety. 'Is all right,' he said, adding that he had a very good driver and the police would help. The prospect of a police escort was comforting and I relaxed. But finally we really did run out of time, cut the coffee stage and left.

The driver proved to be a huge Army Sergeant weighing at least 18 stone. The car was a powerful one with automatic transmission and he drove it with verve. With his left elbow out of the open window and hand lightly on the wheel, right hand almost permanently on the horn, right foot on the throttle and left on the brake, he quickly demonstrated that he was an experienced disciple of the Stop/Go Cult – mainly Go. In Egypt they do not practise the derisory two-finger salute fashionable in Great Britain, they raise a loosely clenched fist; otherwise the degree of insult is similar. Sergeant Ahmed was well versed in the law of Cairo's traffic jungle. His left forearm quickly became permanently raised in the clenched fist gesture leaving his right arm to continue operating the horn while releasing, if necessary, from time to time, a few fingers to apply to the wheel.

I shall never forget that journey. With a fixed ghastly grin of pure terror on my face I endeavoured to keep up conversation with the Commodore while we hurtled towards the airport. Cars, taxis, buses, lorries all shrieked their protest at us, verbally and on the horn. Sergeant Ahmed responded almost caressingly with his raised fist. Lights meant nothing, we shot across them all leaving behind a trail of fury and last-minute braking. Even with a police escort of outriders our progress would have been remarkable; but we did not have one.

Hot and shaking we screeched to a halt at the airport in a spectacular cloud of dust and gravel. Take-off was delayed by three hours.

The summer of 1979 saw the closing operational weeks of *Ark Royal*, the last of the Royal Navy's fixed wing Carriers. I was determined to take leave of the old lady while she was still a fully running ship and not be merely one of the many hundreds standing on the jetty with nostalgic tears trickling down my cheeks watching her final berthing at Devonport. I put the Staff on to arranging this with her Captain accordingly. I knew Ted Anson well. Short, sharp and inscrutable, he never allowed himself to get ruffled by events, however formidable, and always tempered his actions with sound common sense. Himself a dedicated fixed wing pilot, there was little he did not know about operating aircraft from the deck. Behind his rather deadpan exterior lay a warm feeling for people and a delightfully wry sense of humour. I liked him.

When my draft programme arrived it was a disaster. It contained nothing but visits to various parts of the ship, witnessing flying operations, etc; all very pedestrian and more appropriate to an elderly politician than to a Fleet Commander interested in flying. The Staff were summoned. 'Get back to *Ark*,' I instructed, 'and tell them this won't do at all. I'm happy to visit what they suggest but places like the Galley and Machinery Compartments can be done by night. Tell them I want personally to fly with every one of their embarked squadrons, including the SAR (Air Sea Rescue) Flight, and especially to be catapulted in a Phantom which I have not yet done.'

In due course an amended programme was received. It picked up all my points except the Phantom sortie which remained conspicuous by its absence. Clearly there was some reason for this further hiccup and I put my Flag Lieutenant on to finding out what it was. The answer was not hard to discover: the ship thought that I had never undergone 'wet parachute dragging drill' – how to extricate yourself from your parachute harness after you have ejected and ditched in the sea – and were reluctant to catapult me in a Phantom without this knowledge. They were dead right. 'Very well,' I said, 'arrange for me to do this training at Yeovilton and inform *Ark* that this is happening.' A few weeks later to Yeovilton I went.

The Safety Equipment Officer at Yeovilton was an old friend who had been with me in *Albion*. He was an understanding man and I knew I was in good hands. This afforded me some relief as I was rather apprehensive about the whole undertaking. They dressed me in flying gear, complete with parachute harness, and led me to their large swimming pool. There they secured a rope to the back of my parachute harness and invited me to mount the high diving board and stand with my back to the pool below. The other end of the rope was taken by a Physical Training Instructor to the opposite end of the pool.

'Sing out when you're ready, sir,' they said cheerfully, 'and the PTI will pull you backwards into the pool and will go on pulling to simulate the dragging effect of the parachute filled with surface wind. You'll find its quite easy. When you hit the water just spread your legs and arms out wide and you'll find the dragging action will get you up on the surface "on a step" like a boat planing. Once there you can release your harness at your leisure and swim to the side.' (I should add here that to release the harness involved the removal of split-pins from the catches on either side of one's chest, inserting one's fingers under the lip of each spring-loaded catch and pushing first up and then down on the respective catches – which then fall apart.)

Experts always make things sound so easy. With increasing doubts on my wisdom in torturing myself like this I climbed to the high board. Being a very poor swimmer I had never ventured thus far before and it really did seem rather high. Then, facing away from the pool and feeling extremely exposed I signified that I was ready. I was starting to take a deep breath when the rope jerked me backwards, I thumped into the water and went under. As directed I spread out my arms and legs and to my great surprise it worked; I planed up to the surface. Once there with my head above water there was no problem. Out split pin, up with the upper release catches, down with the lower ones and I was free. It took but a few strokes to reach the side of the pool and climb out. I'd done it – and was frightfully pleased with myself. My former anxieties vanished; it was really quite simple.

'Well done, sir,' exclaimed my tormentors, 'that was fine. But now you must do it again using only one arm, simulating having lost the other one when you ejected. Which arm have you lost, sir?' My exuberance evaporated slightly, but after all it *had* been pretty easy and I was sure that I could handle it again. 'I'll only give you a very gentle tug, sir,' said the PTI helpfully and like an ass I failed to spot the fallacy in his well-intentioned promise.

On to the high board again. Signal ready. Don't bother about the deep breath; you'll soon be back on the surface. Topple over backwards. Smack onto the water. Down, down, spread legs and arms. Down, down, down. It's not working this time – that bloody PTI and his 'gentle pull'. Oh why hadn't I taken a deeper breath. Down, down, down. This is too much – I must have air – I'm *drowning*. To hell with the rules, try to get a hand above the surface to indicate I'm in trouble. Too late, too deep, too deep. *Must* breathe, only water, choking and struggling, getting darker, is this the end? What a way to go; what will Mary think of me, and the girls, and the rest of the Navy? Start to come up, break surface, gulp down air and choke again but it's *air* not that cursed water. Someone is pulling me to the side of the pool; it's the diver they have put in to yank me out – just in time. I slither onto the paving slabs alternatively gasping air and spewing water.

'What happened, sir?' they asked. 'You seemed to be in difficulties.'

'Yes,' I replied weakly as soon as I could speak. 'I was – you very nearly drowned your C-in-C.'

The subsequent Phantom sortie from *Ark Royal*'s deck was child's play in comparison.

16

THE BIG FRONT DOOR

'I cleaned the windows and I swept the floor
And I polished up the handle of the big front door.
I polished up that handle so successfully
That now I am the Ruler of the Queen's Navee.'

Sir W. S. Gilbert.

In July, 1979, I took over from Terry Lewin as First Sea Lord and Chief of
Naval Staff. The prospect was exhilarating rather than daunting; the years I
had previously spent in the Admiralty and Ministry of Defence had long
since expunged any traces of apprehension which Whitehall might hold for
the uninitiated. I already enjoyed a very good relationship with all my
Admiralty Board colleagues and the same went for a large cross-section of
the senior Civil Servants and Scientists in the defence field. Thus I could
reasonably look forward to my last command – that of the whole Navy – as
likely to be one of unstinted pleasure. True there would be problems, life
would be dull without them, but in general the way ahead seemed set fair.
Events were to turn out very differently.

At that time the position of First Sea Lord was unequivocal: he was the
professional head of the Royal Navy and ultimately carried the responsibility
for everything to do with his Service. His relationship with other uniformed
members of the Admiralty Board was not unlike that of Chairman of a Board
of Directors though he had the power (rarely needed) to override if necessary.
The head Civil Servant within the Navy Department was at Deputy Secretary
level and was mirrored on the scientific side by the Chief Scientist (RN).
The full Admiralty Board was normally chaired by a junior politician below
cabinet rank – the Under Secretary of State for the Royal Navy. It goes
without saying that such an arrangement called for the closest co-operation
between all Board members, whether uniformed or not; this never presented
a problem in my time.

Within the Ministry of Defence relations between the Services depended,
as ever, very largely on the personalities of the respective Chiefs of Staff.
Basically they were good but when cuts in the defence budget loomed
responsible attitudes tended to be subsumed by parochial abrasiveness and

the philosophy of 'fighting one's own corner'. It has to be said that the Air Force Department was particularly adept at this. Within Whitehall the role of Chief of the Defence Staff (CDS) was analogous to that of a Unified Commander in the field: he was the primus inter pares and carried an extra star in rank to facilitate this. It fell to him to co-ordinate the views of the Chiefs of Staff, whose Committee he chaired, and whenever possible present an agreed opinion to the Secretary of State. If, after very reasonable attempt to obtain an agreed solution, this was not achieved it was usually preferable to present the Secretary of State with a split view rather than with a fluffy compromise – a precept which was not always followed.

CDS's task was not an easy one and called for a powerful mixture of firmness and tact, at times in the face of blinkered obstinacy. The Chiefs of Staff normally did a tour of about three years and CDS rotated in turn between the three Services.

At the political level the Secretary of State was supported by one Minister of State and three Under Secretaries of State, one for each of the Services. Serving as a link between the political and the military and bridging any potential gap between them was the Defence Secretariat headed by the Permanent Secretary (PUS) and several Deputy Secretaries (DUS), of which the two featuring most prominently were DUS (Policy) and DUS (Finance and Budget). In practice and given proper handling at the lower levels, gaps of significance rarely occurred. Where the staffwork was inept or was by-passed, or the divergence of view was fundamental, the gap was probably unbridgeable anyway.

The whole system was stable and well proven in circumstances of both peace and crisis. It worked well but this was not enough to save it from arbitrary and radical upheaval, to which I shall return.

Over the years immediately preceding 1979 the pay of the Armed Forces had progressively fallen behind that in other public sectors. Despite repeated representations at the highest level the former Labour Administration found it all too difficult and constantly turned a blind eye on the problem. The stage had been reached when officers and men were 'voting with their feet' – leaving prematurely or failing to re-engage. Recruiting was poor and dissatisfaction at all levels was widespread. Had such a situation arisen 70 years before it would have led to mass mutinies throughout the Services. But by now the quality of Service people, and their education, rendered them too sensible for that sort of action; it was easier simply to go – and they did. During the run up to the 1979 General Election the Conservative Opposition pledged that if they were elected to office they would quickly and properly redress this sorry state of affairs. They were as good as their word and within two months of taking over the Government they had implemented a comprehensive and fair adjustment to Service pay.

By any standard this was a remarkable performance and it stopped the rot in the nick of time.

Thus by the summer of 1979 the sun shone and there was hardly a cloud on the horizon. But not for nothing does Great Britain enjoy the reputation for her weather being changeable.

In the autumn I attended a NATO Commanders' Conference at Newport, Rhode Island. The setting was new to me and I found it fascinating if rather depressing. On land every quarter of a mile or so was a huge Victorian mansion of massive construction, full of fancy cupolas, towers and castellation – but almost all empty. In contrast the waterfront was packed with the floating real estate of the late seventies: large luxury yachts of untold gadgetry and smartness, some of which occasionally put to sea, but full of life and laughter.

The conference itself was unspectacular and followed a routine pattern. Its finale was scheduled to be a grand banquet on the Thursday night and next day everyone would disperse and return home. Because I had previously undertaken to be the Guest of Honour at the Gunnery Reunion Dinner at Whale Island on the Friday evening, I planned to cut the banquet and fly back from Boston that night so allowing what I thought was a reasonable margin for error. Fate deemed differently.

Having said my farewells I left Rhode Island and drove with my Naval Assistant, Captain John Coward, to Boston. The British Airways flight on which we had booked was delayed by half an hour and would now take off at 2130 – a minor but irrelevant irritation. In due course we boarded and taxied out to the runway; the engines were run up and then we aborted because one engine had failed to develop full power. So back to the apron, disembark, wait hopefully to be called forward, taxi out to the runway, run up the engine and – abort again. By the end of the third performance of this sort it was midnight, Boston Airport had closed and we were informed that there would be no further flight out to UK until late next morning. The two British Airways officials (by now the only sign of life in the entire airport), tired after a long day, found it all too much and simply gave up; the milling crowd of equally tired and more frustrated passengers was left to find telephones and make such alternative arrangements as it could on their own. It was chaotic.

John Coward and I took stock quickly. There was no way in which we could catch up the programme unless we flew out early next morning – that morning. There was no such flight from Boston. The nearest alternative was New York. In a Concorde we could still do it. Penetrating the now-deserted back regions we contacted New York by telephone and teleprinter to discover that there was no eastbound Concorde flight on a Friday, but the next best thing was a PANAM flight due to take off at 0930. In the course of booking that all communication failed and we were left uncertain of success and increasingly desperate for transport to get us to New York in time.

By now four others similarly placed had joined us. A taxi was ordered and on its arrival we all piled into a large estate car and set off. I made a dive for the back corner seat and got it, the others tumbling in afterwards. Last in was a man with an ashen face, rolling eyes, drooling mouth, sweat pouring down his cheeks (it was very cold). He was I think a drug addict suffering from withdrawal symptoms. He squeezed into a corner and apparently died. We set off. By now it was 0200, the air conditioning was not working and we were all pretty tired. Fug and fatigue combined to put us out for an hour or two when we were roused by the cab stopping to fill up at a gas station. It was a brilliant, frosty, starlit night with a full moon turning it almost into day. We overheard an interesting exchange between our driver and the attendant.

'Say, is this right for New York City?'

'No, sir, you're heading straight for Cleveland, Ohio.'

There are occasions when intervention has to be swift and ruthless. Clearly this was one. Basic guidance on the nearest north/south freeway was hurriedly extracted from the attendant. Someone produced a school atlas from his brief case and with the aid of this and the moon we navigated the driver (a nice man who quickly responded to the sporting exhortations of his passengers) towards our proper destination.

'Drive,' we told him. 'Drive hard. We'll help guide you. We *have* to be at the airport by 0900. We'd like to get there alive but don't fuss too much about that. Just *get* there.'

'OK, boss,' he replied cheerfully. And drive he did.

It was a nightmare journey and the person I envied most was the drug fiend who was oblivious to its finer points. As daylight dawned the traffic thickened and so did the risk factor. We made the airport at 0915.

For a time our luck held. All our luggage was still in the British Airways aircraft at Boston and there was nothing we could do about that. A PANAM official met us, hustled us through to the 'plane and half an hour later we took off. Out over the Atlantic the pilot informed us that conditions were good and our estimated time of arrival would be about an hour earlier than we had expected; our spirits rose. But a couple of hours later he came on the air again and said he'd got it wrong – we would now be about an hour *later* than scheduled. John Coward and I discussed whether to try to get a signal through to my office in the Ministry of Defence or whether to leave the system to pick up the bits and do what they could. We decided on the latter.

We landed at Heathrow at 2030. (By now they would have been dining for half an hour but I might still catch up the speeches.) A RAF car whisked me across to the other end of the airport and I boarded a naval helicopter. In the cabin was my full mess kit together with the regalia of the CDS (mine being in the stranded aircraft). During the flight to Lee-on-Solent I managed to change into ball dress despite the fact that the internal lights had failed. Waiting at Lee was the Commander-in-Chief, Naval Home Command's car which took me round to Whale Island. As I flung open the double doors of the Wardroom and slipped into my place on the President's right the clock struck 2200. The tables had just been cleared and the port was about to be passed.

For a moment my entry went unnoticed; then they all stood up and cheered.

March, 1981, was notable for an official visit to the Spanish Navy. This was particularly important in view of Spain's imminent entry into the EEC and NATO. Captain José Aldama, the Spanish Naval Attaché in London, accompanied me. A charming Naval Officer of the old school, I had got to know him quite well. The usual pattern of calls, discussions and social events was well organized but unexceptional, as was a tour of their main submarine base. There were, however, two particular highlights: a visit to their Infanteria de Marina (Marines) at Cadiz; and one to the Carrier *Dedalo* operating at sea off Cape Trafalgar.

For the former I had asked that no formal Guard of Honour be paraded but that I should be allowed to go round units performing their normal training or exercise tasks and talk with them informally. For the latter, having been told that the ship was equipped with Sea King helicopters (with which I was familar) I had asked that I should be allowed to fly myself out to the Carrier, from the left-hand seat.

The day dawned bright and hot. Drawn up on the huge parade ground at the Marine Headquarters was, as requested, no ceremonial guard but the entire Brigade of the Infanteria de Marina. Dressed in full battle order, blackened faces, weapons and the lot. After inspecting this formidable array I walked round the various groups which had split up into smaller numbers for weapon demonstrations. There followed an impressive Drive Past the saluting base by all the vehicles and finally a Double Past by the full Brigade at a brisk run. It was a memorable morning and somehow the whole atmosphere was steeped in a degree of personal intimacy which was remarkable.

And so a short walk through the New Entry Naval Training Establishment to the pad on which were two helicopters with rotors running. But neither was a Sea King. In vain I scanned the aircraft for some familiar feature which would enable me to identify the type. I found none. We reached the leading aircraft and without ceremony I was firmly ushered into the back.

This was a bitter disappointment. I had been looking forward to doing a bit of flying again and was determined not to forego the opportunity without a struggle. Summoning the unfortunate José I looked at him coldly and said,

'What is this? You told me you had arranged for me to fly in the left-hand seat'.

He got the message. With immediate effect the Second Pilot was told to vacate his seat and I started settling in in his place. The seat-belt arrangement was of the old-fashioned webbing type where you had to feed the end of one through a loop in the end of another and so on to a central point. It is a cumbersome method and it took me a little time to remember the drill and get fastened in. Meanwhile I searched the instrument panel for some clue as to the aircraft type – but without success.

Throughout the performance the First Pilot sat slumped in his seat. An elderly man with white hair, he looked bored and seemed disinclined to communicate. Having located the torquemeter and other essential instruments I enquired about the height, heading and clearance for take-off. His replies though monosyllabic indicated that he spoke good English. Gingerly I lifted off, got the aircraft sorted out and we were on our way.

After we had climbed to height and settled on course I had time to search again for some clue as to the type of aircraft, but again without result. 'To hell with this,' I thought and turning to the First Pilot casually asked, 'By the way, what aircraft type is this?'

'Bell 212, Sir,' he replied.

I recalled having made a brief 20-minute sortie in a Bell 212 in Oman some five years previously. (This had been a great privilege in that they only had three such aircraft in the whole country, recently delivered, and were understandably concerned lest I bent it!)

We flew on in silence for several minutes. Then, 'How many hours do you have on this type, Sir,' enquired the First Pilot.

'About 20 minutes,' I replied honestly.

Clearly this reply made a considerable impact. The First Pilot lit a cigarette to steady his nerves and chain-smoked for the rest of the sortie. This loosened his tongue and we chatted happily from then on.

Came the time when we should have rendezvoused with the Carrier but despite the excellent visibility there was no sign of the ship. Nor was there any communication with her. 40 minutes later, when we were beginning to pay rather closer attention to our fuel state, we made contact and in due course I landed on without incident.

The Spanish Carrier Admiral was a charming man who gave me the warmest of welcomes and took me up to his Bridge. He was very tickled that I had flown the aircraft myself and still more so when (against the return flight) I drank the orange juice intended for the First Pilot and the latter quaffed the champagne intended for me.

A junior Indian defence Minister was paying an official visit to the UK. He was accompanied by a small entourage of which the Vice Chief of the Indian Naval Staff (V.C.N.S. – a Vice Admiral) was the senior adviser. Their five-day programme followed the usual pattern of briefings, tours and social events. To help out I offered to give the party lunch on Tuesday, despite it being the normal day for our weekly routine Chiefs of Staff meeting.

It was evident that the timing was going to be tight. The visitor's forenoon schedule did not end until 1300 which left me a bare hour in which to entertain them before having to leave for my meeting. Accordingly I briefed my Chief Steward that whenever I pressed the buzzer for the end of a course he and his splendid team were to remove the old plates and serve the next course as quickly as possible. My wife not being up in London that week, I also chose the menu with particular care so as to be compatible with Indian tastes: egg mayonnaise, fricassee of chicken, fruit salad – safe as a house I thought. From the outset things started to go wrong. My visitors were more than 20 minutes late in arriving. They were hot and thirsty after their morning's activites and badly needed a drink (orange squash). As soon as I decently could I hustled them into the dining room and with the Minister opposite me and the Vice Chief by my side we sat down to lunch. Quickly I became absorbed in conversation with V.C.N.S. who was an old friend and having finished our entree I glanced towards the Minister to see how he was getting on. He wasn't. The wretched man hadn't even picked up his knife and fork, let alone started eating. Desperate, and supposing he disliked or perhaps was allergic to eggs, I learn across the table and asked if he would prefer something else.

'A piece of fruit,' he replied 'and perhaps a little cheese'.

Without thinking I pressed the buzzer. Instantly the door burst open and the Chief Steward and others descending on us like locusts started to whisk away the plates – as briefed.

'Stop,' I said and, summoning the Chief Steward to my side, 'The Minister does not care for eggs. I'm sure you can rustle up an apple or something and a bit of cheese. But hurry.' He disappeared, together with his team. A short time later he returned carrying a dinner plate on which were the largest, greenest cooking apple I have ever seen and a huge hunk of mousetrap (cheddar) cheese. Placing them before the Minister he withdrew. The man gazed at this latest offering with a mixture of incredulity and dismay and diffidently started to peel the apple.

The time was now past 1400 and in less than twenty minutes I would *have* to leave for my meeting. I had no alternative but to press the buzzer and get on with the next course. In came the Stewards again, the plates were quickly changed and the chicken handed round. No more problems I thought and resumed my talk with the Vice Chief.

Not so. Having been handed the fricassee of chicken the Minister remained poised irresolutely with his spoon and fork hovering over the dish. Firmly I caught his unhappy eye.

'What is this please?' he enquired.

'Fricassee of chicken, Minister.'

'I am sorry, I cannot touch the sauce.'

'Would you like some chicken without the sauce?'

'No, No. It might have been contaminated.'

I saw little point in taking the issue further, engaged the Minister in animated conversation and awaited the arrival of the fruit salad with resigned interest. He ate it in suspicious silence.

It transpired that the Minister was a strict vegetarian. This would have presented no problem if only I had known, but no one had had the sense to say so beforehand.

There are some days when you just can't win.

Francis Pym was a charming man but not perhaps the strongest ever Defence Secretary. Small decisions were an irritating inconvenience to him; big ones were more difficult and he preferred to avoid them. Thus it was not surprising that Frank Cooper, the Permanent Secretary and intellectually a much more powerful personality, seized the initiative and resuscitated the Defence Council. This forum embraced all Ministers in the department, the top Civil Servants and Scientists and the Service Chiefs. As such it was too big and amorphous to decide anything of substance; for years it had been moribund and never convened. It was chaired by the Secretary of State for Defence himself but the agenda were skilfully devised by the Permanent Secretary who de facto ran the meetings. The skill lay in selecting matters which needed resolution by decision but which were of so little consequence as not really to matter whichever way the decision went. The meetings were a fatuous waste of time but helped some people to feel important. They exemplified bureaucracy at its worst.

In 1980 there were mumblings of defence cuts and even of a defence review. Over recent years this had been a recurring theme in Whitehall and most had become hardened to it. Pym did indeed initiate a sort of mini-defence review and it was generally supposed that he was under instructions to do so. But as the consequences of significant cuts and the weight of decisions to implement them became evident so too did the assessment that to carry them through would make no political, military or economic sense;

the exercise fizzled and became subsumed into the routine annual Long Term Costing.

Nevertheless two things emerged which were to have profound effects on the future of defence. The first was that Pym himself became finally convinced that his department had reached the lowest acceptable plateau and that no further savings could responsibly be made. This view which he expressed in Cabinet with sincerity and courage was to hasten his replacement and sideways shift to Leadership of the House.

The second was the embargo, imposed by Pym, on any Serving Officer whether inside or outside the Ministry of Defence, having contact with the media without Ministerial approval (which was rarely given). This was designed to stop the exposure of politically unpalatable truths. That senior Service officers were generally more experienced at handling the media than Ministers was discounted. Prior to this it had been the practice for the Service Vice Chiefs to hold unattributable press briefings, at which representatives of other elements of the media were welcome, about every four months. At them the necessary taboos on sensitive subjects like Intelligence or the finer points concerning the strategic nuclear deterrent were respected by the media; a Vice Chief only had to say, 'I may not answer that,' and the questioner would realize he had gone too far and drop it. In this way the media were kept as fully informed as responsible security permitted and over the years a good relationship had been built up to the mutual advantage of both media and defence. Now all this was stopped and by the time of the Falklands War only two years later the relationship had degenerated into positive distrust. Starved of facts the media speculated (they had no alternative) and on occasion the result was wildy inaccurate. Personally I largely ignored the embargo and the only reason I was not sacked is because if I had been the whole truth would have been exposed instead of only small parts of it.

This then was the situation in the closing days of 1980. In the Ministry of Defence there was a certain edginess abroad but on the whole the more important programmes had survived. Francis Pym, convinced now of the imprudence of further defence cuts, was (just) holding his corner in Cabinet with some effect. At which point it was announced that Nott (from Trade) would replace Pym early in the new year.

'What do you think of the impending change of Secretary of State, Sir?' asked Brian Brown my excellent Secretary (later to become the first non-Seaman Officer to hold with distinction the high office of Second Sea Lord).

'Well,' I replied, 'at present we have a charming man but one to whom decision-making does not seem to come easily. I know nothing about Nott but it must be a change for the better.'

How wrong I was. Over the months to come Nott took a number of major decisions and I was to find that I disagreed professionally with nearly every one of them.

January, 1981, saw the start of increasing unease and uncertainty within the Ministry. Nott assumed office with preconceived ideas that the Navy needed to be cut back, the Air Force needed to be built up and the Army was about right. The origin of these preconceptions was never discovered but they persisted throughout the usual round of initial briefings – in which many questions were asked but scant heed paid to the answers – and beyond. Soon afterwards the new Defence Secretary wisely paid a lightning visit to Washington to meet his United States opposite number. It was while returning from that trip, on a wet Sunday afternoon in Bermuda without proper professional advice available, that the main milestones of what was to become the notorious 1981 Defence Review were sketched out.

It is not my purpose in this book to elaborate on the remarkable way in which this review was conducted. At the time throughout Whitehall there was an overriding obsession about money. Public spending had to be drastically cut and how this was achieved was of relatively little concern. The upshot was that the Royal Navy's budget was slashed by more than twice that of the Army's and by more than seven times that of the Royal Air Force. In addition the Navy was saddled with almost the entire cost of Trident, the national strategic nuclear deterrent planned to replace Polaris in due course. Apart from losing between one quarter and one third of its manpower and a number of shore support and training facilities, naval cuts included the reduction in destroyers/frigates (the backbone of the Fleet) from the middle sixties to the low forties, the sale of the new Anti-Submarine Warfare Carrier *Invincible* to Australia at a bargain basement offer, the disposal of the two Assault Ships *Fearless* and *Intrepid* and the final withdrawal and disposal of the Ice Patrol Ship *Endurance*. It is sad to reflect that it took the Falklands War, barely a year later, with all its horrors of destruction, mutilation and loss of life to restore some sanity and balance to defence.

Top of the list in the Bermudagram (as the initial parameters of the Defence Review were irreverently termed) were the disposal of the Assault Ships. John Nott seemed to have difficulty in grasping the significance of surface ships and from the beginning set his mind against them. In this he received some support from the Chief Scientific Adviser (Ron Mason), a clever physicist, lacking practical experience, who concentrated his thinking on the scenario that the maritime element of the next war would be fought by maritime patrol aircraft and nuclear-powered submarines. The wisdom of both these views was to be tempered by the Falklands War.

Accordingly measures were set in hand to arrange for the Defence

Secretary to spend a day at sea in *Fearless* so that he could see for himself the versatility which this ship had to offer. The gambit was successful: the sun shone, the calm sea sparkled, the ship pulled out all the stops to show off her multiple capabilities. The Defence Secretary was converted, stormed back to Whitehall and forthwith sent me a short note enquiring, 'Who is behind this absurd notion of scrapping the Assault Ships?' The reply was even shorter: 'You'. Both ships were saved.

Invincible, however, was a different matter altogether. At a unit production cost of £175m she was brand new and had successfully completed extensive sea trials which had ironed all the bugs out of her systems. She had been operational for barely a year but even in that time had demonstrated her capability beyond her designers' and the Naval Staffs' most optimistic hopes. In a recent exercise her Sea Harriers had achieved more intercepts than the United States Navy's F4 Phantoms. Overall her capabilities within a single hull of that size were uniquely cost effective and I was determined to keep her and her two sister ships *Illustrious* and *Ark Royal*, still building. This would enable the Navy to operate two Anti-Submarine-Warfare Carriers for most of the time while the third was in refit or reserve.

The wrangle was protracted and lasted over some months. During it an Australian delegation came over to discuss terms, headed by their defence Secretary and including David Leach (no relation, but a good friend) whom I had taken through his Sub-Lieutenant's Gunnery Course at Whale Island in 1948. It was a Gilbertian situation. After lunch in Admiralty House we repaired to the Secretary of State's office and took our places on opposite sides of the table. Once seated, John Nott turned to me.

'CNS, would you like to explain the position?' This was ridiculous but if he wanted it that way I saw no reason why he shouldn't have it – straight.

'The position is quite simple,' I said. '*Invincible* has been fully paid for by the Royal Navy, operationally she is a great success, she is an important and integral part of the Royal Navy's future capability and so far as I am concerned she is not on the market.' The Australians were somewhat taken aback and in an effort to regain some initiative tried to make *me* justify the retention of *my* ship. This was the last straw and I said so.

Nevertheless even this was not the end and it became necessary for me to ask for a formal meeting with the Defence Secretary finally to decide *Invincible*'s future. This was scheduled for 1800 on a Thursday evening in November. After being kept waiting for 10 minutes I was ushered in. John Nott was evidently tired and restive.

'I can't see you now CNS,' he greeted me. 'I don't know what it is you want to discuss but I must go back to my constituency and unless I leave at once I shall miss my train.'

I was furious. 'Secretary of State this won't do. My meeting with you tonight, at a time chosen by *your* office was arranged over a week ago. The *Invincible* issue cannot drift on like this. It must be resolved now.'

'I can't do it now. I must go.'

'Very well, I can't stop you. But I shall follow you to Cornwall and have it out with you there – in public if necessary.'

'Don't be absurd, of course you won't. I must *go*,' and he strode off.

Fuming, I returned to my office to simmer down and let the dust settle. Half an hour later I summoned Nott's Private Secretary, David Omand, a very good young Civil Servant who I liked and respected. Sitting him down, 'Now,' I said, 'I meant it about following the Secretary of State to Cornwall. Will you arrange a place and time convenient to Mr Nott for me to see him or must I? One way or another I am going to do this. Since you know his programme I think it would be better and more appropriate if you did. Otherwise I shall have to find out by other means and there may well be another scene.' After some initial reluctance he agreed that this was the best way to proceed and we parted amicably.

He was as good as his word. By early next morning all had been arranged. The meeting with the Defence Secretary was fixed for 1700 that evening at Caerhays Castle, home of Julian Williams (Chairman of Cornwall County Council) with whom he would be spending the night. The Private Secretary would come with me, we would catch the 1200 train from Paddington and a RAF car from St Mawgan would meet us at St Austell and take us to Caerhays.

The previous afternoon it had turned bitterly cold and overnight there was an unusually heavy fall of snow. By the Friday morning a thick white blanket covered the Southern counties. As usual British Rail was caught short and scheduled timetables became chaotic. Our train was an hour late in leaving London and delayed further by more than two hours en route. Cold, tired and hungry we drew up at the front door of Caerhays Castle just as the hall clock was striking 2000.

John Nott was the first to greet us and came right out into the bitter cold. To give him his due he could not have been more charming or apologetic.

'I really am very sorry,' he said. 'I honestly didn't think you meant it. Come inside into the warm.'

The welcome was reiterated by Julian Williams, his wife and one of their sons who was down from London for the weekend. After a quick drink we all repaired to the kitchen for a really good dinner. The Williams family were all delightful and very easy to get on with. Not a word of shop was spoken. However, as the pudding approached I became increasingly anxious about time. The last train left St Austell at midnight and with the icy state of the roads to catch it necessitated leaving Caerhays half an hour before. This left only one hour for the whole purpose of the journey: *Invincible*. I suggested that Nott and I should take our pudding into another room and get on with it. We did – to such effect that when Julian Williams came in at 2330 to tell us that I ought to leave to catch my train neither of us had touched our pudding and our coffee was cold and untasted.

I had rehearsed the full case for retaining *Invincible* yet again but it was evident that the Secretary of State had closed his mind to argument. Indeed there *was* no counter-argument, simply the desire to get £175m from the Australians. I said my grateful goodbyes to the hospitable Williams's and started to leave. 'I'll come with you to the station,' said John Nott. It was a generous gesture which I gladly accepted, a forlorn hope but at least it extended the opportunity (however remote) by another half an hour.

By now the cold was intense and it was freezing hard. The heating system in the car was defective, either full on or full off; we alternated between the atmosphere of a Turkish bath and the rude health of the ski slopes whenever we cracked the window a few inches. In desperation, having regard to her unique capabilities, which I could not see being reprovided by any other means for at least two decades, I went so far as to offer to 'pay for *Invincible* again,' i.e. to find the notional £175m by other means but retain the ship herself.

'That would be absurd,' growled John Nott.

'Yes,' I retorted 'it would; but not so absurd as the present plan to flog her to the Australians who haven't even got any VSTOL aircraft to operate from her anyway.' And off we went in argument again, hammer and tongs. Hearing all this going on in the back seat the young Leading Aircraftman who was driving us was agog.

We arrived at St Austell station and got out. The icy cold hit us almost physically. Nott had no overcoat and I little sympathy for his discomfort. The train was late, the waiting room was locked and we stood shivering on the platform.

Finally, 'What is your answer, Secretary of State'? I asked. 'Is it "yes" or "no"?' But the Defence Secretary would not give it – then. 'I'll sleep on it,' he replied through chattering teeth, 'and let you have my answer through the Resident Clerk (the Duty Civil Servant in the Ministry of Defence) in the morning.' To this day I do not know if Nott's untypical hesitation was due to conscience, misplaced kindness or simply an aversion to saying 'no' to my face. That the answer would be 'no' I had little doubt. Weary and very cold, we parted amicably. I entered my sleeper; the heating system had broken down.

Next morning, as arranged, I got the answer: predictably it was 'no'. I had finally lost the battle for *Invincible*. There was nothing more I could do.

The only reason *Invincible* is still part of the Fleet today is because of the Falklands War. Her role in it was indispensable. The whole country knew this and it would have been political dynamite not to have retained her. When she returned from the South Atlantic in July, 1982, I flew on board in a helicopter as she approached Cornwall the previous evening. Next morning she was greeted by the Queen (who had launched her), the Duke of Edinburgh and Princess Anne. The Royal Family went out to Spithead by barge and came up harbour in her. Literally hundreds of yachts and small craft of all sorts escorted *Invincible*, packed so close that hardly a patch of clear water was visible. It was a marvellous welcome and thoroughly deserved. The whole of South Railway Jetty where she finally berthed was jammed with families and friends. Whether on board or ashore there wasn't a dry eye amongst us.

17

TOUCH AND GO

'If you can bear to hear the truth you've spoken
Twisted by knaves to make a trap for fools,
Or watch the things you gave your life to, broken,
And stoop and build 'em up with worn-out tools . . .'
Rudyard Kipling

The Parliamentary Under-Secretary of State for the Royal Navy was Keith
Speed, an appropriate choice for he had himself spent eleven years in the
Service and knew a thing or two about it. A shortish man with greying hair
he was sincere, devoid of pomposity, loyal to the Service he loved and was
doing a good job as Navy Minister. He did not shirk decisions and tempered
them with good sense. I found him easy to get on with and we quickly
became friends. During our two years together we only disagreed on one
fundamental issue: Wrens serving in ships of the Fleet. At that time had
they done so they could not (by the rules then in force) have been employed
on combat duty and thus would have had to be replaced in any HM Ship or
Aircraft entering a war zone. To me this self-imposed reduction in flexibility
was unacceptable and I would have none of it. We compromised on the girls
being employed in greater numbers on operational duties in shore headquarters. Nine years later the rules were changed to include combat duty,
domestic arrangements in warships were suitably modified and the Wrens
sent to sea.

By now Nott's defence review, though not yet approved by the Cabinet,
was fast being set in concrete. For the Navy the prospects were bleak: on
top of its unbalancing and disproportionate share of the cuts, having to bear
the full cost (less the warhead) of *Trident* was bordering on the crippling.
The latter set an extraordinary precedent. Hitherto the strategic deterrent
had properly been regarded as a *national* instrument, supra single Service
budgets, and an appropriate subvention had been made to the budgets of the
Service responsible. Now all was different and the Navy was simply told to
get on with it alone. Remonstrations that this would impose an intolerable
financial burden were met with the bland response: 'I don't understand –
surely the honour of being responsible for the strategic deterrent is enough

in itself'. Moreover the strains imposed on the rest of the Navy were ignored. It was a dirty trick; honour and glory don't buy frigates.

When the Government announced to an expectant House of Commons that it intended in due course to replace Polaris/Chevaline with Trident, in view of the intense interest from both sides of the House the Speaker, exceptionally, granted 35 minutes' worth of questions. The last of these came from the Opposition benches. (I was in the gallery.)

'Will the Right Honourable Member assure the House that the Royal Navy will not be required alone to pay for the cost of Trident?'

'I can reassure the Honourable Member,' replied the Defence Secretary, 'that the cost of Trident will be borne by Defence.'

The mini-debate then closed. In the accepted jargon of Whitehall 'Defence' in this context meant 'all three Services and the Procurement Executive'.

Ten minutes later I was sitting next to the Defence Secretary on the stage in the main conference room of the Ministry of Defence ready to support him at his Press Conference. As he passed me and sat down he said, sotto voce, 'Sorry about that CNS, but you know how it is.'

'Yes, Secretary of State,' I replied 'I know exactly how it is.'

Not long after this Keith Speed, the Navy Minister, had occasion to address his constituents in Kent over a weekend. As an honest man he elected to do so in honest terms. His form of words was extremely restrained and where he was critical of the way things were shaping up the phrasing was mild. I had helped him with the drafting. That Saturday evening his speech was duly delivered.

The following Monday Speed dined at the Chinese Embassy. He had recently acquired a bleeper, set to call him to the nearest phone and ring his office in the Ministry of Defence. Half way through dinner the bleeper was activated. Being unfamilar with its use Speed spent a little time fumbling around his breast pocket to switch the beastly thing off. Having achieved this he made his excuses and left the table for the nearest telephone. At the other end was John Nott expressing the Prime Minister's disapproval of what he had said to his constituents and saying he had to go, thus asking him to resign. Keith Speed's reply was in the sense of 'Get stuffed' and he returned to the dinner table.

A few courses later off went the bleeper again. This time Speed managed to silence it more quickly. It was Number 10 on the phone and he was asked to step round. The interview was friendly and took some time but the result was inexorable: Keith Speed was sacked. Soon after 2300 he telephoned me in my flat by Admiralty Arch.

'I'm off,' he said.

I was surprised and not a little shocked. We chatted for a few minutes and I thanked him for letting me know so quickly, at the same time expressing very sincere regret. Two days later I escorted him from his office along the corridor lined by the Naval Staff and out through the North door of the Ministry of Defence for the last time. Defence had lost a good man whose only fault was to play it responsibly and straight. It was to take eleven years and a different Prime Minister before his patriotic loyalty was rewarded by a knighthood.

Speed was not replaced and the Navy was left without a Minister as the Defence Review ground its inexorable way to completion. This was no oversight but a deliberate act of political manoeuvring. For the time being the Army and Air Force Ministers were kept in post. The former, Philip Goodhart, had been a soldier during the last part of World War II and then a journalist before taking up politics. He played the Whitehall game wisely and with a straight bat. Very deservedly he was later to receive a knighthood.

Not so his Air Force colleague: Geoffrey Pattie was sharp and ambitious. Lacking the rounded, statesmanlike qualities of Keith Speed, he missed few opportunities to further his Departmental case. One of the more public examples of this had occurred earlier in the year when in an interview with the Air Correspondent of the *Daily Telegraph* (Air Commodore Cooper) he had said, inter alia, that Britain spent twice as much in money terms in providing air defence for its own blue water navy than on the air defence of the United Kingdom. 'In the Eastern Atlantic and Channel,' he had added, 'our resources at sea and in the air are more than a match for the Soviets at every stage of the conflict. In any event a sea campaign would merely be a means to an end, which could be achieved more quickly and effectively by direct assault on land.' Such dogmatic stuff coming from a junior Minister had been too much for me and I had sent him a gentle reproof in doggerel:

> 'Dear Geoffrey Pattie, you really are a one,
> You make it all so simple, such gorgeous light blue fun;
> Your maths are getting quite the rage (if curiously applied)
> You multiply so cleverly when others would divide.
> We know you didn't mean it, that Cooper got it wrong,
> And the Great British Public won't misconstrue your song.
> We love our Airmen dearly, *we'll* not forget The Few –
> Could *you* remember also there are two shades of blue?
> And even if indulging in a mildly selfish dream
> We are, dear Geoffrey Pattie, still members of a team.'

Perhaps not surprisingly I did not get a reply.

Later that year a further reshuffle occurred: the Army and Air Force Ministers were withdrawn, two Ministers of State (Armed Forces – people, and Defence Procurement – material) were appointed instead of the previous one and two Under-Secretaries of State (again for people and material) replaced the original three. Thus at a time when savings appeared to be the only thing that mattered there were none in this area. The political hierarchy was rather more top-heavy and their knowledge of and contact with Forces in the field very much reduced.

The new Minister of State (Armed Forces) was a nice person with a gentle, courteous manner underlaid with a streak of stubbornness. Peter Blaker was a typical politician: he liked to back things all ways. He normally chaired all meetings of the Service Boards. Apart from one rather absurd incident to which I shall refer later we got on well together. His opposite number in Procurement, Euan Strathcona, was a huge 'teddy bear' of a man with great charm, twinkling eyes and an Old Testament beard. Kindly and with a fairly laid-back sense of humour he conveyed the impression of never finding it easy (or necessary) to take the often self-imposed cut and thrust of the Ministry of Defence too seriously. After a year or so he was to be replaced by Tom Trenchard; on hearing of the impending change he is reputed to have felt somewhat hurt and to have remarked to his Private Secretary, 'Good God! I know I wasn't the fountain of all knowledge in the defence field but compared with dear old Tom . . .'

At the lower (Under-Secretary of State) level Geoffrey Pattie took over Procurement and one Jerry Wiggin was brought in for Armed Forces. Tall, broad-shouldered and loose-limbed it soon became apparent that the latter's intellect did not seem quite to match his physique. Not many weeks had passed before I had occasion to attend a meeting chaired by US of S (AF). It was protracted, indecisive and futile and as I walked the corridors back to my own room I improperly muttered darkly 'two planks' to one of my staff. To my dismay it had been overheard by others and was flashed round the front offices in no time flat. Throughout the ensuing weeks, as the Defence Review gathered momentum, periodic leaks of information to the media occurred. Their content was not of a particularly sensitive nature but as a matter of principle they were reprehensible and I deplored them. Most of them concerned naval cuts and were ultimately traced to Civil Servants, not, I am glad to say, to Naval Officers serving in the Ministry. There is little doubt that the incentive to indulge in this undesirable activity stemmed in no small part from Defence Ministers' absolute embargo on any Service Officer having any dealings whatsoever with the media. The perpetrators of such illicit leaks came to be termed 'moles'.

In the middle of all this I experienced growing trouble with the furrier species of mole in my garden at home. In fact I have always had rather a soft spot for these gentle, clever little creatures, but one specimen can quickly wreak untold damage to a lawn which then takes months to repair. From my experience I knew that the only way to get rid of this horticultural nuisance was by trapping.

When I left the Ministry one Friday evening a formidable witch-hunt to catch the latest Whitehall mole was in full swing. On arrival at home it was obvious that my local animal had intensified his activities. Enough was enough; I hurriedly set some traps. Overnight the naughty thought flitted through my mind, 'What fun it would be to tweak the sense of humour of the Establishment by catching a real mole and presenting the corpse to the Permanent Secretary'. With that I fell asleep.

Next day revealed one sprung trap but no victim in its jaws. With infinite care I reset them all and by Sunday I had my prey. Its lifeless body neatly fitted into a small After Eight chocolate box as into a coffin and, together with a covering note to Frank Cooper saying that I understood he was looking for a mole – I had caught one – any use? The package was duly placed on the PUS's desk on Monday morning. It was well received.

By May I was beginning to get fairly desperate about the way in which the Defence Review was going. After very careful thought I decided to exercise my prerogative (hitherto hardly ever invoked) and make a direct approach to the Prime Minister. To this end I minuted No 10, copying it to the Defence Secretary, as a basis for discussion:

'1. There is no need for me to remind you of the stark facts of the increasing Soviet maritime threat. Their build-up, particularly in submarines and high quality surface ships, is relentless and there can be no doubting their aim of achieving worldwide maritime domination over the West. On the other hand NATO's navies are short of ships and although the USN is desperately seeking to reverse its decline there is no sign that the shift in the maritime balance of power in favour of Russia will be halted in the foreseeable future – rather the reverse.

2. As you know the Royal Navy carries the mantle of the maritime leadership of European NATO. It provides the bulk of our ready forces in the Eastern Atlantic and in war they will have to take the brunt of the Soviet attack until such time as the USN elements of the striking fleet arrive. The significance of this role on the US commitment to the defence of Western Europe is cardinal – as the recent *Herald Tribune* article emphasized so clearly. No other European NATO nation could take it over.

3. The Defence Secretary's proposals to OD (Defence & Overseas Policy Committee) involve a shift of defence resources away from the Royal Navy of over £7½bn over the next nine years. They involve

paying off over fifty ships prematurely, cutting back the building programme, abandoning the modernization plans for the rest of the surface fleet and eroding the fighting capability of our ships to the extent that independent operations will become increasingly dangerous. Maintaining even the residual force levels will depend on the realization of some very risky support and manpower assumptions. These include reducing naval manpower by over 20,000, closing three dockyards, twelve naval establishments and ten support depots. The Naval Industrial base will be undermined with much loss of work.

4. Such a step change in our conventional naval capability will cause disproportionate damage both to our National and to our Alliance interests: the former because we are an island dependent on seaborne trade and because much of our political influence in Europe and world-wide depends upon naval power and presence – a principle from which the Soviets and the French continue to derive great benefit; the latter because of its impact on NATO's ready forces to deter and confront the expanding Soviet Navy and because it impacts upon the crucial linkage of the US to Europe. At a time when the capability to deter Soviet aggression outside Europe is becoming increasingly important it makes no sense to slash the only part of our defence capability which can contribute to this deterrence on a continuing day-to-day basis.

5. The cutbacks form a package which is militarily unsupportable, industrially damaging and politically unpalatable. The Soviets would be pleased, but SACLANT, SACEUR and CINCHAN dismayed. The French, who are already gaining much credit with the US for their naval activities, could well claim to be the new maritime leaders of Europe.

6. I do not dispute the continuing need for adjustments in the naval forward programme. The Admiralty Board had already accepted that some reductions would have to be made and that there was a need to go for a much cheaper frigate in the future. The outcome of this Review, however, lacks balance and could be disastrous for NATO in the Eastern Atlantic, leading to a lowering of the nuclear threshold. But is *all* the maritime agony proposed necessary? Even on the basis of the Defence Secretary's second option it is very considerable. I do not believe that the need has yet been proved.

7. Although much Defence Review work has been done in the Ministry of Defence over the past few weeks only one option has been seriously pursued: cutting the Navy. I fully recognize the extent of our economic problem and the need to restrain expenditure but there

are other ways to save money without adopting the equally irresponsible course of just cutting our Continental forces. Some obvious possibilities are:

   a. Before applying further cuts to the front line, drastic reductions should be made in headquarters, especially the Ministry of Defence.

   b. Swingeing and risky reductions are to be made in naval support, training and manpower. These are not at present being contemplated for the Army and RAF.

   c. BFG (British Forces Germany) employs over 2,000 UK-based civilians, 23,000 LECs (Locally Enlisted Civilians) and supports over 70,000 dependents. The cost is huge and much of it (for this year some £680M) is in foreign exchange.

   d. The Brussels Treaty is a particular problem but its protocols have already been amended on occasions and the treaty will have to be renegotiated at some time. There will never be a good time to amend the Protocol II on British Forces Germany but with so many countries conducting Defence Reviews there may never be a better. Amendment would enable us to maintain our present forces' structure – albeit smaller – and also allow us to build up again later if the economy permitted or the threat so demanded.

   e. In addition to the core programme the specialist reinforcement forces cost £1.7 bn over the period. Some elements whose cost approaches £1bn could be cut with less impact.

8. Furthermore, at a time when we know that many of our European NATO partners are also conducting large-scale Defence Reviews is it really sensible to delay 'consultation' until it is frankly too late to affect the issue? For obvious national reasons many of them are likely to look to their Navies for cuts rather than their standing armies (eg the Belgian Navy to finance AWACS – Airborne Early Warning). The overall result in Alliance terms could well be unbalanced and unsound and with the most serious implications for the US perception of their ability to reinforce Europe. Surely now is the time to press forward on burden-sharing and really 'consult' properly – *before* irrevocable decisions are made.

9. A historic and radical reduction is being contemplated in the strength of the Navy in order to preserve at huge cost standing forces in Central Europe accompanied by their families and massive overheads at a level determined 30 years ago. To cut the Navy in haste before a proper, objective assessment has been made, both nationally and with the Alliance, would be to leap into the dark and would involve

taking a grave risk with our national security on an arbitrary basis which has not been fully substantiated. It will markedly reduce our flexibility for tackling the unforeseen and thus reduce options for future Governments. In my view it would be neither wise nor responsible to proceed in this way.

In the event the scheduled meeting did not materialize owing to the pressure of other business. I therefore sent a shorter, sharper minute so that the dust would not settle so easily:

1. I note with regret but understanding that the tightness of your programme precludes your seeing me personally as requested. I am confident, however, that you will at least spare two minutes to read this note from the professional Head of the Navy before you and your Cabinet colleagues consider a proposition substantially to dismantle that Navy.
2. It is proposed to cut the Naval budget by more than £7½bn over the next nine years. This is 62% of the total reduction contemplated for Defence and a quarter of the Naval budget. If implemented it would by 1983 cut our Anti-Submarine Warfare Carriers by one third; by 1991 the Destroyer/Frigate Force, the Survey Flotilla and the Fleet Auxiliaries would be halved and our Anti-Air Warfare and Mining capabilities abandoned; 20,000 uniformed personnel would go, 24,000 civilians and there would be 80,000 job losses in industry; Gibraltar, Chatham and most of Portsmouth Dockyards would close as would ten Supply Depots and 12 Naval Establishments.
3. The proposal has been devised ad hoc in two months. It has been neither validated nor studied in depth. No alternative options have been considered. It has all been done in a rush. Such unbalanced devastation of our overall Defence capability is unprecedented; it must cause serious doubts concerning United States reactions in the context of your own conventional assurances and successful nego- tiation of the TRIDENT project so important to our country.
4. We are on the brink of a historic decision. War seldom takes the expected form and a strong maritime capability provides flexibility for the unforeseen. If you erode it to the extent envisaged I believe you will undesirably foreclose your future options and prejudice our National Security.'

Early in June, some three weeks after they had originally sought a meeting, the Chiefs of Staff saw the Prime Minister at No 10. Present also were John Nott and Peter Carrington (Foreign Secretary). Discussions ranged broadly

30. My first real deck landing of a Lynx from the left hand seat —
HMS *Invincible*.

31. On the occasion of the public announcement that the Navy would
continue to be responsible for the national independent strategic nuclear
deterrent and that Trident would be ordered.

Evening Standard, July 17, '80

"I suppose you chaps will be looking for a civilian club soon!"

32. Preparations for War — early morning scene in the hangar of HMS *Hermes* as Royal Marines Commandos check their weapons, Sea Harriers in the background (reproduced from Norton Cleaver's historic photograph which featured in many of the newspapers).

33. SS *Canberra* — the tremendous and well-deserved welcome home given to "The White Whale" as she returned to Southampton after the Falklands War.

over the general areas of the Defence Review; it took the form of the Chiefs doing most of the talking and Mrs Thatcher listening attentively, occasionally putting a question to elucidate a point. The meeting lasted about an hour and a quarter and was devoid of acrimony and decision; it was in short, an exercise in communication and none the less welcome for it. The main trend of the Defence Review remained unaffected.

Five days later on the morning of 8 June I personally saw the Prime Minister as First Sea Lord. Calling at the Defence Secretary's room before walking across to No 10, John Nott was kind enough to suggest that I should go alone so as not to inhibit the discussion. 'Thank you, S of S,' I said, 'that is generous of you but I really must insist that you come too. I have things to say which you will not like and I would rather that they were said to your face than for you to learn of them second-hand subsequently with all the risks of changed nuances.' He readily agreed and off we went together. Mrs Thatcher was her usual, courteous self; she listened patiently while I briefly summarized the main points of my case (which had not changed since my recent submission), then looking gravely at me she asked:

'What would *you* do instead?'

'Prime Minister, I would start by hiving off £2–3bn to the Army,' I replied.

'To the *Army*? You mean the Navy.'

'No I do not, I mean the Army.'

'Why on earth would you do that?' she broke in.

'In order to reprovide in this country the necessary barracks etc which are currently in Germany with a view to rotating front line units to a frequency selected by the Army (say every nine months, like naval deployments) thereby saving the recurring and crippling annual bill in foreign exchange.'

For a moment the PM looked uncertain and glanced inquiringly at the Defence Secretary.

'We've studied that and it's too expensive,' said John Nott curtly.

The remainder of the meeting was anodyne and inconclusive.

For the benefit of the non-Service reader I should perhaps make it clear that my proposition in no way stemmed from a desire to 'do down' the Army; on the contrary I sincerely believed that it was only a matter of time before recruiting as well as financial considerations would compel a change on these lines. Already disenchantment at the prospect of a 12-year stint in a foreign country where local fraternization was minimal (as faced many armoured regiments) was being increasingly experienced. Some of the more far-sighted senior Army officers with whom I had discussed it fully supported my idea; most opposed it, a few even going so far as to say it would be the end of the Army. Without exception middle-ranking and more junior officers regarded it as long overdue and ultimately inevitable.

That evening the Secretary of State for Defence made a preliminary presentation of his Defence Review proposals to the Cabinet.

At this stage there was not a lot more I could do about the Defence Review except keep the pressure up. The Press gave extensive coverage of 'the naval case' (based on speculation and very incomplete information) and were helpful on the whole. As a final tease before Parliament adjourned for the Summer recess I persuaded a retired friend to cast a fly over Peterborough of the *Daily Telegraph*. Being a sportsman he took it and with only a minor editorial addition printed it verbatim:

'*Nott funny*

As they wait for confirmation of defence spending cuts, expected tomorrow, I understand that Ministry of Defence staff are keeping up their spirits with this adaption of a last war song, smuggled to me past security yesterday:

> Oh Johnny! Oh Johnny! You're on the spot
> Oh Johnny! Oh Johnny! Did you say Nott?
> You make the Russians dance with joy,
> And with your wildcat schemes you
> Emulate the Ayatollah.
> Oh Johnny! Oh Johnny! Please tell the truth,
> What makes you muck things so?
> To defence you are new
> Yet you listen to few –
> Better go, Johnny!! Go, Johnny, go!!'

There was no reaction from Whitehall.

Towards the middle of that long hot summer I was rung up by a former First Sea Lord for whom I had great respect. He wanted to come and see me and to this I readily agreed. Never one to mince his words, no sooner were we seated in my study than he came straight out with it:

'I have been talking with So & So [another predecessor],' he said, 'and we both think you should resign and lay it on the line.'

Here was a bolt from the blue. I thought for a good minute before replying.

'I don't think you are right. I am very conscious of the futility of David Luce's resignation in the mid-sixties over the Carrier débâcle. It attracted little more attention than a one-inch paragraph in only some of the dailies. If then he had taken the full Board with him it might have made an impact but his lone action made none. Today, in my judgement, even if I took the whole Board with me (and I'm sure they'd come if asked to) I am pretty certain it would make no significant impact. Furthermore I believe that resignations by senior Service officers should be based on different criteria from those of, say, politicians and should in fact be on a point of honour, when you're caught with your fingers in the till or in the vestry with a choirboy, not merely in protest.

'So I'm grateful to you for taking the trouble to come and see me, and for your advice. I will certainly think about it very carefully but my present strong inclination is that I would best serve the Navy and the country by staying put and continuing to fight.'

My visitor took it in good humour and shortly left.

Then I telephoned So & So (whom I equally liked and respected) and explained what had gone on.

'Henry,' he said, 'I quite understand. *You* must be the judge of what is best and do exactly as you think fit. You carry my best wishes whatever you decide to do.'

So that was that, at least for the moment. I must confess to feeling a little hurt that two such distinguished brother officers and personal friends had seen fit to proffer the advice they had. It felt rather like a kick in the crutch. But the more I thought about it the more convinced I became that to go would be to take the cowardly, easy way out.

Not long afterwards I chaired the usual half-yearly meeting of uniformed Admiralty Board members and Commanders-in-Chief to decide on the next Flag promotions. After completion of normal business I briefed my colleagues on the advice in respect of my resignation (as described above) and told them I wanted their hard-nosed views on the subject, stripped of loyalty and sentiment. To facilitate dispassionate debate I then handed over the Chair to Desmond Cassidi (Second Sea Lord) and left the room.

As I tramped the rather barren corridor outside the conference room I wondered if I had overcalled my hand. Having gone through so much it was only natural to *want* to finish the job and perhaps even to think boastfully that I could do it better than anyone else. But was this perhaps being *over* self-confident? The leaden minutes ticked by; I had imagined that my colleagues would only take a few and it occurred to me that the longer they took the more likely was the conclusion 'go'. Certainly I had 'laid it on the line' but not perhaps in quite the way my distinguished visitor had had in mind. What in fact I had done was to put *myself* on the line and now I must stand by others' decision. Rather morbidly I began to wonder if this was like walking the plank.

They took 20 minutes and on my re-entry I was told they were unanimous that I should stay.

God knows what they were talking about for all that time and I never thought it fair to find out!

*

A few weeks later the Argentine naval sail-training ship *Libertad* (3,720 tons) moored in the Thames opposite Greenwich. I was invited to visit her, walk round the ship and have lunch on board. Their Naval Attaché in London accompanied me. On arrival by car at Greenwich pier it quickly became apparent that they had laid things on in a big way. They had manned all the masts and yards; drawn up on the starboard side of the quarterdeck were all the officers; on the port side they had mounted a guard of 48. I was welcomed most genially and having inspected the guard asked if, while I was meeting the officers, they would unman-ship and lay the ship's company aft so that I could thank them for their handsome gesture. Whereupon they went to Divisions (formal parade by parts of the ship on the upper deck). All this took a little time and it was clear that a most friendly spirit prevailed and that the sailors appreciated notice being taken of them in this way.

After drinks in the wardroom we repaired to the Captain's cabin to enjoy a prolonged and extremely good lunch. All present spoke good English (fortunately for me) and there was a really happy atmosphere with much merriment. When lunch was over I was presented with a singularly nice bronze model of an Argentine sailor, standing some 18″ high and beautifully moulded. Since *my* model of a British sailor, which George Tullis my Naval Assistant hardly ever moved without, in case of eventualities, stood at best no more than six inches I quietly told him to keep his head down with a view to getting something more nearly equal on return to Whitehall. After the friendliest of partings and my promise to visit one of their British-built Guided Missile Destroyers in the autumn, before she left UK waters, we returned to London. By chance I had a pair of quite nice silver-plated candlesticks available; these were quickly wrapped up and sent down to the *Libertad* as she was sailing that evening. With this act I thought perhaps I had scored 'plus one', which was about right.

In October I did indeed visit their GMD at Portsmouth after she had completed working up at Portland. This time I was given a rather over-pastried tea in the Wardroom with all officers present before being taken to the Captain's cabin. Once again 'Father Christmas' appeared and I was given a beautifully engraved electric chronometer clock in an exquisite, folding, brassbound mahogany case. I am afraid I gave up the unequal struggle. They had won, game, set and match.

I mention these delightful if unimportant little incidents as a measure of the friendly relationship then enjoyed. Less than six months later we were at war.

18

WHO WOULD VALIANT BE

'Thrice is he armed that hath his quarrel just
But four times he who gets his blow in fust'
Henry Wheeler Shaw

The Falkland Islands lie 400 miles north-east of Cape Horn, the notorious tip of South America. Captured by the British in 1833, they are today the most remote of our remaining overseas territories. There are two main islands in addition to lesser ones; East Falkland, on which are situated the main centre of population, Port Stanley, with its associated airfield and harbour, and West Falkland, smaller, even more thinly inhabited and composed almost entirely of sheep farms. The two islands are separated by the Falkland Sound, a strip of water some ten miles across at its narrowest. The combined area of the islands is about the size of Luxembourg. The total population is around 1800.

Associated with the Falkland Islands are their Dependencies: South Georgia in Antarctica, some 800 miles south-east of the Falklands; and Southern Thule in the South Sandwich Group a further 600 miles to the south-east. Neither is inhabited on a permanent basis but the British Antarctic Survey team usually has up to a dozen scientists or research workers in South Georgia.

There is no strategic or commercial importance attached to either the Falkland Islands or Southern Thule, though some test drilling for oil off the former has been carried out with, as yet, unconvincing results. But the Falkland Islanders are British citizens and as such are entitled to British administration, law and defence.

South Georgia, on the other hand, has all the exciting potential of the unknown. Strategically it is a foot in the door to Antarctica. It is known to be rich in mineral deposits but their cost-effective extraction from this glacial wasteland is a matter for speculation. It has been aptly described as the end of the world and the weather conforms to that title.

For the first half of this century it had been the British practice to deploy a South Atlantic Naval Squadron, normally based on Simonstown in South Africa. This was deemed appropriate to support the many British interests in both South Africa and South America and the vital shipping routes through the South Atlantic. But the United Kingdom's progressive retrenchment of the 1960's disbanded this Squadron and thereby removed effective *deterrence* from the area. From then on reliance was placed on a *tripwire* in the form of a single Ice Patrol Ship (initially HMS *Protector*, later *Endurance*) at sea for only six months in the year; and a small party of forty Royal Marines as the garrison at Port Stanley.

For many years (but especially during the last sixteen) Argentina had laid claim to the Falkland Islands (Malvinas) in varying degrees of strength and validity. An incident calculated to probe the UK's resolve, if not to provoke her irritation, had been contrived almost annually. Over the years periodic talks between the two countries had been held at junior Ministerial level. The pattern had developed of the Argentines demanding and the UK stalling. More recently the issue of *sovereignty* had featured with increasing prominence. The Argentine demands had become more pressing and the Falkland Islanders' rejection more obdurate if less rational; but because of their British citizenship it was politically difficult not to support their views. Nevertheless by the end of 1981 there were growing signs in Whitehall that at the next round of Anglo-Argentine talks, due to be held in June the following year, de facto sovereignty would be transferred to Argentina under some form of lease-back. The view was held in many quarters that in practical terms the Islanders would not experience any adverse effects from such an arrangement and that adequate safeguards to preserve their rights as British citizens could be written into the agreement. Britain's standing in the eyes of the United Nations Organization, as well as with one of the most powerful countries of South America, would be enhanced. And the UK would be effectively rid of a distant encumbrance which contributed nothing but difficulty and expense.

Two other factors arose in 1981 which were to have a profound influence on events to come: the UK's Defence Review, and the internal situation in the Argentine.

I have briefly covered some of the more ridiculous aspects of the Defence Review in the previous chapter; it was conspicuous neither for its wisdom nor for its statesmanship. So far as the South Atlantic was concerned it was planned to emasculate the Navy and withdraw the Ice Patrol Ship. To the objective observer of the world scene this astonishing performance by an island nation, still dependent on the sea for more than 97% of its imports and exports, could have only one rational interpretation: the UK's growing disinterest in maritime matters in general and the South Atlantic in particular. And so it was deduced in the Argentine.

Domestically Argentina was in a mess. Public feeling against the 'Dirty War', which had involved the forceful disappearance of thousands and the suspected liquidation of many, had risen to a peak. The economy was in a shambles, as was widely evident. The Administration lacked competence and direction. Public confidence in the Government was at rock bottom. By the spring of 1982 there was rioting on the streets in Buenos Aires. *Some* immediate panacea was needed to divert attention until a more lasting solution could be devised. In terms of its magnitude and popular appeal, one thing *only* met this requirement – the Malvinas. That the next round of talks was only two months away and that all the portents were that they would be highly satisfactory for Argentina was just too bad. Two months are too long to wait when the mob is howling at the gate.

This, then, was the backdrop to the closing weeks of March, 1982. Once more the Falkland Islands situation seemed to be blowing hot. In Whitehall yet again the military options were reviewed – and endorsed – and Intelligence updates called for. It was known that the Argentine Fleet was at sea and that it included a sizeable element of amphibious troops; but it was also known that every year at about this time it was usual for the Argentine Navy to conduct a major amphibious exercise with the neighbouring Uruguayan Navy. In January *Endurance* had paid a routine visit to Ushuaia in the Southern part of Argentina and reported that, unusually, her reception had been cold to the point of hostility; but shortly afterwards when she paid a similar visit to Mar del Plata all seemed normal. Understandably, in view of the forthcoming talks, in Whitehall overriding political importance was attached to a policy of non-provocation and this tempered every activity in the early days.

On 19 March one Davidoff with a party of men landed on South Georgia from an Argentine naval Support Ship. He himself was a scrap merchant who had obtained permission from the British Embassy in Buenos Aires to dismantle and remove the unwanted remains of the whaling station at Leith in South Georgia, abandoned since the middle sixties. But once ashore the Argentine flag was hoisted and it became clear to the watching British Antarctic Survey scientists that an Argentine toe-hold had been established. This was duly reported to the Governor of the Falkland Islands and in turn to London. *Endurance* was ordered to embark extra Royal Marines from the Falkland Islands Garrison and proceed to South Georgia.

In the course of the next few days further incidents occurred in the South Atlantic. The Argentine Naval Support Ship re-embarked most, but not all, of the landed men and sailed from Leith. The Argentine Airline office in Port Stanley was broken into by night and some of its contents defaced. A French yacht in the vicinity of South Georgia was discovered to be in direct contact with the Argentines. There was growing evidence that Davidoff was being directed by the Argentine Navy. The Argentine Foreign Minister began to reveal the pressure he was under from Admiral Anaya, Head of the

Argentine Navy; this was confirmed by Intelligence reports. *Endurance* was instructed to wait at Grytviken (a few miles away in South Georgia) and not to proceed to Leith. Meanwhile a second Argentine Naval Support Ship berthed at Leith and was seen to be working cargo.

On 25 March it became known in London that two Argentine frigates equipped with Exocet anti-ship missiles had been deployed to the sea area between the Falkland Islands and South Georgia. It was also learned that Argentine Forces were being kept informed of the movements of *Endurance* and of the Falkland Islands Garrison. There were indications that the Argentine civilians still in South Georgia would remain there and shortly afterwards this was formally confirmed by the Argentine Foreign Minister. The hawks in Argentina were assuming the ascendancy.

Meanwhile Whitehall initiated discreet moves against the possibility that on this occasion the Argentinians meant business. The avoidance of provocation continued to dominate all decisions. The withdrawal of *Endurance*, now imminent, was cancelled. To resupply her and enable her to remain on station a Royal Fleet Auxiliary was sailed from the Gibraltar area. The previous Falkland Islands Garrison, due to be relieved by the fresh Royal Marines Contingent recently brought from the mainland by *Endurance*, was held, thus effectively doubling the size of the Garrison and bringing its strength up to eighty. A nuclear-powered Fleet submarine (SSN) was withdrawn from exercises off Gibraltar, loaded with her war outfit of torpedoes and stores, and despatched to the South Atlantic. Instructions to deploy a second SSN were issued and a third was earmarked but not yet withdrawn from her current operational task. Consideration was given to sailing a force of destroyer/frigates from the Gibraltar area in the general direction of the South Atlantic but was rejected on the twin grounds of inadequacy and provocation. Whitehall knew the approximate positions of the Argentine naval ships in the vicinity of South Georgia and also of the Naval Task Force including the Attack Carrier *25th of May*, four destroyers and an amphibious landing ship exercising some 800 nautical miles north of the Falkland Islands. It noted that no change in the readiness of the Argentine Air Force had been directed and that the Argentine air service to Port Stanley was operating as usual.

By longstanding arrangement I was due to visit the Admiralty Surface Weapons Establishment on Portsdown Hill on 31 March. Three times in the previous fourteen months defence review considerations had caused me to cancel my visit. This time, if I could responsibly do so, I was determined to go through with it. By flying a naval helicopter from Northwood I could be in almost continuous communication with the Ministry of Defence and within 1½ hours' notice of recall if necessary. I went. It was a useful day and there were no emergency calls from London.

By 1800 I was back in my office. There I found the latest Intelligence Report and a number of briefs, all relating to the South Atlantic. The former indicated without equivocation that an Argentine invasion of the Falkland Islands seemed likely in the early hours of 2 April. The latter consistently advised that further naval deployments were unnecessary and undesirable. *Endurance* would remain on station and be resupplied, two SSN's were on the way; to deploy further units in circumstances which were potentially no more serious than on many previous occasions – indeed arguably less so in view of the forthcoming talks – would have damaging effects on our other commitments.

To me the two, Intelligence Report and Briefs, were incompatible. There was a clear, imminent threat to a British overseas territory. It could only be reached by sea. What the hell was the point in having a Navy if it was not used for this sort of thing? Even as I decided that the briefs were upside down I learned that my Secretary of State was being briefed from them at that very moment. I strode down the corridor to his office. He was not there.

'The Secretary of State is holding his briefing in his room in the House,' explained his Private Secretary, adding, 'he must be nearly finished by now'.

Snatching a House of Commons pass I jumped into my car and was whisked to the main entrance. Being still in ordinary day uniform and moving as quickly as I could among the milling throng waiting to enter the Galleries or see their Members caused a bit of a flurry. But not so with the splendid Police Officer at his desk in the Central Lobby. Years of handling silly questions from crazy cranks had hardened him to courteous stone. An impatient First Sea Lord, though in uniform and urgently seeking the Defence Secretary, was chicken-feed.

'I'll ring his room, sir,' he said with unruffled calm. 'Hmm. No answer. Would you care to sit on one of the benches over there sir, and I'll try to locate him for you?'

I sat. Various MP's and officials who I knew passed and exchanged a few words. Then I was collected by one of the Junior Whips and taken to the Whips' Room. They were a nice lot, nearly all ex-soldiers and rather intrigued to chat over a much-needed whisky with the Head of the Navy. After ten minutes or so the search for the Defence Secretary was successful. He was with the Prime Minister in her room and I was asked to go up.

'Good evening, Prime Minister,' I said on entering. 'Is there anything I can do to help?'

She was her usual charming, purposeful self. 'Come in Admiral,' she said. 'You are very timely. We are of course discussing the Falklands situation and what we should do about it.'

Present also were the Defence Secretary and the Permanent Secretaries from the Ministry of Defence and Foreign and Commonwealth Office (FCO),

Ministers and officals from the FCO, and the Prime Minister's Private Secretary. Discussion was fairly general, the FCO pressing for the despatch of a third SSN and the Defence Secretary reluctant to initiate any further action. The reality or otherwise of the threat, the importance of not prejudicing the forthcoming talks with Argentina, and the courses of diplomatic action open to us predominated. In due course I had my chance.

'Admiral, what do you think?'

'On the basis of the latest Intelligence,' I replied, 'I think we must assume that the Falkland Islands will be invaded and that this will happen in the next few days. If it does there is no way the Garrison can put up an effective defence against the amphibious force known to be embarked in the Argentine Fleet. Nor, now, is there any effective deterrence that we could apply in time. Therefore the islands will be captured. Whether we take action to recover them or not is not for me to say but I would strongly advise that we did. To do so would require a very considerable Naval Task Force with strong amphibious elements. I believe we should assemble such a force now, without further delay. To be seen to be doing so in sufficient strength might conceivably cause the Argentines to hold off from landing, though I doubt it. Arguably such a move would be too late to provoke them into doing something on which they already seem bent.'

'The Task Force, that would be *Invincible, Fearless* and some frigates?'

'Yes. It would also include *Hermes, Intrepid* (which is currently being put into reserve), a substantial proportion of the operational destroyers/frigates, very considerable afloat support from the Royal Fleet Auxiliaries and the taking up from trade of a number of merchant ships. The whole of 3 Commando Brigade Royal Marines would be required, supplemented by at least one additional Army Unit.'

'What about the third nuclear submarine?'

'Contrary to the advice I gave my Secretary of State yesterday when I opposed this suggestion, in the light of today's information I think we should sail a third SSN as soon as practicable. For other operational reasons this would not be for a few days but I don't think that would matter.'

'You talk of *Invincible* and *Hermes*; what about *Ark Royal*?'

'The old or the new? The old is in the throes of being scrapped. The new, regrettably, will not complete building for another three years or so.'

'Shall we have enough air cover?'

'We shall be entirely dependent on the Sea Harriers embarked in *Invincible* and *Hermes*. No, we have not really got enough Sea Harriers. But the Sea Harrier is a highly capable aircraft and I believe it to be more than a match for anything the Argentines could put up. Provided we deploy every single aircraft that can be made operational, including those normally used for training, we should be able to inflict sufficient attrition on arrival in the area to achieve at least local air superiority before the landing. I won't pretend that it will not be an operation involving considerable risk; but in my judgement it is, on balance, an acceptable risk – and anyway there is no better alternative.'

'You keep on about the Sea Harriers. What about the Buccaneers and the Phantoms?'

'They were all transferred to the RAF when the old *Ark Royal* was paid off. They cannot be operated from *Invincible* or *Hermes* and they cannot get there on their own.'

'How long would it take to assemble such a Task Force?'

'Apart from the Merchant Ships, which would be subject to an Order in Council and then depend on their whereabouts and the time needed to modify or equip them, and *Intrepid* whose precise state I would need to check – 48 hours.'

'And how long would it take to get to the Falkland Islands?'

'About three weeks.'

'Three weeks, you mean three days?'

'No, I mean three weeks. The distance is 8,000 nautical miles.'

'Could the preparations be carried out without it becoming generally known?'

'No. Something on this scale would be bound to get out fairly quickly.'

'Could we really recapture the islands if they were invaded?'

'Yes, we *could* and in my judgement (though it is not my business to say so) we *should*.'

'Why do you say that?' snapped the Prime Minister.

'Because if we do not, or if we pussyfoot in our actions and do not achieve complete success, in another few months we shall be living in a different country whose word counts for little.'

The Prime Minister looked relieved and nodded.

Discussion then turned to other aspects: a telephone call to Al Haig, the American Secretary of State, in Washington; the drafting of a personal message from the Prime Minister to President Reagan; messages to our Ambassadors to the United State and the Argentine and to the Governor of the Falkland Islands. All this lasted well into the night.

When the meeting finally broke up I left with full authority to sail a third nuclear submarine when current tasks permitted and to assmble and prepare the Task Force on the lines proposed, but not to sail it pending further instructions. One thing was certain: faced with a crisis we had a Prime Minister of courage, decision and action to meet it.

I returned to the Ministry of Defence, issued the necessary instructions and telephoned the Chief of the Air Staff who was Acting Chief of the Defence Staff (CDS himself was in New Zealand on an official visit but was keeping in close touch) to inform him of what had happened.

Next day Whitehall was busy. There were meetings of the Cabinet, the Defence and Overseas Policy Committee and the Chiefs of Staff Committee. Diplomatic activity was further intensified in Buenos Aires, in the United Nations Assembly in New York, and in Washington. Everywhere the Argentine representatives presented an atmosphere of impasse. In this hardening and worsening situation the assessment from Washington was that it seemed likely that the Argentines would now go ahead with a military operation. They could be in Port Stanley in 24 hours. President Reagan would personally telephone General Galtieri.

Invasion of the Falkland Islands now seemed imminent. An advance Task Group of seven destroyers and frigates exercising in the Gibraltar area was sailed towards the South Atlantic under the command of Rear Admiral Woodward, Flag Officer First Flotilla. This was still in the nature of a precautionary move; the Group would later join up with the main Task Force in mid-Atlantic if the latter was deployed.

That evening I had a long-arranged dinner party in my Mall House Flat by Admiralty Arch. It included the Permanent Secretaries of the Foreign and Commonwealth Office and the Ministry of Defence. To an extent it was a last desperate attempt to muster sense and curb implementation of the more extravagant absurdities of the 1981 Defence Review – of which the impending sale of *Invincible* was a prime example. Despite the gathering war clouds it was a convivial evening, though not entirely without analogy to a certain game of bowls at Plymouth 400 years previously or to the Duchess of Richmond's Ball on the eve of Waterloo. Our wives had withdrawn and the port had just been circulated a second time when, by prior arrangement, I had to leave my own table to attend another meeting called by the Prime Minister with the Foreign and Commonwealth Secretary and the Secretary of State for Defence.

The discussions in No 10 Downing Street lasted far into the night. Yet again all possible options were reviewed but no panacea other than continuing high-pressure diplomacy identified. There was considerable debate over what instructions should be sent to the Governor of the Falkland Islands. A message of confidence? Of exhortation to fight to the last? Of restraint on such heroics to reduce bloodshed? After a period of heavy drafting a message in the sense of 'complete confidence in your ability to handle the situation . . . realize you may be faced with impossible odds . . . know you will exercise your judgement in avoiding needless loss of life . . . our thoughts with you at this critical time' was shaped up. To me it seemed at worst backseat driving and at best a package of platitudes. Evidently I displayed my distaste for the Prime Minister spotted it.

'You're shaking your head, Admiral; you don't agree?'

'Prime Minister, I can only say what I, as an operational commander, would do were I on the receiving end of such a message.'

'What?'

'Put it straight in the wastepaper bin and lose my remaining confidence in Whitehall.'

'What would *you* say then?'

'Nothing. At this late stage I should leave it to the man on the spot.' And so it was.

During these long night sessions the Prime Minister was at her very best, exhibiting no sign of the gruelling 16-hour day which normally preceded them. Indeed such were her stamina and resolve in a crisis that I believe she rather enjoyed them. At one stage she rounded on me sharply:

'Admiral, supposing we did send the Task Force, what would *you* do if you were C-in-C of the Argentine Navy?'

'I should return to harbour, Prime Minister, and stay there,' I replied.

'Why?'

'Because I should appreciate that although I could take out some of the British ships, they would sink my entire Navy. It would take years to recover, if indeed it were practicable to do so.'

In the early hours of Friday, 2 April I returned to the Ministry of Defence with authority to sail the Task Force. The Naval Operations Staff were poised awaiting the outcome of the meeting at No 10.

'Signal C-in-C Fleet to prepare and sail the Task Force,' I instructed. I then telephoned Admiral Fieldhouse personally.

I knew John Fieldhouse very well indeed. Over recent years we had been Flotilla commanders together; he had been an excellent and far-sighted Flag Officer Submarines when I commanded the Fleet, and an outstanding controller of the Navy during my earlier time as First Sea Lord. I could not have wished for a better C-in-C Fleet in a crisis nor one whose thinking so completely matched my own. We were 'in each other's minds'. Behind his unruffled calm and almost urbane manner lay a keen mind, resolute determination and a fund of good sense.

'The Carrier Task Force must sail on Monday,' I said.

'Could we not have a little more time, First Sea Lord,' the Commander-in-Chief reacted. 'We could then improve the preparation so much.'

'No,' I replied. 'I'm sorry but they *must* sail on Monday.'

'Understood,' said the C-in-C. And they did.

At dawn on 2 April the Argentine invasion force landed and by 0830 the Governor of the Falkland Islands had surrendered. Another chapter in maritime history had been opened.

19

SHEEP MAY SAFELY GRAZE

'Before the battle proper is fought it is decided by the
Quartermaster'

Field Marshal Rommel

I make no attempt to give a detailed account of Falklands War itself nor of
the many brave actions at sea, on land and in the air which ultimately led to
victory. These sagas have been chronicled elsewhere by those on the spot at
the time. As wars go its scale was less massive and its duration less protracted
than most preceding conflicts. It was, in fact, short and sharp. Nevertheless
it was the first for many years, in the course of which technological and
tactical developments had been significant, and it was fought some 8000
miles from base. There are some interesting conclusions to be drawn and I
discuss a few of the more important ones below.

If one were to select the single most dominant factor above all others it
would be the continuing value and flexibility of sea power and the total
relevance of surface ships. Without them the land force could not have been
put ashore, there could have been no air cover, no airborne (helicopter)
mobility and no naval gunfire support. The same goes for logistics: without
adequate surface shipping there could have been no re-supply of food,
ammunition and essential stores. Even the main field hospital was afloat.
The part played by the Merchant Navy in all this needs special mention; it
was crucial. Never before had the Royal Navy/Merchant Navy liaison been
surpassed.

Merchant ships were needed for many duties: additional tankers, troop-
ships, hospital ships, aircraft ferries, solid stores support ships, repair ships,
despatch vessels. Some fifty were taken up from trade and, after rapid
conversion, fulfilled a key role in the recovery of the islands. Stability
standards were a major concern and in some cases it was necessary to limit
loads or fit additional watertight sub-divisions. Examples of the necessary
modifications were the design and fitting of helicopter pads and flight decks,
extra fresh-water-making plants, power generators, weapon and communication fits, replenishment at sea gear, additional fuel tanks, accommodation
and workshop facilities.

The majority of the work was carried out in the Royal Dockyards to very short timetables, typically in the order of four days. The greatest credit is due to a host of engineers in industry and the Merchant Fleet: at all levels from managing director to shop floor they worked long hours with commendable skill and enthusiasm. 24-hour working was maintained seven days a week and a sense of dedication and loyalty shone through, reminiscent of 1939–45. Such was the speed of events that divers were still in the recompression chamber in *Stena Seaspread* when she arrived in port; *QEII* was fitted with satellite communications in five days when normally this would have taken five weeks; *Uganda* was taken off her Mediterranean cruise and fully converted to a hospital ship in $2\frac{1}{2}$ days. Trawlers were converted to minesweepers while still with fish in their holds.

Whenever possible small teams of experts flew out to the ship concerned and checked modification design details during the final passage to conversion ports, signalling ahead the main parameters of the work to be done. A sense of urgency, professionalism and determination surmounted obstacles which might ordinarily have seemed intractable.

After the war was over the ignorant and those still ill-disposed towards our country maintaining a proper maritime capability persisted in their blinkered dogma. 'Marvellous achievement but not a basis for Defence Policy,' they bleated, or, 'Of course never again will there be another war like it so let us not get led astray by conclusions drawn from a very particular scenario'. Never yet in history has anyone correctly predicted the course of the next war and I have still to meet the divine genius who can do so. Ten years after the Falklands was the Gulf War: different in many detailed aspects and, being closer to home, predominantly an air battle, but once again a conflict in which a very significant part was played by maritime forces.

In the previous chapter I briefly described some of the critical events leading up to the sailing of the Task Force. This was the first of three major decisions leading to our repossession of the Falkland Islands. It was at once the greatest and the most difficult. At that time the UK's stock in terms of world opinion was not at its highest: as a nation we were increasingly regarded as long on advice but short on muscle to back it. Probably about half the world thought we *wouldn't* attempt to retake the Falklands and the other half thought we *couldn't*. In international terms the despatch of the Task Force caused astonishment in some quarters but served as an earnest of intent to all.

To some the sailing was seen as sabre-rattling. During the 3-weeks' passage south some settlement would surely be negotiated and the whole risky undertaking called off. Even within the Task Force itself there were those who thought it was likely to turn out to be just another sort of exercise, though the intensity and nature of their training while on passage gave cause for doubt. To those at the heart of things it meant *war*; true, negotiations had to be played out to the last card but the prospect of responsible success seemed remote.

And it is a regrettable fact that nothing is more unifying than a war. Led by the Prime Minister, a natural leader, overnight the 'B' was put back into 'Britain'. Most of the routine party-political bickering temporarily ceased, Trade Union squabbles were suspended and overtime pay stopped being a pre-condition for major extra effort by the workforce. After it was all over I visited British Aerospace: young and old alike were rightly proud to tell me how they had heard the 'call to arms' and immediately switched to an 18-hour day, the overtime to be sorted out later. This was typical of all connected with the defence industry, the shipbuilders and owners, the dockyards, and others. That well-worn historical phrase 'The British are never at their best until at their last ditch' was borne out yet again.

The second major decision was to sail the Assault Force from Ascension Island. There they had gathered, re-grouped, cross-loaded stores and equipment and generally refined the contents of each ship which had not been possible (there had not been time) before sailing from UK. In placid hindsight the critic may ask, 'What was the problem, why so difficult?' In real terms there was more to it. There was a limit to time. To delay that sailing was politically attractive in that it bought further time for political negotiation. But militarily this was unattractive because of the impending onset of the Antarctic winter with all its hazards for an effective amphibious landing and essential follow-up support. Of course the Assault Force could be sailed and if (unlikely thought it then seemed) subsequent diplomatic negotiations achieved a breakthrough, it could be recalled. But this option, in the *absence* of such a problematic achievement, would have been detected by the watching world and perceived as a backdown.

The third decision was to authorize the Task Force Commander to carry out the assault landing on the Falklands to a precise timing of his choice. Although perhaps the most cataclysmic in its immediate potential results, this was in fact the 'easiest' most straightforward decision of the three. Paradoxically it was taken by the full Cabinet. Having got the Task Force in position off the islands and the Assault Force poised to land, it was inconceivable that we, as a country, should back down at the last moment unless the Argentines demonstrated their immediate and total evacuation. Predictably they expressed no such intent.

As the Task Force got closer to the islands the risk of it being subjected to surprise attack from aircraft or submarines increased and it became necessary to relax the rules of engagement despite the continuing diplomatic negotiations. In Whitehall the predominant theme was still the avoidance of provocation and it was at this point that the value of war experience by senior ministers was brought out. Most notable was Michael Havers, the Attorney General, who had served as an officer in the RNVR during the Second World War. He understood clearly the feeling of utter nakedness when at sea in a hostile air and submarine environment with inadequate means of defence. His professional legal advice on such issues was consistently sound and pragmatic and the safety of the Task Force in those early days owed much to his influence in the War Cabinet.

Another instance of where war experience showed up to advantage was in the matter of ship losses. At the final Cabinet meeting held to approve the landing I had fully expected to be asked how many ships I thought we would lose in action and what losses I would regard as the acceptable limit. I had speculated at length on this and reached the broad conclusions that we would probably lose about six destroyers/frigates and could, in the circumstances, afford to lose at least double that number. Where the assessment became more complex was over the possible sinking of one or both of the Carriers; here additional factors such as the state of the air battle, whether the landing and build-up had been successfully accomplished and the availability of helicopter and VSTOL operating sites ashore became relevant. In the event I was questioned on none of these aspects. When the first ship loss (*Sheffield*) occurred the waves of emotion that spread through Whitehall were almost tangible. Ministers and Officials were deeply shocked and indeed it seemed that for many this was the first real comprehension that the country was *at war*.

Three weeks later news of the sinking of the *Coventry* came through in the early evening. For some time little more was known beyond the fact that the ship had been sunk by air attack; no details of casualties were given and indeed were probably not then known. This was a sad blow but not entirely unexpected and there was absolutely nothing to be done about it until more was known. I remained in my flat by Admiralty Arch. At about 2130 my Vice Chief (William Staveley) telephoned to say that all hell seemed to have been let loose in the Ministry of Defence and he really thought I should go in. I did. Half-way up the quarter-mile corridor from the south door there came a loud shout from behind me; it was the Defence Secretary returning from reporting the loss of the ship to the Prime Minister. As I retraced my steps I could see that he was in a rather agitated state.

'We can't go on like this, CNS,' he said, 'losing all these ships.' He repeated this several times and I became irritated by his manner; it had been a long day for us both, but he did not have the benefit of war experience or the ability to face up to the trauma of major losses at a critical time.

'What are you saying, Secretary of State?' I asked coldly. 'Are you saying you want to call off the operation? I doubt that it would be practicable at this stage or that the Prime Minister would wear it any more than I would.'

'No, of course I'm not,' he snapped.

'Then what *are* you trying to tell me?'

Still striding along the corridor, we lapsed into silence until we reached the Chief of the Defence Staff's room where Terry Lewin and others had already gathered. The discussion quickly centred on when a public announcement should be made. John Nott was for making a statement at once but Terry Lewin and I strongly opposed this on the grounds that we still had no details of casualties and in the absence of this knowledge the telephone exchange at the Fleet Headquarters at Northwood would be jammed throughout the night by enquiries from the 280 families of the *Coventry*. At length the Secretary of State accepted this and no public statement was made then. As events turned out the Northwood exchange was indeed completely jammed – not only by *Coventry* families but by those of *the entire Task Force*. Nott had been right, Lewin and Leach wrong.

One last point concerning the public announcement of setbacks relates to the person charged with this difficult and unenviable task. The individual selected from the Public Relations Department within the Ministry of Defence to make such announcements was a middle-grade Civil Servant called Ian MacDonald. He was a nice person, totally sincere and loyal, if not perhaps obviously destined for the head of his profession; in other capacities I had known him well over a number of years. Unfortunately he had not read the prudent advice proffered in the naval parade training manual for those responsible for conducting a Service funeral: 'assuming an aspect cheerful but subdued . . .' Weighed down by the solemnity of what he was about to reveal to an expectant public, MacDonald's otherwise handsome face assumed an aspect of stark tragedy bordering on abject horror and his voice was matchingly sepulchral. Such was his impact on the anxious families at the receiving end that, after some initial experience, they could no longer bear it and switched off their TV sets, so largely negating a prime element of modern communications. Rather late in the day Ian MacDonald was replaced by a presentationally less gloomy spokesman. Another important lesson had been learned.

Satellite Communications (SATCOMS) were extensively used by our forces for the first time in war. They permitted reliable, secure, near-real-time communication between Northwood/Whitehall and the front line. They constituted a breakthrough in terms of knowing what was happening so far away and knowing it without much delay. They also facilitated 'back-seat-driving'. Some adverse comment on this has been made by certain senior officers in recent TV programmes; their strictures were inappropriate as they themselves *needed* to be prodded into action.

Such a communications facility also made possible the tight, centralized control of Rules of Engagement and understandably this was synonymous with tight *political* control during the period of tension preceding hostilities – at a time when diplomatic negotiation was still being vigorously pursued. Thus when one of our nuclear submarines contacted the Argentine Carrier *25th of May* at an early stage in the confrontation when the US Secretary of State was still forlornly shuttling, the Chiefs of Staff denied approval to sink her and did not even pass the request to the War Cabinet. But when, later, a similar situation occurred over the cruiser *Belgrano*, War Cabinet approval was obtained from Chequers within a very few hours.

One problem resulting from SATCOMs was responsible control of media representatives in war, not helped by the fact that it had never been properly exercised in peace. Not surprisingly, correspondents and broadcasters wished to get their messages back to UK fast when incidents were occurring, as often as not precisely when military commanders needed the SATCOM facility for operational purposes. Moreover, censorship presented a problem unless the reporter was limited to a pre-censored set piece. Readers may imagine my feelings when at 0700 on the *Today* Programme one morning I heard a BBC man say, 'I am standing on the upper deck of the *QE2* watching 5 Infantry Brigade transfer to the *Canberra* and the *Norland* against the magnificent glacial backdrop of South Georgia'. This was at a time when the Argies desperately needed some internationally recognizable success such as the sinking of the *QE2* and the ship had been deviously and meticulously routed accordingly. Later, similarly irresponsible disclosures were made concerning the assaults on Darwin and Goose Green.

I have touched on the importance of a proper, trusting relationship between the Services and the media elsewhere. The Falklands war pointed up the acute lack of this liaison. The preceding years of political constraint inhibited the early establishment of mutual trust even under war conditions. It is long overdue that realistic problems of political and security sensitivity were written into peacetime major exercises and Defence Correspondents and Broadcasters and relevant Ministers as well as Military Commanders were practiced in their handling. To assume that things will be 'all right on the night' simply will not do. It is to be hoped that the editors of *The Times* and *Daily Telegraph* will draw on their personal experiences in the Falklands War to give a lead in this; I wonder if they will. I wonder, too, if Ministers will ever surmount their inherent apprehension that senior Service Officers will be insufficiently economical with the truth.

No commentary on the Falklands War would be complete without adequate tribute being paid to the Naval and Army Medical Services. Often working under difficult conditions, they constantly maintained the highest standards of retrieval, recovery and skill. Many of those wounded in action but alive today owe their continued existence to the tireless expertise of the doctors and nursing staffs. It is a pity that their selfless work went largely unrecognized by the media and the public.

Nine years later, by courtesy of the Admiralty Board who generously sponsored my trip, I paid a brief visit to the Falklands for the first time. Seen from the air the islands looked very much as expected: barren, craggy, undulating peatland from which rose steep mountain peaks, water everywhere in myriad inlets, rivers and lakes – not unlike the Outer Hebrides or the remoter parts of Sutherland – and with that rugged beauty associated with wild places. A haven of quiet peace on a still evening when the sunset flames; a challenge for survival only a few hours later when storm-force winds sweep the treeless wastes, horizontal rain lashes the quartzite outcrops and thick cloud blankets the uplands.

After so many hours spent pouring over maps and charts during the war itself I had imagined that I knew the various scenes of action fairly well. What I did *not* realize was the steepness of the mountain crests, the size of the boulders in the outcrops and the jaggedness of their edges, and the general difficulty of making any kind of fast progress. Add to this winter bogginess, darkness, landmines and being under fire from a well-concealed enemy on the crest, and a rather more realistic understanding of what our assault troops achieved begins to dawn. I can only reiterate what I had often thought in World War II: thank God I am a sailor.

20

FINISHED WITH MAIN ENGINES

'There must be a beginning of any great matter, but the continuing
unto the end until it be thoroughly finished yields the true glory.'

Sir Francis Drake

By the spring of 1982 it was becoming imperative to inform the whole Navy
of the Admiralty Board's plans for implementing the cuts and closures
required by the previous year's Defence Review. An immense amount of
work had been necessary to formulate an orderly rundown with the minimum
hurt to people (there was going to be more than enough of that anyway). I
had discussed this in some detail with Minister of State (AF), Peter Blaker,
and obtained his concurrence to my releasing the information in time for its
receipt, comprehension and promulgation within ships and establishments
before their companies went on Easter leave, so enabling them to discuss
their personal futures with their families over the Easter break. In practical
terms this meant despatching the letters early that week, and this was done.

To my amazement there followed a considerable scene. The Minister
suddenly realized that the letters would be received before an announcement
had been made in the House and, further, because of some protocol the
latter could not be brought forward. He promptly rang up the Prime
Minister and No 10 Press Office issued a statement on the 1200 news to the
effect that I had 'embarrassed the Government'. This was relayed to me by
my Royal Marines driver on my way to lunch. It was an astonishing
performance and I couldn't help feeling that it was time *everyone* went on
Easter leave to restore a sense of proportion!

I was asked to write a short, not-too-serious description of the Service Staff
Colleges; I called it 'Birds of a Feather':-

'To my knowledge Clausewitz never suffered from ulcers. Yet his
wisdom seems to have struck the founders of our English Staff Colleges
as something pretty indigestible. Why else should the common theme
of some bird pervade the heraldic motif of all our centres of military
intellectual excellence unless it be that a gizzard is better than a stomach
to assimilate all that hard stuff?

Roll to the dark blue depths of Greenwich and you will be received
with comfortable irrelevance by a Pelican.

> 'A strange bird, the Pelican –
> Its beak holds more than its belly can.'

The subtle significance of this is apparent only to those holding an Ocean
Navigation Certificate. Yomp across to the khaki drives of Camberley
and all is different. There you are greeted by an owl. The greeting is at
once courteous, a little formal and perhaps tempered by just a touch of
superiority (after all, Wellington did become Prime Minister).

> 'A wise old Owl sat in an oak.
> The more he saw, the less he spoke;
> The less he spoke the more he heard:
> Wasn't that a wise old bird?'

But there's more to it than that. From his lofty perch the owl dispensed
advice to the animals: he told the squirrels to store nuts for the winter,
the horses always to face the wind, the cows to back into it, and so on.
After a while it occurred to the animals that the owl was teaching them
their business; and they accused him of it. The owl contrived to raise
one heavy eyelid a fraction and murmured: 'I only make policy'.

Then swoop on to the light blue skies of Bracknell. The welcome
there is from a hawk. I know no nursery nonsense about this bird
beyond its name rhyming with 'cork' and that it is recognized to be a
sharp customer. It seems constantly to be trying to get to some star or
other and finding it all rather hard work.

At this stage you are certified as 'P*ssed' and a small black mark is
noted against your name in the List of Club Members.

Later you may weave your way to the green swards and lakeside of
Latimer, where the colours of the native fauna and flora are more
varied. But what quirk of nature, what curiosity of creature is there to
mutter a gibbering greeting? Dirty blackish green in colour, scrawny of
frame, lank of leg and webbed of foot, this caricature of a living thing is
normally to be seen staggering about twixt wind and water and beach in
a condition describable only as thoroughly well oiled. This is the
Cormorant (only the P*ssed call it such; the rest of the world knows it
for what it is, the Shag).

> 'The common cormorant or shag
> Lays eggs inside a paper bag;
> The reason you will see no doubt –
> It is to keep the lightning out.

But what these unobservant birds
Are unaware of is that herds
Of wandering bears may come with buns
And steal the bags to hold the crumbs.'

The relevance of this erudite stanza is discernible only to those additionally certified as N*rsed.

Finally, if your state of dypso decline merits it you may reel across that handsome portico in Belgrave Square. Here your host is beyond adequate ornithological description. Who ever heard of a Lion that flew? Maybe Dr Spock or Mark Thatcher – or of course a meticulously selected few of the N*rsed. Yet there in the imposing hall stands the King of Beasts with a serviceable aerofoil sprouting from either flank and holding in his stick-hand a Fisgig (semanticists sometimes prefer to call it a Trident but that gets them into trouble with certain Field Marshals and the CND). The company in these hallowed halls is titillating in the extreme: all shades of colour, creed and sex are there assembled. And after a jolly calendar year of living, eating and sleeping together you can hardly not be R*used.'

One day in May, 1982, while waiting in his outer office to see Minister (AF), my eye was caught by a huge pile of foolscap sheets headed 'The Royal Navy' lying face upwards on the Private Secretary's desk. Interested, I examined the top sheet further without making it obvious that I was doing so. To my surprise and concern the opening sentence read 'Talk of running down the Navy is nonsense;' at that point the door opened and I had to go in to the Minister. Our business did not take long and on my way back through the outer office I picked up the top copy of the pile and walked out with it. Immediately the Private Secretary started to remonstrate but I assured him that I was certain the Minister would not wish to deny me an unclassified paper on my own Service, and with a sweet smile I left. What I had acquired is reproduced at Appendix 1 and I subsequently discovered that it had allegedly been produced by Conservative Central office and given nationwide circulation. Having consistently voted Conservative all my life I felt I had been stabbed in the back and my repugnance was not lessened by reading the misleadingly selective tissue of half-truths (or worse) contained in the paper.

Accordingly I gave instructions for the Navy Department Secretariat to prepare a brief factual counter to the points made without resorting to selectivity. The result was also given a wide circulation (including the Minister's Office) and is reproduced at Appendix 2.

I never heard another word on the subject.

*

Shortly after I had got home one Friday evening the telephone rang. It was some fellow from The Naval & Military Gallery in Albermarle Street. He was trying to form a small committee to select 'the 10 most distinguished military commanders in the field since 1740'; would I join? Having ascertained that I was the only sailor he had so far approached (or wanted to) and who my fellow selectors from the other Services would be (I knew them all) I thought it might be rather fun so I said 'yes'. In due course it turned out that the others in the team were Shan Hackett (General), Christopher Foxley-Morris (Air Chief Marshal) and three military historians: David Howarth, Michael Glover and John Terraine.

We met at the In & Out (Naval & Military Club, Piccadilly) and after introductions, a photograph and a glass of sherry sat down to an exceptionally good working lunch 'chaired' by our man from the Gallery. Business started immediately. The first three slots were filled unanimously and with little debate: Wellington, Nelson and Marlborough. Thereafter it was not so straightforward; it became necessary to clarify 'command' and 'in the field'; a particular difficulty emerged in the case of the Royal Air Force in that for nearly two hundred years of the allotted time span they had not existed and their commanders commanded not 'in the field' but 'from base'. Concessions were made and minds became more concentrated by the time the fish had been eaten and with the roast pork Haig, Cunningham and Dowding had been added to the list and Trenchard, Fisher and Churchill excluded. By the completion of the pudding stage a form of 'rationing' had been agreed as a means of narrowing the issue: there would be five soldiers, four sailors and one airman. Hawke, Jervis and Slim gained places. That left only the tenth place, for a soldier, to be resolved. The port was now going round (a little erratically) and all tongues had been fully loosened. It was Alex ('he was a *gentleman*, but that doesn't make him a good *commander*,' 'such a nice person and he was a Governor General', 'Irrelevant') versus Monty ('little upstart', 'but he did win battles', 'really rather nasty', 'but horribly *right* most of the time'). Then was revealed the fallacy in the selection process: there was an even number of selectors and they were evenly divided; the historians voted for Alex, the Military for Monty. The port had long been finished, the afternoon was far spent and some of us had other things to do; by unanimous agreement it was decided to seek the view of Brigadier Peter Young, military historian and librarian at the Army Staff College at Camberley. He chose Montgomery.

The arrival of foreign Heads of State paying a state visit to this country usually takes one of three forms: at Victoria Station having travelled by train from Southampton or Dover; at Westminster Pier having come up river in Royal Yacht or warship and landed by barge; or by flying in direct to

Heathrow. For the former two venues a full Royal Guard is paraded and the Queen accompanied by Prince Philip receives the guests; for the latter the guard is provided at the palace in use for the occasion and Prince Philip only receives. In all cases the Prime Minister, Foreign Secretary, certain other Members of the Cabinet and the Chiefs of Staff are part of the receiving line, as are the relevant Ambassadors.

Early in June, 1982, the President of the United States and Mrs Reagan paid such a visit. The Queen was in residence at Windsor Castle and the visitors were due to arrive by air at Heathrow in the early evening. Al Haig, US Secretary of State, was scheduled to fly in at about the same time but in a separate aircraft. Because of the uncertainties of flight times at a busy commercial airport those forming the reception party arrived early and stood about in random groups chatting. Nobody seemed to know which of the two aircraft would land first, or when, or even precisely to what apron it would taxi for disembarkation; so we all milled around in the general area of probability.

Suddenly a likely looking aircraft appeared, taxiing towards us. Hastily we formed ourselves into some semblance of a line and Prince Philip and his equerry took up position. But at the last minute the aircraft turned away and disappeared in the direction of the cargo area, covering us with dust as it did so. Presumably that had been Al Haig. Minutes passed. Just as the reception line was beginning to break up in disorder again a second aircraft approached. This came right up to us and looked promising. Yes, it was indeed Air Force One. Engines were shut down and after a slight pause the door was opened at the head of the landing steps. But instead of the President out stepped two of the most thuggish looking hoods it has ever been my lot to behold. Despite the warm summer evening they were dressed in double-breasted mackintoshes which protruded in various unlikely places due to the ironmongery underneath. Having surveyed the scene from the top platform they clumped slowly down to ground level and stood facing outwards either side of the steps. Moments later the President and Mrs Reagan appeared and started to descend. Shortly before they reached the bottom Mrs Reagan evidently spotted a chum in the small crowd, clutched her husband by the arm and stopped, pointing. The unfortunate Prince Philip standing waiting to receive them, only some three steps down, eventually had to administer a 'Jeeves cough' to attract attention and get the show back on the rails again. As they came down the line the President shook hands firmly and had a word ('good evening' or 'how are you') for everybody; Mrs Reagan shook hands limply and said nothing.

Back in the ante-room at Windsor Castle after a sumptuous royal banquet later that evening the Queen presented me to the President and left us chatting together. This was during the final stages of the Falklands War and although we had not yet re-entered Port Stanley and heavy fighting was still in progress it seemed highly unlikely that anything could now prevent the successful completion of the operation (in fact the surrender was signed six days later). Somehow it was a very happy, relaxed evening and a certain air of restrained euphoria could be detected; we really did seem to be 'over the hump'. Nevertheless I did not think this was an entirely suitable topic for the President and instead I opened up on NATO matters (having recently been a Major NATO Commander, with Al Haig) and especially the vexed problems of out-of-area operations. We talked for a good ten minutes and the President was charmingly attentive, if contributing little to the conversation. Then a member of The Household rescued him and led him away to meet someone else. I could not escape the impression that he hadn't had the foggiest notion what I was talking about; maybe he was dead right!

In due time the programmes for the closures of the more important naval establishments in compliance with the 1981 Defence Review were taken by the full Admiralty Board. On this occasion the controversial closure of the Royal Naval Hospital Stonehouse (Devonport) was due for consideration; its demise was favoured by Minister (AF) (Who had fielded a rather narrowly subjective paper) but opposed by my uniformed Board colleagues. As usual Peter Blaker was in the chair with me next to him on his right; it was my useful prerogative as First Sea Lord to speak last on the subject under discussion. On my right was the Vice Chief of the Naval Staff, then Minister (AF), Chief of Fleet Support, Controller, Second Sea Lord and so on.

In a few crisp sentences Peter Standford (VCNS) pointed out the short-sightedness and foolishness of closing Stonehouse, the undesirable loss of flexibility if reliance had to be placed solely on Haslar (Gosport) (it was already planned to close the entire Chatham complex), and the nugatory cost and inconvenience of having to travel from Devonport, where the majority of the Fleet was based, to Gosport.

Jerry Wiggin took up the challenge. He spoke loudly and with considerable belligerence and he went on, and on. It was also largely irrelevant. Muttering my intentions under my breath to the Chairman I decided to break precedent and intervene early, to save wasting further time.

'Stop,' I said peremptorily, 'You have said more than enough. You have made it quite clear that you do not know the first thing about what you are speaking. You talk about war as if it was just another exercise; it is not. It's not your fault you are too young to have experienced it and indeed I hope for your sake you never do, though I'm surprised you haven't picked up more of its flavour from recent events in the South Atlantic. So I'll *tell* you what war is: it's extremes of heat and cold, and wet and dry; it's noise – hideous noise, explosions, shouting, screaming; it's smoke and dirt and

236

squalor; it's limbs and heads blown off, guts hanging out, blood everywhere; it's death. And I'll tell you something else; unless they have a very high level of assurance of the best possible facilities for retrieval and recovery we in the Services will not in the future continue to enjoy the exceptionally high quality of fighting man we have today. Now can we please get on with responsible Board business.'

We did and Stonehouse was not closed.

As touched on in the previous chapter the Falklands War generated a remarkable sense of urgency and priorities throughout the Country as a whole and perhaps especially within the Ministry of Defence. Within a few days of the despatch of the Task Force the normal (and considerable) circulation of papers virtually dried up. Apart from a nameless few who had nothing better to do than continue to scratch away at Defence Review cuts, at all levels people concentrated on the job in hand – winning the war – and got on with it. Some three weeks before the final surrender by the Argentines it became clear that nothing short of an adverse miracle could prevent our victory and the flow of papers started to build up again. By VF Day it was back to full strength. Hardly had the cease-fire been signed when all the old internecine bickering on Defence Review cuts recurred in full strength. Or stronger, because now the Army, the Air Force and the Treasury were fearful that the Navy, having fought a highly successful war but suffered not inconsiderable losses in ships and demonstrated critical shortcomings in equipment, would mount a recovery bandwagon which could only be at the expense of the others.

I was determined to redress the gross absurdities of the Defence Review and to this end decided to stay on for a few months beyond my nominal three years as First Sea Lord. (After all the Chief of the Air Staff was doing five for less compelling reasons!) The range of options for me to exert further pressure was now strictly limited and indeed the only one with real potential was to generate support for the Navy's case in Parliament. Accordingly I invited David Owen (an ex-Navy Minister) to lunch and John Silkin (Shadow Defence Secretary) and, separately, Jim Callaghan (who had served in the Navy during World War II and always held it in high regard) to dinner. In each case nobody else was present and we were free to speak our minds. Over after-dinner coffee with Jim Callaghan the telephone rang; it was John Silkin seeking another meeting; he was all set for a long chat then and there but I told him who I had with me so he sent his regards to my guest and rang off. His message was duly passed on and soon afterwards Mr Callaghan left as he wished to drop in at the House on his way home. All these meetings had gone well and my guests had promised to do everything they could to stop the rot; I could not have asked for more.

0900 next morning, Jim Callaghan rang me in the Ministry of Defence. 'Thank you so much for that delightful evening last night, First Sea Lord,' he said. 'I thoroughly enjoyed it. By the way, when I got back to the House I bumped into John Nott.' A cold shiver started to run down my spine, 'so I gave him your message.'

'*What* message?' I asked sharply.

'Why that you'd be seeing John Silkin again,' was the reply.

What a cock-up and I said so.

'He didn't seem very pleased,' went on Callaghan; 'said he'd be sending for you. I thought you ought to know.' The shiver had now become a rivulet.

'Thank you Mr Callaghan,' I said and put the receiver down.

Days passed. Nott never sent for me. He asked Frank Cooper (PUS) to tell me off. When the latter, clearly rather embarrassed by the situation, had finished I gave him my sympathy for his impossible position, thanked him for his courteous handling of it, added that I had no regrets and assured him that I would continue to do whatever was necessary until the dire circumstances confronting my Service were corrected.

We parted friends and he sent a cleverly worded note on 'heavy briefing' to all the Chiefs of Staff a day or two later. It was very even-handed.

By prearrangement, over the period May-July all three single Service Chiefs had been asked to deliver lectures on their respective Services at The Royal United Services Institute in Whitehall. These lectures, like all others, would be printed and released to the public in September. This presented a dilemma: how much or how little to say about the Defence Review and all that. I decided to be absolutely factual and play it straight. I gave my lecture on 9 June and it is reproduced at Appendix 3. When released subsequently it made a really big impact. All the responsible Press took up my criticisms of the Defence Review and gave them extensive coverage. The whole exercise achieved more than I had dared to hope for. The only snag was the increasing speculation on whether I would be sacked; I wasn't. Furthermore, back in July on the very day the Defence (Review) White Paper was to be debated in the House of Commons, *The Times* had run a first leader under the heading 'Too much on the Rhine' expressing almost identical views to those I had put to the Prime Minister a year earlier. This is reproduced at Appendix 4. Was the tide at long last beginning to turn my way?

The Egyptian Chief of Naval Staff was paying me an official visit and that evening was to be the Guest of Honour at an Admiralty Board dinner at Admiralty House in Whitehall. Minister of State (AF), Jerry Wiggin, was to preside and had asked to be briefed on the procedure. I had nearly completed this and had got to the stage of the Loyal Toasts.

'After the port has been circulated,' I said, 'you should get everybody up and propose the toast "The President of Egypt". The band will play the Egyptian National Anthem on completion of which we all toast "The President". Immediately afterwards, while still standing, the Egyptian Chief of Naval Staff will propose the toast "Her Majesty the Queen", the band will play our National Anthem, we all toast "The Queen' and then sit down.'

'But that's the wrong way round,' exploded the Minister. 'I'm not toasting some bloody foreign blighter before our Queen.'

Patiently I explained that this was standard procedure, not peculiar to the Navy, long practised and showed proper courtesy to our distinguished guests.

'I won't have it,' grunted Wiggin.

I was disinclined to indulge in further argument on this score and, having quickly finished the briefing, left. Subsequently I did just mention to the Bandmaster and to my guest (an extremely nice and understanding man) that, picking my words with loyal care, it was conceivable there would be some slight variation from the normal drill (with which both of them were of course as familiar as I was) and they should be prepared to adjust their response accordingly.

Dinner and drinks beforehand passed off pleasantly enough. The table was cleared, the port passed, the Minister knocked with his gavel and rose. Knowing his propensity for maintaining a steady course regardless of charted hazards I awaited the next step with interest.

'Chief of Naval Staff, Gentlemen "The Queen",' intoned the Minister.

There was a fractional pause, then the Band struck up the Egyptian National Anthem.

'The President,' we toasted; we were back on the rails again.

When finally seated conversation picked up again quite easily; a little care was necessary to avoid catching anybody's eye.

In the autumn of 1982 Nott held a meeting to consider the future responsibilities of the Chief of Defence Staff and the method of selection for that post. Hitherto, as explained earlier, it was incumbent on CDS to forward a consensus view on major issues while reserving the right to add his personal opinion if it differed from the majority. Each Service in turn filled the post for about three years following completion of his tour as head of his Service. The faintly disparaging but useful shorthand jargon for this system was 'Buggins's Turn'. Its great merit lay in its predictability, enabling a Service to groom its CDS (Designate) with appropriate background experience (not least being head of his Service) some years previously – together with a 'runner-up' in case of accidents. It had been generally accepted (and practised) that no one could become CDS unless he *had* been head of his Service for at least six months.

Some 14 months previously *The Times* had printed a leader entitled 'Time to say goodbye to Buggins' but this had been effectively countered by Marshal of the Royal Air Force Sir William Dickson, the first-ever Chief of the Defence Staff and one of the best. He did not have the lust for power displayed by Earl Mountbatten (and some later successors) and though small in stature he was very large in wisdom. As he put it in a letter to *The Times*:

'Most reluctantly I feel compelled to write to you again on the subject of defence. I can understand the feelings of your readers: he is old, out of date and out of touch. Why not lie down and leave it to those who serve today?

'But they are not free to speak. So someone like myself has to decide whether the strong views you express on defence organization need to be challenged. I think they do. I refer to the leader that appeared on June 2 under the title "Time to say goodbye Buggins". It started by commending the Government's recent ministerial adjustment within the Ministry of Defence, but it went on to urge the Prime Minister to "finish the job" while she "had the chance".

'The job it saw was to suppress the pressures of the Service Staffs and the voice of their chiefs by giving greater power to the Chief of the Defence Staff. This may sound like a logical conclusion, but it is not as easy as that, and since you mention surgery I would remind you that drastic and over-ambitious surgery is not always the answer. It can finish the patient as well as the job.

'What is at risk is the invaluable asset which our constitution has in its Chiefs of Staff Committee and its supporting organization. It was the wise concept of Lord Hankey. It proved its value in the war and subsequently and it is a model which most democracies have copied.

'It brings together the expertise of the three Services and the functions of sea, land and air power and it forges and submits joint military advice to the Government. The strength and value of the Chiefs of Staff Committee is that jointly and individually they are responsible for carrying out the advice they present.

'I have served closely under nine Ministers of Defence and from Churchill onwards there was not one who did not value and respect the Chiefs of Staff Committee. They prodded it, they argued with it and often overruled it, but there was not one of those ministers who would have been happy without it or would have wished to emasculate it.

'Of course the Chiefs of Staff have difficulty in presenting agreed advice in the course of urgent reviews of defence policy involving major changes in the shape and size of the Services, and their reactions may cause irritations. But a wise minister knows how to make the best use of those reactions by judicious questions put to the committee by the Chief of the Defence Staff. This helps him to weigh the pros and cons of the many options he has to consider.

'The Chief of Defence Staff has an essential coordinating and advisory role, but the strength and value of his advice derives from his membership and chairmanship of the Chiefs of Staff Committee. It is a dangerous suggestion that he could be someone who has not previously served on the Chiefs of Staff Committee and that he be given overriding powers.

'It may seem a logical conclusion to tidy minds to narrow the base to a strong minister and one military adviser, but what might befall if they happened to have the wrong ideas or were not quite the right men for the job? It should be the constant endeavour to improve the working of the defence machine, but we must not remove its central cog.'

Now it was proposed to change all this. CDS would become principal adviser to the Secretary of State on *all* defence matters. His would be the view forwarded from Chiefs of Staff meetings with a differing view expressed by a Service head only if he insisted. The effect of this change of emphasis was not subtle. Furthermore a new CDS would be selected solely on the basis of his being considered the 'best man for the job', without necessarily having been head of his own Service.' Surely it must be right to pick the best man for the job,' the argument ran. The fact that, taken over a period of time, the existing system did precisely that was glossed over. So too were other considerations: that the Defence Secretary of the day could more easily reject a nominee who robustly stood up to Ministers reaching unwise decision as *not* being the best man for the job; that some adjustment to a candidate's confidential report could readily be made to improve his chances; that if after several tours it were found that a particular Service had not yet filled the post human nature would incline the Defence Secretary to 'give that Service a run' despite its candidate perhaps not being really the best man for the job. And so on.

From the start it was clear that the outcome of the meeting was pre-ordained. The Defence Secretary knew that it would be easier to deal with one man than with four. The Permanent Secretary scented a shift of power back towards the Civil element of the Ministry. The current CDS, though about to retire, an intelligent and active person, would have welcomed more to do. His sucessor (designate) had little option but to sit on the fence if he wanted the job – so he sat on it. That left only the third head of Service and myself to oppose the scheme. Predictably nobody wanted to hear us.

At the time of writing CDS has recently changed. The new incumbent is said to be outstanding in every way. Yet he has neither commanded a major force in the field nor been head of his own Service; the best man for the job?

★

For the First Sea Lord the events of Remembrance Weekend in November followed a fairly set pattern. On Saturday evening to the Albert Hall for the traditional Massed Displays, short service with well-known hymns and the release of poppies from high up in the dome. The Queen, The Queen Mother, The King of Norway and other members of the Royal Family present, also the Prime Minister, several members of the Cabinet and Opposition Front Bench. The entire hall packed to capacity and all quietly determined to pay their personal and collective tribute to the fallen in two World Wars and since and 'to remember them'.

A very moving ceremony indeed with many a damp eye and sober reflection. Then off to the Dorchester for a good dinner with memorable speeches by the Prime Minister or Defence Secretary and the National President of the Royal British Legion and away by midnight.

Next morning, Sunday, the traditional short service at the Cenotaph conducted by the Bishop of London and the wreath-laying by the Royal Family, Political Leaders, Foreign Diplomats and the Chiefs of Staff. The first time I did this I was a little concerned about who would produce my wreath and where and when. 'Don't worry, sir, it just happens,' I was assured. Having confidence in a well proven organization I probed no further, though my mind was not entirely at rest. But sure enough just before we stepped out of the Foreign and Commonwealth Office a little man emerged from the shadows and handed me my wreath. Little did I think that immediately after the ceremony the Chief of the Air Staff would round on me and complain that my wreath was bigger than his and what was I going to do about it? Amazed that such pettiness could reach such levels I muttered an insincere, 'How dreadful, I'll see it doesn't happen again,' (without the least idea how I injected this into the anonymous systems) and the moment passed.

A short reception in the FCO, hosted by the Foreign Secretary followed and then there was just time to return to the flat by Admiralty Arch, change out of uniform and away to the Bishop of London's charming house behind Westminster Abbey for a delightfully informal family, self-help lunch with the Prime Minister and half the Cabinet present.

Remembrance Weekend, 1981, followed this format precisely save for one important incident. Saturday morning dawned bright and still and clear, a perfect winter's day. At home briefly, I was refitting one of those whirlygig things which rotate in the wind and dry the laundry. The heavy plastic lines had become slack with usage and I was tightening them. To get them really taut involved some muscular effort and this I applied with such enthusiasm that I parted the line and drove my right knuckle hard into my right eye. It was rather painful and by the time I had completed the task I could feel my eye swelling up quickly. Going indoors I glanced in a mirror and saw that

34. With Mary in Guildhall after receiving freedom of the City of London.

35. Sent along the corridor to me by my old friend Dwin Bramall, Chief of the General Staff.

Evening Standard, October 27 '80

"Miss Wilkins, take another leak!"

London Express Service

36. The Author on leaving active service in December, 1982.

37. Final send-off from the Zoo (MOD). A most moving turnout. At the explicit request of the Naval Staff we all wore uniform.

already my eye and its surroundings were steadily going a rich blackish purple. In short I was rapidly developing an absolute 'shiner'. How unfortunate, I thought, that it should happen on this of all weekends when I have to be rather in the public view. But there was nothing to be done about it and I pressed on normally.

That night the Albert Hall presented little problem for me, the lighting was dim and all eyes were centred towards the arena. Similarly at the subsequent dinner though some explanation was needed. The crunch came at the Foreign Office reception following the Cenotaph ceremony next morning. As I stepped forward to shake the Foreign Secretary's hand Peter Carrington let out a loud guffaw.

'Oh no!' he shouted. 'I can't bear it. I know – it was John Nott.'

By this time conversation in that part of the room had ceased and all glances were turned in my direction. John Nott was standing some six feet away. He was not amused.

By far the best feature of the entire Ministry of Defence was the efficiency of its lifts. These were self-operated but, partly for status reasons and partly on good compassionate grounds, one lift at each of the North and South ends of the quarter-of-a-mile-long building was manually controlled by a disabled pensioner and took you direct to the sixth floor which housed most of the top management. One such pensioner was Bill.

I had known 'Bill The Lift' for more than 10 years. He was short, stocky, arthritic, very Irish and a dypso. Sometimes in the afternoon he was barely capable of coherent speech; sometimes he disappeared for weeks to be dried out; at all times he was a pretty rough diamond but absolutely loyal to his friends.

When the time finally came for him to retire I invited him into my office for a farewell glass of grog. I had laid on a photographer and we were snapped together, enabling me subsequently to send him a signed memento of our association. For his part Bill graciously introduced me to his successor, Edmond – shy, soft-spoken, rather broken English and as black as night.

It so happened that for the next few days I did not often have occasion to travel with Edmond so that our relationship had not developed much beyond our initial, brief meeting. Then one afternoon I returned from a delayed official lunch, further held up by traffic and in a tearing hurry to grab my papers and go to a Chiefs of Staff meeting. All the automatic lifts were away but Edmond's lift was at bottom floor level and Edmond himself, feet well apart, was standing firmly in front of its open door. As I made to pass he thrust himself sideways to bar my entry.

'No, no,' he said, 'I must wait.'

'Nonsense,' I snapped, 'take me at once to the sixth floor.'

'No, I cannot,' wailed Edmond, visibly upset, 'I am waiting for de Lord.'

And I? Heaven forgive me 'I *am* de Lord' I growled and up we went to the sixth floor.

At about this time the Defence Secretary decided to issue a white paper on the Falklands War. To this day I am not sure why it was done nor what purpose it was intended to serve. Work on it began at once. The first six chapters were drafted by Civil Servants; though uninformative they were innocuous and factually correct. The seventh (final) chapter was largely prepared by the Defence Secretary himself; it dealt inter alia with the intended replacement, if any, of forces lost in the recent war. It was thus important for the future. But as initially drafted it was inaccurate, misleading and in places incorrect.

Towards the end of November I paid my final, farewell call on John Nott. By then the earlier chapters of the white paper had been suitably polished but the significant final chapter remained largely unchanged. Having arranged five interviews with different elements of the media for the day the white paper was published (and that day having been postponed several times so that I began to wonder if it were not being deliberately delayed until I had left office), I had given some thought as to whether or not to have a last up-and-downer with the Defence Secretary over the objectionable chapter seven. I had decided not to on the grounds that it was inappropriate for our last meeting and anyway amendments could easily be reversed after I had gone.

In I went to John Nott. It was 1830 in the evening; he greeted me with friendly charm, gave me a large whisky and sat beside me on the sofa. Hardly were we seated when he asked, 'What do you think of the white paper?'

'The first six chapters are all right,' I replied. 'They don't tell anybody much about anything but they're harmless. The seventh chapter is simply not true and unless it is changed I shall expose it for what it is worth.'

I added that I had five interviews booked with the media, to coincide with the day of the white paper's publication; that this date had already been postponed two or three times and that I now had an open-ended agreement with the media that the interviews would take place on the actual day of publication irrespective of when that day might be.

'Finally,' I said, 'you have my word that nothing would please me more than to be able to say "I support the white paper" when, as they inevitably will, they ask me what I think of it. But I cannot and will not support it with chapter seven in anything like its present form'.

John Nott gave me a long, hard look; then we got down to a detailed discussion on the objectionable passages.

My final months following the successful completion of the Falklands

Campaign (covered in other chapters) were busy ones. Much of the time could have been spent walking the corridors saying 'I told you so' but there were better things to do. Ministers had at last woken up to the fact that warships needed effective self-defence against air attack and that Airborne Early Warning radar integral to a Force was necessary for its survival. *Invincible* was saved, it being tacitly accepted that her planned sale to Australia had become politically unacceptable – one of the greater ironies of that year. Also the Treasury was being typically and calculatingly obtuse about the replacements of warships lost in action.

December came all too quickly. Earlier that week the Admiralty Board and Commanders-in-Chief had kindly honoured me with a splendid farewell dinner on board *Bristol*, moored off Greenwich and wearing my flag as an Admiral of the Fleet. Now it was time for me to leave the Ministry of Defence, in which I had spent most of my previous 25 years when not at sea, for the last time. At the request of the Naval Staff everyone who could wore uniform. After a final drink with Board colleagues in my Vice Chief's office they escorted me down in the lift and out of the North door. There to my astonishment the steps and the entire approach was packed with people – Naval Officers and Civil Servants, some of whom had come up from Bath and Portsmouth for the purpose. I said goodbye personally to as many as I could and then stumbled rather blindly down the steps to my waiting car, door held open by faithful George Tullis my Naval assistant. As I turned to give a final wave I caught sight of Mimi, the Matron-in-Chief of the Queen Alexandra's Royal Naval Nursing Service, standing on the top step and looking unhappy; I had missed her in my farewells. Nipping up the steps again I gave her a quick hug, and then into the car and away.

It was some time before I could steady my voice to speak to Chippy Wardle, my devoted Royal Marines Sergeant driver, indeed it was just past Harrods. The plan agreed with my family had been that I drove to my daughter Henrietta's little house in Fulham, changed out of fancy dress and pulled myself together over a family lunch.

'Steady on,' I exclaimed as we suddenly turned sharp left off the normal route, 'where are you going?'

'Sorry, Sir,' replied Wardle 'but you've been hijacked'.

We stopped outside the Capitol Hotel of which my son-in-law's Best Man was Manager. The venue had been switched. After a quick change and a much needed bottle of champagne I was given the lunch of my life.

Later as Mary drove me home through the chill winter's fading light, I recalled one of my favourite sayings of which I had made much use: 'Always expect the unexpected'.

The Falklands white paper was published on 14 December. I went to London early and was assured by my successor (John Fieldhouse) that although the contentious chapter seven was still not quite right it was very nearly so and the greatest help I could be to him would be to support it. I undertook to do so.

In the twelve hours between 1100 in the forenoon on that day and 2300 that night I had eleven separate interviews. At each my questioner asked, predictably, 'What do you think of the white paper?' And to each I replied 'It doesn't tell you much but I support it.' The media were furious.

My final session at the end of that day was with Peter Snow on Newsnight. I had done interviews with him before and knew him to be languid and charming off the air but, necessarily, sharp as a needle when on the job. Also present was Julian Critchley MP. A contemporary controversy current at the time was over the optimum configuration for a frigate: should it be 'long and thin' as conventional expertise had it or should it be 'short and fat' as unscrupulously plugged by some who had pretensions to being able to design small craft. The latter theory, though fundamentally unsound and impractical, gained limited support in some quarters (including a few in high places who ought to have known better). Peter Snow had warned me in advance that he wished to resolve this controversy once and for all and I was delighted to do so. To this end I had had a long talk with the Chief Naval Architect, a fine man who more than confirmed all my own professional instincts.

The interview started briskly with my being quizzed fairly searchingly on the issue of frigate shape. In the course of the next ten minutes or so I was able to shoot down the absurdity of the 'short and fat' pretty conclusively. It was now Julian Critchley's turn to be probed on a different subject but just before working on him Peter Snow asked me a final question about the country's position in the world and whether Armed Forces were still relevant. It was an easy one to answer and I ended by reminding him, 'After all, England won the Falklands War'. He turned to Julian Critchley. As he did so the telephone by his side buzzed; he picked it up, listened for a moment before replacing the instrument and glancing back to me said, 'I think you ought to know that the entire telephone exchange is jammed by incoming calls of complaint from the Scots, the Welsh and the Irish about your having said *England* won the war. I'll give you a chance to retract your words before the end of the programme.'

'Oh Lord,' I thought, 'here is a googly.' Although it must have been obvious to all except racist prima donnas that I intended the word 'England' to be in the general sense, in retrospect it was an unfortunate choice of words. But what could be done about it? If I retracted that statement it would impair my credibility and undo the good I had done earlier in ridiculing the 'short and fat' frigate lunacy. But clearly I had to say *something*. I also had to pay some attention to what was going on between Snow and

Critchley because at any moment I too might become involved. Try as I did to find some convincing way out of the impasse, no solution came to mind.

The Critchley interview ended. Still no inspiration. As promised Peter Snow turned back to me.

'Admiral, earlier in the programme you said, 'England won the Falklands War' and as you know we have since had a number of complaints from all over the country. Would you care to retract your statement?'

This was the moment of truth. I had still devised no solution to my predicament but knew that I must retain the initiative and attack; if I went on the defensive my case would crumble. Jacky Fisher's famous dictum 'Never apologise, never explain' flashed unhelpfully through my mind.

'No,' I said, 'I will not retract anything. The spirit in which I said and intended my words must have been crystal clear to all but the meanest and most small minded . . .' and then in the nick of time inspiration came.

'During the Second World War,' I continued, now with confidence completely restored, 'there was a popular song the theme words of which ran "There'll always be an England". It did not say "there'll always be an England, Scotland, Wales and Northern Ireland", or even "there'll always be a Great Britain and Northern Ireland", it said "there'll always be an *England* and everyone accepted the underlying spirit.'

The programme ended.

I only had three letters afterwards. The best was from an unhappy Welshman. It sentenced me, with erratic literacy, to be court-martialled, flogged round the fleet, keel hauled and reduced to the rank of Midshipman. Stirring stuff – I have it in my Scrap Book still.

I wished I could have complied and become a Midshipman again.

APPENDIX 1

POLITICAL HANDOUT

THE ROYAL NAVY

Naval Budget

Talk of running down the Navy is nonsense. This financial year we will be spending £½bn more in real terms on the Navy than was spent in the year before we came to office. As to the future we will *still* be spending more on the conventional Navy, even when expenditure on modernising the strategic deterrent is at its peak, than we were in 1978/79.

Ship Numbers

There will be more major ships and submarines operational in 1985 than there are today. A massive modernisation programme for the fleet is in hand. The principal threat to our peace and freedom will continue to come from the Soviet Union and we will be increasing the numbers of our nuclear submarines – which will be the main strike threat to the Soviet fleet – from 12 to 17.

Recent Orders

Last year we placed naval orders with British Shipbuilders to the value of over £400m. In the past few months we have decided to order the Heavyweight Torpedo, improve Sea Wolf and procure Sea Eagle. A further Type 22 frigate was ordered in February and last month we invited tenders for a further nuclear submarine and 4 minesweepers. The total programme for torpedo procurement alone amounts to more than £2,000m.

Carriers

It was made absolutely clear in the White Paper on the Defence Programme (Cmd 8288) that 2 carriers will be kept in service. ILLUSTRIOUS will join the fleet later this year and the construction of ARK ROYAL is progressing satisfactorily.

APPENDIX 2

FACTUAL COMMENT ON THE POLITICAL HANDOUT

Naval Budget

There can be no certainty about what we may be able to spend on the conventional Navy in the future but an indication of the Navy's financial cutback is that today its budget represents about 38% of the total Defence budget whereas by the end of the decade it will have fallen by several percentage points. Furthermore the cost of ships and weapons (the life blood of the Navy) rises faster than the rate of general inflation; thus the problem towards the end of the decade is exacerbated.

Ship Numbers

The term 'operational' is open to several definitions and by being selective in dates and semantics substantially different interpretations can be placed on the figures.

But, leaving aside these nuances, in terms of the total number of major warships in the conventional Fleet, we are facing a steady decline. When the present Government took office we had a total of 98 major warships (that is, frigates and above and submarines other than Polaris). By April 1982 this was down to 86 and current plans show a further decline by the end of the decade. It follows that the statement made by the Secretary of State in the House of Commons on 7 April 1982 (Official Report Col 1050) that 'We cannot be criticised for cutting back the conventional Navy, when it is far larger today than it was when we entered office, and it will be in the late 1980s' is not true.

The handout also refers to the 'massive modernisation' programme. Certainly new ships are entering service but, as explained below, almost overwhelmingly this is the result of orders placed by the last Government. The planned numbers of carriers, destroyers/frigates, nuclear submarines, Sea Harriers, Royal Marines Commando Groups, assault helicopters and Royal Fleet Auxiliaries are all less than those inherited from the previous Administration. Air defence capability has been particularly hit by the decision to abandon the third carrier and its Sea Harrier air group, the termination of the Type 42 destroyer programme, its planned improved successor class and the Sea Dart improvements, and the planned premature disposal of HMS BRISTOL and County Class guided missile destroyers. Furthermore the decision to abandon mid-life modernisation will result in increasing obsolescence in the surface flotillas' weapon systems, and the reduced dockyard capacity will make it very difficult to implement improvements to capability in the future.

Recent Orders

The shipbuilding figures in the handout are highly selective. Of the 27 major warships that have entered service since April 1979, or will enter service over the next 5 years, only 4 (2 Type 22 frigates and 2 nuclear submarines) have been ordered by the present government. Furthermore this government has so far placed orders which average only about half the value per year achieved by its predecessor.

Carriers

The handout adds nothing to Command 8288. The facts are that in May 1979 there were 2 carriers (HERMES and BULWARK) in service, 1 (INVINCIBLE) on sea trials and 2 (ILLUSTRIOUS and ARK ROYAL) being built. Future plans were based on maintaining 3 carriers in service (INVINCIBLE, ILLUSTRIOUS and ARK ROYAL) with the option of keeping a fourth (HERMES). This Government has disposed of BULWARK prematurely, announced the sale of INVINCIBLE to Australia, and decided to pay off HERMES in 1985 (when ARK ROYAL enters service); their plans are to keep only 2 carriers in service. With only two carriers there would be only 1 immediately available for a significant proportion of the time. If 3 carriers were retained in service, with one of them always in refit or reserve, 2 would always be operational and the third could be brought forward in an emergency. (The wisdom of this option is being underlined now as ILLUSTRIOUS is currently being brought forward early from the builders in order to be available for service in the Falklands to supplement HERMES and INVINCIBLE).

APPENDIX 3

BRITISH MARITIME FORCES: THE FUTURE

A lecture given at the RUSI on 9 June 1982
by Admiral Sir HENRY LEACH, GCB, ADC, Chief of the Naval Staff and
First Sea Lord

General Sir HARRY TUZO, GCB, OBE, MC, MA, in the Chair

*THE CHAIRMAN welcomed CNS to the Institute on the occasion of the second
of three lectures to be given by the Chiefs of Staff*

Some 2,400 years ago Themistocles said 'he who controls the sea controls
everything'. In the last three years I have served two Secretaries of State for
Defence and neither has been a Greek scholar.

You might reasonably suppose that the value and use of maritime power
for a country such as ours with its seafaring background and geographical
position would need no explanation. I regret you would be wrong – as events
of the past 18 months have proved. More recently you might contend that
the situation in the Falkland Islands has served as a stark reminder of
realities of the truth. You would be right – but to an extent which remains
to be translated into action.

I intend to discuss the maritime defence requirement in general. I shall
try to do so from what I hope is a responsible overall defence viewpoint and
not a narrow, parochial naval one. I shall address the question of whether
we still need a strong Navy and Maritime Air capability, and I shall end with
a personal view on the future.

Let me start with a few BGOs (Blinding Glimpses of the Obvious). First,
we are an island race, dependent on our sea lines of communication for more
than 95 per cent of our trade, and with over 600 merchant ships at sea on
any one day. Our Merchant Navy may or may not pick up again after the
present recession ends but it still contains 1,000 ships of over 1,000 tons.
Over many years we have developed a seafaring expertise which is second to
none and internationally recognised as such.

Second, the defence of this country is rightly based on the support of

NATO – of which the Atlantic is by definition at its very heart. It might be (but it is not) the Central Region Treaty Organisation; it is the North *Atlantic* Treaty Organisation. It is the Atlantic which forms the link between the two main partners, Western Europe and North America. The strength of the Alliance depends on the partnership of these two power blocks; one without the other would destroy the effectiveness of the whole. North America would survive alone but few would seriously doubt the dependence of Europe on the USA. Nothing would please the Soviets more than to see America decoupled. They continue to work vigorously to this end and on occasion some European countries come perilously close to doing their job for them.

Third, because of our geography and demonstrated maritime capability the UK is accepted as the maritime leader of NATO in Europe. Without wishing to make a party point, we provide 70 per cent of NATO's Eastern Atlantic Ready Forces at a cost of 23 per cent of the UK defence budget. This compares with our provision of 10 per cent of the allied forces in the Central Region for some 41 per cent of our defence Budget.

Let me now look at some of the fundamental wider issues which should condition this country's strategy.

Other than religious war, virtually all conflicts of history have had as their basis a competitive struggle to gain control of economic resources which would enable the homeland of the victor to enjoy a high standard of living. The shorthand term for this is imperialism. In our anxiety to ensure the integrity of the NATO area there is a danger of misunderstanding this underlying cause of conflict between the Soviet Union and Western countries. Secure behind a stalemate position on the Central Front – which engages so much of our resources and energies – we risk adopting a Maginot Line attitude and pay insufficient attention to our flanks.

By flanks I do not mean the Northern and Southern Flanks of NATO, important as they are, but the worldwide economic flank. The countries of the West are dependent not only on the oil reserves of the Middle East – over half a billion tons of crude oil are imported into NATO Europe each year – but on importing other scarce commodities: Copper, Tin, Chrome, Potash, Manganese, Bauxite – to name but a few critical raw materials on which we are nowhere near self sufficient. As well as the Middle East, countries and continents such as India, South-East Asia, Africa, South America and Indonesia provide the geography of this economic flank. None of these areas is notable for its stability and all are vulnerable to political social, economic and military pressures. The Communist ideology is based upon the centralisation of these four factors and by their combined use to extend the creed throughout the world and thus ensure the imperialist wellbeing of the Soviet Union.

So what is the more likely strategy of the Kremlin planner? Not an attack on the Central Front with all the attendant risks of nuclear escalation destroying the homelands of both Russia and the United States – the 'both lose' scenario. Nor a military attack on NATO's Southern and Northern Flanks, unless there should be sufficient NATO disunity or lack of will to make it possible to pick these plums, without risking a major conflict. Far better a strategy based on peaceful exploitation backed by military strength to gain control of the economic resources on which the West relies, yet which are geographically situated outside the defensive circle around the NATO area.

Faced with a strong Alliance in Europe, the hard continental NATO boundaries, the Soviets are trying to outflank it by probing the soft and ill-defined maritime boundaries around the rest of the world. Was it Lenin who said 'probe with bayonets; if you find mush – proceed: if you encounter steel – withdraw'.

In pursuing such a strategy, the Soviets have suffered some expensive rebuffs, for example Egypt. But they have remorselessly pressed on, continuing to learn from their mistakes (for example the Cuban crisis in 1962) as they turn to more long-term and safer methods of achieving their aim. This is what lies behind the support given to Admiral Gorshkov in building up Russia as a major maritime power, a policy which is expensive yet which is clearly seen as an essential requirement.

The ships, submarines and aircraft needed to project maritime power take time to develop and deploy but the Soviets have made great strides over the past 15 years. We are now facing an acceleration of the build-up of their already powerful Soviet fleet. It is not my purpose today to give you a detailed exposition of Soviet maritime capabilities; but to illustrate my theme, consider the following categories:

- Ahead in submarines – one nuclear every six weeks
- Alfa class – Faster/deeper
- Oscar class – only slightly smaller than *Invincible* – 24 SSNX19 cruise missiles with a range of 500 km
- Typhoon – the size of *Hermes* – Nuclear Battleship – Battleship Submarine
- Four classes Cruisers/Destroyers – one 28,000 ton Battle Cruiser, nuclear powered
- VSTOL Carriers – Fixed Wing Carrier
- Soviet Naval Air Force – Backfire
- Capability – Defence of homeland/through sea denial/to sea control

Overall we see a reasonably balanced fleet with modern and heavily armed ships and submarines; there are shortcomings in afloat support and organic fixed-wing air but these are being remedied. In the air, they possess a large shore-based long-range Naval Air Force and are well advanced in the use of satellites.

They also now have by far the biggest fishing fleet in the world, a large number of oceanographic and research ships, and the fifth largest merchant fleet which is still climbing the league table; there are clear signs of undercutting freight rates which is a way of using economic means to gain a monopoly control of certain trade routes – the classic tactics of maritime powers throughout history. These three fleets (as well as the Navy proper) are all under central, national control; Gorshkov calls them his four fleets; together with the Naval Air Force they form the maritime strength of the Soviet Union.

What is it all for? Not just defence of the homeland. Nor can it be because of Russia's dependence on sea trade and sea lines of communication; unlike Western Europe, shipping is an economic convenience, not vital to Russia's survival. It enjoys interior lines of communication for food and oil and what it gets by sea could be replaced; its natural wealth is such that there is no absolute need to secure raw material reserves overseas.

The Soviets see their maritime power as an ideal tool for furthering their fundamental aim of achieving world domination and economic advantage.

Our rigid NATO boundary is relevant for only one reason: that relating to Article 5 of the Treaty, 'an attack on one is an attack on all'. In all other respects the conflict between NATO and the Warsaw Pact needs to be considered in global terms, not only in war, but also in tension and peace – and it is in this context that the presence and flexibility of maritime power comes into its own.

Now you might say that is all very well. No one would disagree with what you have just said but we must look at what the UK can afford and what it can contribute towards defence in the context of the NATO Alliance as a whole, and taking into account the maritime balance between East and West compared to the continental imbalance, particularly on the Central Front and Northern Flank.

The maritime balance

When comparing the numbers of hulls on each side, the West still has numerical superiority in surface forces but the underlying trends show our numbers to be reducing whilst those of the Soviet Navy are increasing. A year ago SACLANT assessed that on present trends the balance will tip towards the Warsaw Pact by the mid-1980s. Matters have hardly improved in our favour since then and some would argue that the balance has already tipped. Remember, it takes some 10-years to produce a new major weapon system or a ship. Furthermore, although totting up numbers used to be a straightforward way of presenting the relative strengths when like was being compared with like and the maritime problem was comparatively simple, the technological advances of this century have changed the nature of war at sea beyond recognition.

For example, at the start of World War II, on a straight numerical comparison, Germany was heavily outnumbered at sea by at least four to one. Yet, by possessing a relative handful of surface ships and some 50 diesel-engined submarines which had to spend much of their time on the surface, it was able to make an almost successful challenge to our control of vital sea lanes. Compare this with the Soviet Navy today with over 500 submarines, many of which are nuclear propelled with vastly superior underwater speed, and operational endurance limited only by the human factor. It is the ever-growing quality inprovement in the offensive capability of the Soviet Navy which is our major concern and which makes a nonsense of any straight comparison of total numbers.

Again I believe people are sometimes misled by the accepted principle that, on land, to take the offensive you need a superiority of about 3 to 1. But at sea, the opposite applies and it is the defence that requires the numerical advantage, particularly for anti-submarine warfare in which a mix drawn from MPA (Maritime Patrol Aircraft), organic helicopters, surface ships and submarines is needed for success against a single nuclear submarine. At onc time in 1943 those 50 German submarines were being opposed by something in the order of 25 carrier types, 800 escorts and 1,100 maritime aircraft. The West cannot take comfort in parity, but needs a substantial superiority to defend our interest at sea, let alone carry the offensive to the enemy.

The UK contribution

At one extreme of the UK maritime contribution to NATO we could just concentrate on defence of the UK base, mainly in the form of mine countermeasures, offshore and fishery protection, and perhaps some contribution to the anti-submarine warfare (ASW) battle in the Eastern Atlantic, and leave the rest to the Americans. After all, the US Navy is the only one able to operate large strike carriers. But the US Navy is itself force poor. President Reagan has reversed his predecessor's decision and given approval to build more nuclear-powered carriers, but they could be the last. CNO has said that at present they are trying to meet a three ocean requirement with a one and a half ocean navy and there is a real need for other NATO navies to plug the gaps. The only other NATO navy that might do more is the Federal Republic Germany which has recently extended its operating boundary up to the Norwegian Sea. But does it make sense for the Germans with their limited coastline to build up their Navy and take on a greater EASTLANT role so that we in this country can reduce the size of our Navy and make savings to build up our forces in German homeland – particularly now that the offset agreement has ended?

Surely the sensible and cost-effective thing for NATO to do is to build on what already exists: for countries such as West Germany with their continental expertise and geography to concentrate on the Central Front – after all it is their own soil – and for the UK with its maritime edge to maintain its lead at sea.

Geographically Britain is ideally placed, adjacent to the Greenland/Iceland/ UK Gap, through which the Soviet main naval forces have to deploy to reach the Atlantic. In the early stages of a war, especially if there had been little warning, UK maritime forces would have to bear the brunt of operations in the North Atlantic. Here we can provide defence in depth against the maritime operations in the Atlantic. Military loss of the Northern Flank would be very serious indeed: the threat against allied shipping would be greatly magnified by the enemy's acquisition of forward sea and air operating bases; control of the North Sea would be in jeopardy; and the direct threat to the UK base increased.

Last but by no means least a word about the protection of reinforcement and resupply shipping for Allied Command Europe. Even if all the currently envisaged pre-positioning is achieved, 90 per cent re/re will still be seaborne. This is a huge task involving something in the order of 1 million men, 11 million tons of military equipment and 17 million tons of Petrol/Oil/ Lubricants; it will need the support of all NATO blue water navies and is essential if war on the continent is to be sustained. Here we could enter the argument of short versus long war. There are those in this country who find it convenient to support the short war scenario but it is a view vigorously refuted by our American allies and not accepted in NATO. In his annual report earlier this year, the US Secretary of Defense points out the fallacy of the 'short war assumption – the notion that in planning our strategy and designing our forces we could rely on the assumption that a conventional war would be of short duration. Common sense', he said, 'and past experience tells us otherwise.'

Any strategy which weakens NATO capability to reinforce across the Atlantic will inevitably lower the nuclear threshold, and unless a viable reinforcement capability is discernibly maintained the United States will not forward-deploy forces, especially ground forces to mainland Europe. Decoupling of the US is a prime Soviet aim. We must keep options open and avoid committing ourselves to an assumption which, if proved false, would be disastrous. In 1914 and again in 1939, no one thought the war would last longer than six months; look what happened.

So I see protection of the reinforcement routes in tension and war as fundamental to NATO's deterrent posture and an important (though not the prime) commitment for maritime forces. All three Major Nato Commanders (MNCs) are agreed that NATO does not have a viable strategy in Europe without the assurance of reinforcement and resupply, and this capability is the principal insurance of US commitment to European defence.

1981 Defence Review

Against this backcloth of why I believe we need strong maritime forces, I turn now to the future – commencing with the outcome of last year's Defence Review. The informed recognise that it was done in a hurry, involved prejudgment, and was driven by short-term politico-economic expediency rather than long-term strategic sense.

The effect on the Royal Navy was dramatic coming as it did so soon after the cuts imposed during the 1980 mini Defence Review. In addition to being saddled with virtually the whole of the bill for Trident (for which project, *en passant*, I am an unequivocal supporter), cuts of several billion pounds were applied to the Naval Programme over the next nine years. To put it in perspective, these amounted to more than twice the cuts applied to the Army and over seven times those applied to the Royal Air Force, on top of substantial and unbalanced reductions the previous year. Our overall military balance will be consequently impaired and our flexibility to meet the unforeseen eroded. I put it to you that a good deal of the future is, and is likely to remain, unforeseen. Forecasts are necessarily assumption-based and are often proved wrong. We really should have learnt this lesson by now. The Cod War, Beira Patrol, the Gulf of Oman requirement and now the Falkland Islands crisis are all examples of operations which arose at short notice and with little or no warning. They demonstrate typically the flexibility of maritime power – by its presence and the wide range of options it can offer in support of our diplomacy. There is one other matter of principle which merits a mention before I summarise how the Navy handled this situation. It is quite simply that once a major capability is given up, and the associated industrial base lost, it is almost impossible to recover. Here again short-term expediency can wreak havoc.

You will be familiar with the Government's main decisions concerning my Service and I will rehearse them only briefly. Mid-life modernisation of destroyers and frigates are to be abandoned; a large number of ships are being disposed of before their time; the new construction programme for destroyers and frigates is to be sharply curtailed in favour of a new smaller, cheaper class; the submarine and mine-counter-measure programmes are to be broadly maintained albeit with some reductions; certain dockyards and support depots are to be closed: some, 8000–10,000 officers and men are to be reduced by 1986 with a further, similar number in the last half of the costing period; reductions in civilians are also to be made.

Faced with these parameters the Navy had few options. The aim set by the Admiralty Board was the retention of the most effective fleet we could afford. Little more could be done in the fields of support or manpower. The choice thus effectively narrowed to the training sector: if a significant proportion of our training, hitherto (and for good reasons) conducted ashore, could be transferred to ships of the fleet it should be possible to close a number of shore establishments and make consequential financial savings.

Such decisions are not without penalties. Abandonment of mid-life modernisations will increase a ship's seagoing availability but at the expense of progressive obsolescence. Periodic weapon system updating is fundamental to effective countering of the threat and provision for it, whether more or less cost effective than the criticised modernisations, will have to be made. And shifting a substantial part of the training load to sea will save on shore training costs but will reduce the time ships are at their full operational capability.

The Falkland Islands

That, in broad terms, was the position reached by Easter this year. Then came the Falkland Islands crisis. I will not dwell on the Intelligence of this event nor on the assessment of it on yet one more of the many blow hot/blow cold occasions relating to these islands over the past 17 years. But now the worst had actually happened and the quickest possible reaction was required. I will make two comments only: first, as a professional sailor I am proud of the response; and second, I doubt that at any time in history an operation of this magnitude has been conducted in the onset of an Antarctic winter from a base 8,000 miles away. There may be a disaster tomorrow – there certainly have been losses and may be more – but there can be few more convincing demonstrations of the flexibility and effectiveness of seapower. Nothing else could have done the job. The very same forces appropriate to peacetime presence worldwide and the exercise of deterrence within the NATO area were now to be put to the test of war outside it.

Fortuitously the crisis occurred before the cuts in the Navy's front line capability were too far down the road. And this brings me to a very unsavoury aspect. Nothing would have been easier than to have made cheap mileage of the need to take up such a quantity and variety of ships from trade on grounds of the irresponsible rundown of the Navy. This was not done – not least because there were more important things to attend to. But at the height of the crisis a party political handout was printed and circulated to MPs. By dint of selective quotation it sought to show that the doubts increasingly being voiced were groundless and that last year's Defence Review had given the Navy more money and better capability and so on. The handling of this was not without resemblance to that of the Defence Review itself: it was a major con-trick or, not to put too fine a point on it, a catalogue of half-truths.

Here are the whole-truth facts of current plans. The ASW carriers are to be reduced by a third as is their organic Sea Harrier capability. The destroyer/ frigate force is to be reduced from 65 to 42 operational plus eight in reserve and there will be a consequential 20 per cent decrease in the overall availability of these ships. The previously planned total of SSNs will drop by three. Out of the 27 major warships and submarines that have entered or are entering service between April 1979 and 1987 (which is when the last currently ordered enters service), only four have been ordered by the present Government achieving an average expenditure of £300m per year on new ships compared to £600m per year during the previous administration. Furthermore a large number of existing ships are to be paid off earlier than planned.

Two absurdities in particular stand out from the Falkland Islands operation so far. First, the projected sale of *Invincible* at a knockdown price to a friendly Commonwealth country the other side of the world. Without *Invincible*, the present operation would not have been possible; and with the change of Australian attitude coupled with its Prime Minister's assurance that we need feel under no obligation to proceed with the sale it is surely inconceivable that we shall do so. Indeed remarkable efforts are already being made to accelerate the completion of *Illustrious* so as to provide a much needed third deck.

Second, the weapon system to come under most criticism is Sea Dart. Its performance in action has been entirely as expected. The planned improvements to correct its known shortcomings were cancelled as part of the cuts.

The future

So how lies the future for the Navy? The roles and tasks will remain essentially unchanged. We will continue to bear the responsibility of being the leading maritime power in Europe and the largest Navy after the superpowers. Our primary task, with our allies, is to deter; that is to maintain peace by preventing war. But should this fail we must then, again with our allies, win the war. Effective deterrence involves maintaining a high state of readiness, being well equipped and trained, and operating and deploying wherever and whenever the situation demands. It means making clear to any potential enemy that escalation to conflict would carry too great a risk to make it worthwhile for him. The Royal Navy and the Royal marines will continue to have unique responsibilities for maintaining peace and stability: by being responsible for the British strategic nuclear deterrent force; by deploying ships and personnel both within and outside the NATO area as required; by being ready to counter Soviet naval dispositions through surveillance operations at short notice; and, at the lower end of the spectrum, by routine patrols to protect our offshore resources and other interests.

In tension or war, we would have to make a major contribution to the Alliance's overall maritime effort. After the strategic deterrent, the most important tasks for the Royal Navy would be to provide ASW support for the US carrier battle groups in the NATO striking fleet Atlantic and to contribute both directly and through forward operations to the protection of the huge amount of reinforcement and resupply shipping which would cross from the United States, and to a lesser extent from our own country to Europe. We would also have to keep open and safe the ports and shipping routes in the shallow waters around the United Kingdom and would deploy the UK/Netherlands amphibious force to its operating areas as early in tension as possible. The retention of the Assault Ships will mean that this force retains its flexibility for amphibious operations, both in support of NATO and out of area. This is a demanding list of tasks involving surface ships, submarines, Royal Fleet Auxiliaries, helicopters and maritime VSTOL as well as RAF shore-based aircraft. To meet them we will still be maintaining a substantial and balanced fleet and will be introducing a range of new weapon systems. But two questions must be asked: will this be enough? and are the shape and size of the future fleet the best we can afford? My answer to both is an emphatic 'no'. A year ago the financial pressure on the defence budget, short and long term, was the overriding factor in Ministers' minds. But defence is now in a markedly different financial situation and I have no dobut that extra resources could be made available for the Navy without grave impact elsewhere. Based on this financial perception and drawing on 45 years of experience in war, tension and peace – endorsed by the present operation in the South Atlantic – I see three clear needs for the Navy.

- We must retain three ASW carriers. For reasons of life-expectancy, economy in manning and running, and logistic support, they should be the *Invincible* class.
- We must improve the weapon system effectiveness in our destroyers and frigates and continue to do so in the future.
- We must hold on to (and in due course replace) a more viable number of operational destroyers and frigates.

All these aspects are within the sensible and balanced limits of the current defence budget. Unless they are implemented we shall be dangerously deficient at sea in the future.

Let me end on a broad note which affects all three Services. It concerns the age-old dichotomy of quality versus quantity and never was it more important to get the balance right. In recent times criticism has tended to focus on what has been described as excessive sophistication (and hence cost); 'gold-plating' has been a recurrent accusation. Let us be absolutely clear about this matter. It is not only the Russians who possess modern, high performance weapons. The *Sheffield* was sunk by a single Exocet missile – a weapon possessed by a number of countries but not Russia. There is nothing clever about complexity for its own sake. But equally there is nothing more ridiculous than simplicity which is ineffective but forced through because it is cheap.

In conclusion let me remind you of the telling remark once made by Edmund Burke:

> The only thing necessary for the triumph of evil is for good men to do nothing

'or' he might have said – 'not enough'.

(Reprinted by permission of The Royal United Services Institute for Defence Studies from *The RUSI Journal*, Vol 127, No. 3, September, 1982.)

APPENDIX 4

The Defence White Paper which is to be debated in the Commons today is the final product of that hurried Defence review which was set in motion eighteen months ago when Mr Nott went to the Defence Ministry. It was brought to a preliminary conclusion by the end of last summer. It was never explained what caused the hurry, and certainly the review suffered from the need for such haste, since a whole raft of essential strategic questions was swept aside and left unanswered in the process.

Mr Nott's financial task seems to have been to cut forward costings by about eight billion pounds over the next ten years, saving half of that sum in the process, and reserving the other half in a central uncommitted fund. His political task was to leave our continental European forces effectively untouched so as not to disturb Britain's relationship with her European allies at a moment of sensitivity in the EEC. Militarily this left virtually only one option, which was to let the main burden of cuts fall on the navy, since both the army and the RAF were featured more specifically in the formal force commitment to NATO. The navy, by its very nature deals in a less precise operational environment than the geographical sectors of West Germany or the provision of that country's air defence.

As a result of his review Mr Nott proposed to cut the navy by twice as much as the army and by seven times as much as the RAF – to the tune of some five billion pounds over ten years. This was to be achieved by reducing the active surface fleet of frigates and destroyers from a current figure of about 65 to one of 42; selling the carrier *Invincible* to Australia; eliminating the need for warships to undergo mid-life modernization which normally helps long-life hulls to accommodate changes in more rapidly obsolescent weapon systems; and the closure of naval dockyards. The fleet of frigates and destroyers would ostensibly be backed by another eight ships on stand-by – not the kind of stand-by which this summer enabled ships to be quickly activated for service in the South Atlantic, but one in which the ships would be unable to put to sea without substantial refits – a state nearer stand-down than stand-by.

There was some laudable cost control in these decisions, taken against the background of lamentable strategy. The strategic effect of concentrating so much of our military effort in that North German plain is that the military machine becomes obsessively concerned with that area, to the exclusion of the rest of the world. The 'short war' enthusiasts in the Army and Royal Air Force dedicated to the territorial trip wires of NATO military planning, seem once again to have won the day in the Defence Ministry. Just because our ultimate security lies with the preservation of peace in Central Europe, it does not follow that the main threat to that security will come in Central Europe. On the contrary, most strategists now accept that the very stability of the force-jam each side of the Iron Curtain has led Soviet strategists to pursue an indirect approach through massive naval expansion and the encouragement of indirect threats to the Western position through proxies far from central Europe, in South East Asia, the Middle East, Africa and Latin America. With all that going on there is no need to ask why things are so quiet on the Rhine.

Mr Nott should be asked two questions. The first is to explain why he did not fully examine the financial consequences of a military alternative to his programme of savage naval cuts – by saving on the cost of our peacetime commitment to maintain force levels in Germany. The second would be to explain why, given that great savings could be achieved without impairing our war-time commitment to the defence of Germany, there is such coyness about initiating discussions with our allies to bring about a more equitable sharing of the defence burden.

Britain maintains 60,000 soldiers and nearly 11,000 airmen in West Germany. They are accompanied by as many wives and children. The Defence Ministry rents or owns some 45,000 married quarters, educates 28,000 children and provides medical services for the lot. The cost of education, health and housing for these service families is at least £450 million a year which would not fall on the Defence budget at all if those troops were stationed in Britain, with adequate plans to deploy them in Germany whenever it was necessary both for operational training and for real emergencies. On top of that Rhine Army employs nearly 25,000 local people in servicing its peacetime establishment, costing probably another two hundred millions more.

The purpose of our troops in Germany is to deter an attack and be ready to fight should such deterrence fail. The existing strength of sixty thousand soldiers is barely half what Rhine army would comprise on a war establishment, and even now is often nominally below our Treaty level of 55,000, with units serving in Northern Ireland though listed on the strength of Rhine army.

It would be possible militarily to bring home many of our army and air forces from Germany, while equipping them with the capacity for rapid redeployment. After the initial capital cost of refurbishing barracks, and arranging for new married quarters, it would save hundreds of millions of pounds on the Defence budget. Some of that could go to repair the damage which Mr Nott's plan will progressively, and seriously inflict on the fleet from 1986 onwards, with fewer ships at sea, fewer hunter-killer submarines on order, and the prospect of a further savage contraction in the early 1990's when the full effects of this year's decision will be felt.

These matters should be put fairly to our allies with a request for an adjustment to our Treaty commitments. Perhaps those who have misgivings about such a transfer of resources would have a stronger case if they spent as much per head on defence as Britain does; but none of them does. Before that can happen, however, the British defence establishment itself must reach a concerted view. Mr Nott may have successfully split the Chiefs of Staff Committee, so that he can claim he is not ignoring their concerted advice. Certainly the Army and RAF chiefs seem to have sat back – like shadows 'yawning at the mass' – and watched, indeed connived at, the axe falling on the Navy, with no apparent concern for the unbalanced way it was done.

They should consider the possibility that they are wrong. The certainties of the 'short war' theory – which lead to such an obsession with Central Europe – are an unsound basis on which to calculate future strategy. Any British government must consider that the possibilities for harassment or minor aggression are infinitely more varied and numerous at sea than they are on that frontier in West Germany. It is vital therefore that Britain should be able to deploy forces at sea which could match each phase of a potential escalation, and that must include an adequate fleet of surface vessels as well as submarines, and carriers. That is not preparing forces to fight the last war (in this case, the Falklands); it is preparing, as best we can, for the unforeseen.

INDEX

Glover, Michael, 234
Goodhart, Sir Philip, 205
Goose Green, 229
Gosport, 58–59, 62, 236
Gozo, 79
Grand Harbour, 49–50
Grantham, Admiral Sir Guy, 119
Great Pass, 46
Greenland, 181–184
Greenland/Iceland/UK Gap, 41
Greenock, 4
Greenwich, Royal Naval College, 56, 245
Griffin, Admiral Sir Anthony, 146
Grytviken, 218
Gulf War, 225
Gundersen, General Zeiner, 172–173
Gutta Sound, 43

Hackett, General Sir John, 234
Haig, Earl, 234
Haig, General Alexander, 172, 180
Hamilton, Admiral Sir John, 136–139
Hankey, Lord, 240
Harrier, GR3 Aircraft, 168
Haslar, Royal Naval Hospital, 66, 165, 236
Havers, Lord, 227
Hawaii, 96–98
Hawke, Admiral Lord, 234
Heathrow, 192–193, 235
Heraklion, 115–117
Herald Tribune, 207
Herbert, Admiral Sir Peter, 156
Hermes, HMS, 220–221, 251
Heron Aircraft, 165
High Wycombe, HQ RAF Strike Command, 163,
Hoare, Commodore Broady, 139
Holy Trinity, Brompton, 106
Honeywell, Captain Dick, 98–99
Hong Kong, 96, 105, 161–163
Honnington, RAF Station, 166–168
Horn, Cape, 215
House of Commons, 219
Howard, Lieutenant Commander Julian, 135–136

Howarth, David, 234
HS 125 Aircraft, 169, 183–184
Hunt, Admiral Sir Nicholas, 136–137
Hutchinson, Lieutenant Commander H, 50–51
Hvalfjord, 27

Iceland, 181–184
Illustrious, HMS, 199, 249, 251–260
Indomitable, HMS, 6
Indonesia, 128
Infantaria de Marina, 193
Intrepid, HMS, 198–199, 220–221
Invincible, HMS, 198–202, 220–222, 245, 251, 260, 263
Isle Class Danlayers, 72–73
Izmir, 75–78

Jackson, Surgeon Captain Mike, 149
Jaguar, Aircraft, 168
Jamaica, HMS, 37, 39
Jane's Fighting Ships, 151
Janes, Lieutenant (E) Harry, 74
Japanese threat, 6–9, 12–13
Javelin, HMS, 42–54, 62
Jenny Side Party, 161–163
Jerusalem, 50
Jervis, Admiral Sir John, 234
Jervis, HMS, 47, 49
Johore, Sultan of, 94
Johore Strait, 100, 122
Joint Planning Committee Far East, 123–124

Kennedy, Air Chief Marshal Sir Jock, 181
Kidd, Admiral Ike, 172, 180
Killick, Sir John, 181
King George V, HMS, 15–18
Kinloss, RAF Station, 181, 184
Kola Inlet, 36–38, 40–41
Korea, 96–96
Kuantan, 9
Kure, 96
Kuruvila, Vice Admiral Chandy, 57–58